OLD NEW WORLD

OLD NEW WORLD

LUCINDA LAMBTON

HarperCollins*Publishers*

HarperCollins*Publishers*

77–85 Fulham Palace Road,
Hammersmith, London W6 8JB

Published by HarperCollins*Publishers* 2000

1 3 5 7 9 8 6 4 2

We are grateful for permission to reprint the
following copyright material in this book. John
Fowles: extract from *The Maggot* (Jonathan Cape,
1985), reprinted by permission of Sheil Land
Associates Ltd. Avery Architectural and Fine Arts
Library, Columbia University in the City of New York
for elevation of The New York Yacht Club by Warren
& Wetmore, reproduced in Robert A. M. Stern,
Gregory Gilmartin and John Massengale, *New York
1900* (Rizzoli, 1983).

A catalogue record for this book is available
from the British Library

ISBN 0 00 257093 9

Set in Albertus and Bembo

Designed by Design Principals, Warminster
Printed in Great Britain by
HarperCollinsManufacturing Glasgow

CONTENTS

INTRODUCTION XI

THE UNITED STATES OF EUROPE

WALDOBORO 2
MARBLEHEAD 8
COLUMBUS CHAPEL 14
SABBATHDAY LAKE 20
RUGBY, TENNESSEE 25
SEAMEN'S BETHEL 32
McSORLEY'S OLD ALE HOUSE 37
SHIRLEY PLANTATION 45
CHRIST CHURCH 51
THE SEELBACH HOTEL 55
ANHEUSER-BUSCH BREWERY 59
GRACANICA, ILLINOIS 65

AMERICA PRESERVED

HONOLULU HOUSE 70
CASTLE TUCKER 77
THE NEW YORK YACHT CLUB 83
MOHONK MOUNTAIN HOUSE 89
TREMONT NAIL FACTORY 95
NEW ORLEANS GARDEN DISTRICT 100
THE CRITERION THEATRE 106
NOTTOWAY 110
THE WAGNER FREE INSTITUTE 114
PENN'S STORES 119
A. SCHWAB 123

ROOTS AND OFFSHOOTS

THE LIVINGSTON TRAIL 132
LAMBTON WITH A 'P' 147

SELECT BIBLIOGRAPHY 168

INDEX 171

ACKNOWLEDGEMENTS

Heartfelt thanks are due to the following people for their help, kindness, patience and encouragement:

Perry Worsthorne, my dear husband who has suffered twice as much as all the here acknowledged put together, enduring days, weeks and years of my worries with devoted support and understanding, whilst over and over again applying himself to helping me along the way; Will Burlington whose exhaustive photographic assistance, as well as his cheerful and cosy, funny and altogether delightful companionship, turned a drive of over 9000 miles with thirty back-breakingly heavy suitcases of camera equipment into an adventure of pure joy; Lucius Lampton, without whom little of this would have been possible, his wife Louise, Crawford and Garland Lampton – my new family; Louis and Tippy Lyell who sowed the first seeds of the Lambton-Lampton saga and who, over the years, have shown such wondrous family affection; Dinwiddie Lampton, king among men and his daughter Nana, my beloved new kin; Michael Fishwick for entrusting me with this tremendous task; Kate Johnson, who like a golden shaft from the heavens sliced through at the end, editing my often idiotic words with sympathetic brio; Sue Freathy for her rock-like support, humour and encouragement against the ever-battering ocean of my worries; Claire Allan for her sterling support during the closing stages; Sarah Teale whose friendship I most lovingly value and who with her company Teale Productions's often sorcery-like solving of problems paved many a happy way forward; Ann, who I love as a sister, Marc, Sarah, Joel, Wilson and Gabbie Savoy for giving me a real home from home in Louisiana; Richard Kaplan and his wife Edwina Sandys, my pals who made the alarming unmanageability of these schemes manageable and gave me the happiest of bases from which to work in America; Sheila Rennie whose assistance, spiced with Scots humour, saw the book off to a flying start; Jenny Barraclough for her constant support during the making of the films; Mark Thompson for commissioning the films for the BBC; Jane Root for her belief in these schemes; Alex Harvey, and the film crew of Jeremy Pollard, Merce Williams and Charles Moss – of whom I grew inordinately fond; George Carey who got the whole show on the road and without whom the *Old New World* films would never have been made.

Great gratitude is also due to the following few who gave this journey a helping hand!

Ricky and Ania Aldrich whose kindness knew no bounds; Winty Aldrich, new kin and kindred spirit with glittering golden knobs on; Max Allen; Doreen Anderson; Judy Anderson who welcomed us on our first night in America and sent us on our much soothed way; at Anheuser-Busch: Dr William Volmer, Kim Stettes; Emily Ann of Teale Productions; Larry Ashmead for his wildly wonderful good nature; Jim Baker; Baldwin Powell; Vicky Bates; Mimi Beckwith; Darla Blazey; Joshua Bloom; Mrs Edward Blum for her great generosity; Susan Bourne; Joel Brown; Bruce Bradbury, a dear old friend ever ready with advice, of Bradbury & Bradbury whose remarkable wallpapers smother houses all over America; Peter de Brant, today's 'Hereditary Lord of the North Bay' – an Englishman in Cornwall; Eleanor Braslow; Kimberly Brigance; Ashley Bryan, as fine and funny a man as you could ever meet; Bill and Pat Buckley for their laugh-a-minute friendship, and to Bill for enabling me to enter the hallowed precincts of the New York Yacht Club; Karen Bulley; Carolyn Bunting; Dot and Perry Byrd; Arthur Cantor, a friend and saviour amid the splendours of the Dakota Building; Cinny Carothers; Buddy Carr; Lorna and Tom Lyell Chain; Charles Hill Carter II, one of the great highlights of this great adventure; Christopher Chute; Judith Chute; Susan and John Collins for their overwhelming kindness; The Crickets: Sonny Curtis, Jerry Allison and Joe B. Mauldin and their wonderful wives who cheered us on our way with a gala dinner in Nashville, with Sonny battling to sing his great song 'I fought the law' against the loud chirruping of his budgerigar, gave us weeks of renewed strength; Criterion Theatre: Betty Morrison for so proudly displaying her cinema and Jim Morrison for his help and advice; Amy and Kendal Cox; Lynn Craig; John Cunning, director of Missouri State Museum; Joan Davidson for her sympathy; Michael Davis, a hitherto unknown spirited sweetheart of a cousin; Ruth Davis of the Mark Twain Birthplace for her welcoming sweetness; Dennis Damon for his innumerable kindnesses; Kate Dixson; John Dobkin; George and Donita Edwards; Laurent Dupal; Elmira College: Gretchen Sharlow, director of Mark Twain Studies and Mark Woodhouse of the Mark Twain Archive Library for turning out on a Sunday to allow me to luxuriate in Twain's first editions; Reg Ennas; Dr Charles Fairfax; Desmond Fitzgerald; Jimmy Flowers; Fritz

Flury and Tina Sitz; Oliver Foot for his ever-cheerful forbearance; Pat and Cassie Furgeson; Evelyn Livingston Furman for allowing me to explore her opera house in Leadville and Sharon and Bill Bland; Richard Gamester who saw me through many a harrowing computer horror whatever the time of day or night; Jane Gelfman; Phil and Sherry Geyelin who introduced me to the marvels of Maine; Sarah Gowers; Gracanica, Third Lake: Father Tom Kazich, Sister Angelina for welcoming us without a moment's notice; Janet Graham for her advice and promise of firm friendship; Desmond Guinness; Anne Hale; Bob Hector whose company, encouragement and camaraderie were a constant cocktail of delight; Rebecca Henry; Grall Herne; John Heron; Karen Hibbet; Nancy Hoover; John Huffman, Historic Site Administrator at the Mark Twain Birthplace, his welcome and winning ways were some of the highlights of the year; Sister Idelphonse and the sisters of the Benedictine Monastery in Ferdinand, Indiana; Norman Ishler; Laska Jimsen of Teale Productions whose help was often invaluable; Ingersoll Jordan; Dolly Jordan for her constant sweetheartry; Ally Jullens; James Kelly; Roger Kennedy for his generosity in the wake of my badgering him for information; Roger H. Kolar; Davilo Konvalinka; Deola LaHaye; Sarah and the late and great Bob Lampton who was responsible for keeping the 'Lampton with a p' story alive in Mississippi; Dr Jane Ann Lampton Moore; Katherine Landrineau; Father George Lane; John Lawton for his wise advice; Zac and Alice Leader; Christopher Lee, his love for the Columbus Chapel was a tonic as was his company; Susan J. Lisk; Bill Little; Dennis Lowe; Amy McDonald and her husband Thomas Urquhart who were some of the fountain forces of encouragement and kindness itself, cheering me on my way; Mary McDougall; Revd Hugh Magerf of St Andrews Episcopal, Fort Worth for his initial encouragement; Mr and Mrs Russel Manoog; Mr Matte and his delightful museum at Oppulsas, Louisana; Rebecca Maxwell; Florence May; Mary McGlolhin who was responsible for building the smallest library in America; Dan McMichael of Das Deutsche Haus-Athenaeum, Indianapolis; McSorley's: Michael Maher whose preservation of the place should be cheered to the echo, Pepe who encouraged the hours of photographing with a joke a minute, and Richard Welsh; Rosalind Michahelles; Sophia Michalellis of Superior Concept; Beth Millward, a true friend; Mohonk Mountain House: Nina Smiley to whom I will be eternally grateful for a myriad of kind acts, Sandra Smiley for her friendship and inspiring love for the place, Joan la Chance, archivist, Kim Ladanyi for her endless acts of kindness, Jim Clark for his admirable knowledge of the Mohonk Barn Museum and Wayne Smith for shivering away a winter's night as we photographed there; Barry Moreno; Grover Mouton; Alberta Moynahan; David Muhlena, expert on Czech life in Cedar Rapids, Iowa; Peggy Murphy; New York Yacht Club: Andrew Curtis, Joe Jackson; Nottoway Plantation: Cindy Hidalto, Mary Teresa James and Annette Montalvo; Jill Osterhaven; Pamina for keeping my pecker up with her architectural jewellery; Lucy and Walter Parlange for breaking bread in Louisiana; Penn's: Alma Tincy Penn Lane, Jeanne Penn Lane, Dava Penn Osborne; Dawn Penn Osborne Graas – friends for life; Kathy la Plante; Nancy and Eben Pyne for allowing me to invade their summer camp and for giving a good deal of advice; Lorna A. Reimers for welcoming us with open arms; Mr and Mrs John Reinhardt; Cherie and Randall Riser; Mildred and James Robinson; Booker Rucker, Department of National Resources, Missouri; Rugby, Tennessee: Barbara Stagg and her husband John Gilliat, Barbara was electric in her response to my disbelieving inquiries that Rugby could exist and thereafter was generous and helpful in the extreme; Sabbathday Lake: Sister Frances Carr who allowed me to photograph the Meeting House, Sister Marie Burgess for her help, Leonard Brooks for looking after us; Jay Sadler for his terrific funniness and friendship; Kenneth Santos; David Schneider; Vivienne Schuster for her fighting battles; Schwab's: Abe and Elliott who, with their hilarious ways, were one of the dazzling highlights of the journey; Adam Seger of the Seelbach Hotel who gave us such a happy adventure; Patty Seiter; Jeanette Shepherd; Victor Simmons; Steven Sitton; Gene Slivka of Rosedown Plantation; Kennedy Smith of the National Trust; Tom and Harriet Soble for their constant interest and support; Mark Speer; Carole Spiegel of British Airways in Chicago whose helpfulness saved us from collapse on the final lap; Laura Sprague of the Victoria Mansion at Portland who put everything aside to help; Roger Stapleton; Jeanne E. Stinson; Fred Storer; Alison Stouse who put herself out to an alarming degree; Henry Sweets; Mrs Gwynne Tayloe; Mike and Chrissie Teale for introducing me to one of the kings of all men, Ashley Bryan; the Tremont Nail Factory: Bill Driscoll, Tony Hanson who turned out for a whole Sunday to reveal and relish an astounding factory; Michael Tshudy; Castle Tucker: Jane Tucker; at Mark Twain House, Hartford, Connecticut: Marienne Curling, David Bush and Karen Miller; George Unangst; Diane Viera of SPNEA; St Volodymyr Ukranian Orthodox Cathedral in Chicago; Wagner Institute: David Dashiell, and Susan Glassman, new friends who allowed me in after five minute's notice; Ben and Lori Watts; Mary Frances Watts; Pat Weber; Pastor Fred Weiser; Peter Weyland; Frolic Weymouth; Ann Wilkinson; Dr Williams; Robert Wolterstorf of the Victoria Mansion in Maine, who, with his help and advice became a friend.

To
Lucius Lampton
from
Lucy Lambton
with love

INTRODUCTION

When Charles Dickens first came to the New World in 1842 he wrote that he felt like 'The Emperor of Cheerfulness on a cruise of pleasure… From top to toe, every fibre of my body was unrestrained and alert… on fire and alive' – my feelings exactly whenever arriving in America!

I have been consumed with love for the country for as long as I can remember. While thumping renditions of 'God Save The Queen' or 'Land of Hope and Glory' kindle but a few sparks, just a passing mention of either 'America the Beautiful' or 'The Battle Hymn of the Republic' sends me into a rapturous (and I am proud to say word-perfect) roaring. As for the sight of the Stars and Stripes, my emotions are unsuitable for one who lives under the Union Jack – if I am warmed by the reflected glow of American patriotism then I give America three cheers for that!

Whereas most of those who go to the United States expect to see a vision of the future, of a country still pioneering a path into the great unknown, what few realize is that the same energy and optimism that makes America so successful in shaping things to come also revels in cultivating the continuities and customs of the land, offering an unique combination that is at once both exhilarating and nostalgic.

The United States is, for me, Utopia; thriving and alive in the traditions of the Old World, set within the fresh and invigorating framework of the New. Far from being a mighty or monstrous marvel of modernity, America is replete with miraculous survivals of its European past, often with buildings that are more evocative of that past than their counterparts in the motherlands today. So it is too with the traditions, customs and cultures that have grown out of the very body of America which have often been preserved in a way that puts parts of Europe to shame.

But the most constant source of delight is the country's architecture: from the modest charms of a 'shotgun' house – so small that a gun can be shot clean through the building – to the great and grand State Capitols that stand proud throughout the land. In Jefferson City, Missouri, the Capitol's dome (lined with magnificent murals by Englishman, Sir Frank Brangwyn) rises out of the un-skyscrapered body of the town, a sight most mournfully reminiscent as it looms over the rooftops in the distance of the once unsullied views of St Paul's in London! Then there is the cosy beauty of such small towns as Belfast in Maine and Marshall in Michigan, which, thanks to the perseverance of the local people, put many a British equivalent to shame. Opera houses survive and thrive in the tiniest towns throughout America,

---

Opposite: *The essence of seventeenth-century Sweden, sandwiched between a roaring dual carriageway and an interstate in Philadelphia: Gloria Dei, the Old Swedes' Church still stands as pure as the day it was completed in 1700. The Swedish pastor between 1744-1801 was a friend of Benjamin Franklin, and one of the earliest lightening rod conductors in the world is still affixed to the church's brick exterior. Inside on the walls and floor are tablets to the early settlers, whilst hanging from the ceiling are models of the ships – the Fogel Grip and Kalmar Nyckel that brought them to the New World.*

'Forty Acres' in Hadley, Massachusetts – one of the most startlingly pure examples of old America. The house is still filled with eighteenth-century furniture, books, china and other paraphernalia, including the sword of its builder, Moses Porter, handed through the window by his Indian servant after his master had been killed in the French-Indian War of 1755. Just outside the door of the unadorned attic bedroom is a 1770s brick, smoke oven for cooking hams and salmon. The Prophet's Chamber, with its wide, whitewashed boards and trundle bed, was slept and studied in by the future Bishop of New York, Frederick Dan Huntingdon – great-grandson of Moses Porter, who had acquired the land 'Forty Acres and its skirts' in 1752.

while even such down-on-their-luck cities as Detroit can boast of a wealth of still glittering architectural gems.

There are many millions of 'Victorians' too – fairy-tale-like houses with their gingerbread trim – great and small, throughout the United States. Matching them building for building are the symbolic splendours of American classicism. As for the Art-Deco style, which has become America's own, where else would you expect to find its forms so flamboyantly displayed than with the house-sized chandeliers that hang above the longest water bar in the world, at the working spa baths of Excelsior Springs in Missouri!

Such thoughts of America had lurked – or rather magnificently marched about – in my mind for years,

A German legacy that is gorged throughout the land: it was in this oven dating from 1784 at Lititz in Pennsylvania that the first pretzel was baked in the United States, from a recipe given by a German hobo – in exchange for food – to Julius Sturgis, whose descendants still run the bakery today.

when suddenly I was to hear fantastical rumours of Lampton kith and kin living throughout America: of Lucius Lampton, Renaissance man in Mississippi and of Dinwiddie Lampton, octogenarian carriage-driver supremo in Kentucky. It was even whispered that Mark Twain's mother was a Lambton. It was all too much to countenance. For years I have been able to proudly proclaim that Princess Pocahontas is my seven-times-great-grandmother; it was thanks to her intervention that the English settlers in Virginia were the first to successfully survive. But now it seemed that there was more, much more in store, so I set off

on a mission to find my American kin. What an adventure-and-a-half it turned out to be. The emotion was an elixir I had never tasted before; indeed I was to feast on it, loosing a walloping three stone in weight! And what more piercingly personal proof too of the Old New World.

Having yearned for years to trounce those who do not see the distinctive grace of America, and to cock a snook at its everyday critics who claim that the skyscraper and shopping mall is all, I therefore embarked upon this enough-for-ten-men-to-tackle odyssey, determined to give credence to the bewildering turning-you-inside-out realization that the New World is now in many respects more elegantly old-fashioned than the Old.

After months of mounting excitement I was given the go-ahead to produce this book, as well as three films for the BBC, in one heart-pounding year. It was to be an immense journey, hauling thirty photographic suitcases through twenty-one states, then plotting and filming the same route twice over again – a handsome total of 27,000 miles!

Of course I had to wear blinkers through the hundreds of miles of blighting blandness in the suburbs, as well as through the villainous and spirit-sinking miseries of the 'strip'. Rose-tinted spectacles had to be cemented onto my nose too when

confronted with sadly dead downtowns, with inner city decay and with piecemeal developments on a truly monstrous scale.

No more poignant example of these American abominations could be found than the view from Pikes Peak in Colorado. It was here, in 1893, that Katherine Lee Bates, a professor of English Literature, was inspired to write 'America the Beautiful':

Oh beautiful for spacious skies,
For amber waves of grain:
For purple mountain majesty
Across the fruited plain.
America, America, God shed his grace on thee,
And crown thy good with brotherhood
From sea to shining sea.

Today, cars by the thousand glint forth from that fruited plain, row upon row, upon row of them, parked in dealerships of the ill-developed Colorado Springs, from which rear dull and dumpy blocks.

Stretching off in every direction from these foothills of the Rocky Mountains, there is a new suburbia which has a sterility that smashed even my rosy specs to smithereens, indeed it drove me to shouting and screaming out loud – anything to immediately infuse some spirit into the air!

These sorry aspects of the United States are all too well known; the purpose of my quest, though,

The most flamboyant of all New World survivals: (Above) *The Mallory Neely House in Memphis, Tennessee, built by grocer and cotton factor James Columbus Neely in 1852, and redecorated in 1883.* (Opposite) *The Morse Libby House in Portland Maine, built by hotelier Ruggles-Sylvester Morse in 1860. Two most luscious cherries on an already rich-enough-to-kill-you cake — both houses are arranged with stupefying extravagance. In America the 'Victorian' past is their great past which is both restored and revered. Such exuberantly, and exhaustingly overdecorated buildings are being preserved by their thousands from California to Maine, from Michigan to Mississippi, often replete with the bourgeois swagger of their creators. These were the homes of the monied middle-merchants, displaying the overblown opulence of the nineteenth-century bigwig. There are, however, no such extant examples in Britain. Throughout the land, from Ealing to Edinburgh, there were once such handsome villas, crammed and coated with splendour by burghers. Today they have all gone, having been gutted out and geared up to their new incarnations as nursing homes, flats and guest houses. Now, the only way that you can peer into that past is at the movies, with such stars as Ingrid Bergman surrounded by their amplitude in* Gaslight *or Bette Davis amid their fringes and flounces in* The Little Foxes.

was to seek out and show off the extraordinary, often surreal survivals that are to be found throughout the land. Being an architectural photographer, buffed up with a passion for buildings – indeed seeing them as the very flesh and blood of a country – I had to develop this theory through architectural evidence rather than through people and their customs, sadly having to leave those wonderfully rich fields to historians and sociologists.

I had been certain that in this country of colonists – once flung into the perils of a vast and unknown continent – there would be many a preciously-preserved enclave of the Europe that they had left behind. And so it proved to be.

Whereas in our little island the waves of modernity have been able to reach and swamp almost everywhere, in giant America this is by no means the case. Thanks to the scale of the country, as well as the sensibilities of so many Americans, there is a myriad of nooks and crannies – places that to Old-World eyes seem archaic and scarcely credible.

Vestiges of the Old World such as the Amish are, of course, well-documented, although that makes not a scrap of difference to the spook shock of seeing them hoving into view in their horse-drawn buggies, like ghosts from the past, in the Pennsylvania countryside. Then there are the Mennonites. I met the 'Black Bumper' sect – so-called because, having eschewed the buggy for the more convenient car, they paint out all the brash chrome. In Tipton, Missouri, I met the serene and sweet Nancy Hoover, dressed in a white bonnet that she said was a 'prayer veil' so 'that we can be in prayer at any time'; it was a bonnet that also denoted 'the woman as the weaker vessel'.

Late one night in December in Lindsborg, Kansas there was but one figure on the street: an old lady, dressed as 'tomte-nisse' – a little Christmas helper – who spoke only Swedish! Here too, on the Western plains of America, they eat potato sausages that are no longer seen in Sweden; for while in the Old World they represent the poverty of their forbears, in the New they have come to symbolize their pioneering spirit.

Ex-patriot love of the old ways of the motherlands, or fatherlands, may of course account for some of this. But a thought worth airing is that America was new from the start, without the inertia of centuries of tradition and customs. After the Revolution (as Americans refer to the War of Independence) there was no regime to rebel against. While in Europe modernization has seemed the only way to shed the shackles of an unjust past, so it is contrariwise with America; fully at ease with its modernity, it has no inhibitions about preserving its past. In Europe classical architecture may speak of autocracy, but in America it denotes democracy. Thus in the United States good manners do not denote servility: think of the many millions of Jane Austin-like encounters enacted both in American movies and still more remarkably in life today, when the hat is doffed, the head briskly bowed, always with the Old-World address of 'Sir' or 'Maam' unfailingly murmured. Eighteenth-century manners still hold hard in America.

If you find this stiff to stomach, then try going to Tangier Island in Virginia, settled in 1686 by the Cornishman, John Crockett (one third of the population still have the name Crockett!) and you will hear sixteenth-century Cornish tricks of the tongue

Opposite: *Shoties Camp, Mount Desert Island, Maine. As America revved up to ever more riches at the end of the nineteenth century, affluent Americans turned to the simple life. 'Savage meccas for pale pilgrims', such 'camps' gave the impression of roughing it in a rustic wilderness. Many still survive with their bucolic sensitivities intact; from the Adirondacks and the giant Mohonk Mountain House in Upstate New York to the miniature Shoties Camp, this architecture of 'the great outdoors' has ardent followers to this day.*

still being spoken in the twenty-first century. Or take yourself off to the upper-mid-South to hear vestigial Jacobean English, where until the Second World War the only book in the house was the King James Bible, and so its language still lives on to this day. The late and great V. S. Pritchett once told me – albeit when he was ninety-five – that as a young man strolling into a small town in Tennessee, he had been asked by the first person he met: 'And where does you all expectation to end?' – meaning 'What are you up to?'

Else just try listening to everyday talk about you, to words that are still pronounced as they were in seventeenth- and eighteenth-century England. 'Baar' was the old English pronunciation of what has now become 'bear' in Britain; likewise in America you hear the old English 'vaarmin' which has changed to 'vermin' in the British Isles. 'Gal' predates 'girl' and 'critter' was the old English for 'creature'. Conversely short 'e's such as in 'sergent' were originally English, as were the 'a's as in 'ant' rather than 'aunt'. 'Rooster' and 'skidaddle' are but two of the many hundreds of regional English words that were borne off on tongues to the New World, where they would survive, having perished in the land from whence they came. Most delightful of all is 'sassy', the old English pronunciation of 'saucy'.

Much of this, you may say, is a far cry from architectural adventure, but once you realize that, along with the survival of so many remarkable buildings in America, there are manners, customs and language that have endured in the New World long after they have died in the Old, then the scene is most satisfactorily set for my theme of 'Old New World'.

THE
UNITED STATES
OF
EUROPE

WALDOBORO

Waldoboro in Maine, originally known as Broad Bay, was first settled by German immigrants in the 1740s, although 'settled' would be too sweet a word to describe the lives of the wretchedly-persecuted Lutherans of the Rhineland who were to find life as arduous in the New World as that which they had fled from in the Old. Now they and their descendants lie in the Protestant Cemetery, which surrounds their Meeting House, the beautiful bedrock of their faith, a building so unaltered that the air alone seems to have retained the breath of the passions that built it in the eighteenth century.

German immigration to America – a force that became so formidable – started in 1682 when a little booklet offering religious asylum to persecuted splinter sects, was printed by William Penn's Quakers of Pennsylvania. Also, the English government had decided that rather than people the Colonies with able British bodies, they would be better off populating it with the longing-to-be-liberated persecuted Protestants of Europe. Pamphlets by the thousand were printed to entice, with alluringly gilded letters and a portrait of Queen Anne. The 'Golden Books of Queen Anne' promised a glorious life. And so the surge began, one that was eventually to grow into the most tremendous swell of all immigrant nations.

From the start the German adventurers were to suffer many and bitter blows, firstly at the hands of the 'soul sellers' (as the unscrupulous agents sent to gather in the gullible were called), and then at the hands of the ship owners, captains and crews of the boats on which the emigrants, 'packed like herring', would have to endure up to eight months of a living hell. One religious refugee, Gottlob Mittelberger wrote an account of his journey to America in 1750:

The filth and stench of the vessels no pen could describe, while the diverse diseases… dysentery, scarlet fever, scrofula, cancers etc., caused by the miserable salt food and the vile drinking water are truly deplorable, not to speak of the deaths which occur on every side… Forlorn though as this situation is, the climax is not yet reached. That comes when, for the space of two or three days, all on board, the sick and dying, as well as those in health, are tossed mercilessly to and fro, and rolled about on top of one another, the storm tossed vessel seeming each moment as if in the next, it would be engulfed by the angry, roaring waves… Even those who escape sickness sometimes grow so bitterly impatient and cruel, that they curse themselves and the day of their birth, and then in wild despair commence to kill those around them. Want and sickness go hand in hand, and lead to trickery and deception of every kind… The wailing and lamentations continue day and night, and as one body after another is committed to a watery grave, those who induced their unfortunate companions to leave their old home in search of a new one are drawn to the verge of despair.

The sufferings of the poor women who are pregnant can scarcely be imagined. They barely live through the voyage and many a mother and her tiny babe is thrown into the water almost ere life is extinct. During a severe storm on our vessel one poor creature, who owing to the trying circumstances, was unable to give birth to her child, was shoved through an opening in the ship and allowed to drop into the water, because it was not convenient to attend her…

Food is so filthy… that the very sight of it is loathsome. Moreover the drinking water is so black, thick

They 'emigrated to this place with the promise of a populous city, instead they found nothing but a wilderness'. The Meeting House at Waldoboro, Maine built 1772; rebuilt 1792.

and full of worms that it makes one shudder to look at it, and even those suffering the torture of thirst frequently find it almost impossible to swallow it.

It was said of one boatload who had disembarked in Boston in 1730 that 'no dying Criminals look more piteously'. But improvements to passage conditions were said to be considerable when the ships were 'purified' twice a day with juniper berries and vinegar.

That the first swathe of settlers came to Broad Bay in Maine is thanks to an Englishman of German descent, General Samuel Waldo, a grandee merchant, politician and land speculator who had styled himself as the 'Hereditary Lord of Broad Bay'. Having amassed vast tracts of land on this eastern seaboard,

he set out to colonize them, distributing enticing terms and conditions throughout the Rhineland. On land that was 'very healthful' and with soil that was 'exceedingly fruitful', Waldo pledged to pay for houses to be built and 'to lay out for the said Palatinate emigrants... a suitable area of land for a city'. They would be able to buy an acre for a mere halfpenny. A preacher was be paid for, as well as a physician, a surveyor and a schoolmaster. Lastly Waldo obligated himself 'to provide... for the period of a year... one hundred and twenty thousand pounds of beef, twenty thousand pounds of pork, sixty thousand pounds of wheat flour, sixty thousand pounds of coarse and unbolted flour, four thousand bushels of Indian corn, four thousand bushels of salt... and further to furnish and deliver to each family... one cow and a calf, a pregnant sow'.

'These and other advantageous circumstances' it was said, would be assumed to influence 'certain Palatine and German folk to emigrate to such a fruitful country… which belongs to such a powerful and gracious Lord.'

The first immigrants to arrive in the New World were to have their spirits somewhat bogusly buoyed by a lavish reception, held in their honour, at Marblehead. Whatever horrors they had endured on the voyage, their fervour for the frontier must have been encouraged by this welcome; even Waldo himself was there with his daughters, to cheer them on their luckless way.

When the settlers finally arrived at the site on the Medomak River in late October, it was to see all their dreams turned to dust, for there was nothing, nothing but 'a waste Wilderness' with 'few Necessaries and not one Accommodation of Life'. Nor were there any buildings in which to shelter from 'the Injuries of the weather at the most inclement season of the year… the Winter'. Amid interminable forests, the wretched settlers were straightway reduced to 'the utmost penury and want'.

The ministers in charge of the settlers, the Reverend Doctors Kast and Kurst, drew up an impassioned petition on this 'deplorable case', a petition that, in Waldo's defence, may well have been unreliable. Both men had axes to grind: neither had been paid by Waldo; Kast was owed the sinful wages of a recruiting officer, and he was later to abandon the immigrants – leaving Waldoboro 'a flock without a shepherd'. Kurst was said to be 'a man of even coarser caliber' who swindled his way through the Colonies – 'cutting a goodly number of dirty capers'.

The petition accused General Waldo of causing 'uncommon hardships' and of him having 'failed in every part of his contract'. But history was to partly exonerate the Hereditary Lord of Broad Bay. A combination of unfortunate circumstances contrived against the settlers. They had arrived many months later than they should have, at the onset of winter rather than spring, and Waldo had in fact provided them with some food and tools, although no shelter.

Surrounded by unending forests and soon to be engulfed by snow, the settlers tried to establish themselves on the barren banks of the Medomak – their artery to the outside world, so soon to be stuck solid with ice. The Germans' lot was indeed a desolate one. They had no contact with a living soul for miles around. Their firearms were few, so they were unable to feast on the living larder of deer, bear, hogs, moose and game. 'Life' it was said 'was an affair to cause the stoutest heart to quail.'

To add alarming insult to their already unendurable injuries, within months of their arrival the settlers were flung into the fray of the French and the Indians fighting against the British, with the local St Francis tribe most unjustly on their trail 'smarting under great wrongs and lusting after a great revenge'. Having no help to turn to, save some English fellow settlers eight miles away, the immigrants were at the mercy of the 'Tigers of the North' as the local tribe were called. 'Woe it was to those who could not understand their subtle and savage tactics', with the Indians suddenly and silently appearing from the snow-clad forests. Such was the seriousness of the threats to do 'mischief', that in 1743 companies of 'snow-shoe men' were assembled by Governor Belcher in Boston. The companies, comprising fifty men, each with 'a good gun… a hatchet and an extra pair of shoes or Moggasons to travel thro the snow', scouted around the settlements in search of marauding tribes.

Despite these defences, the Germans of Waldoboro were to become embroiled in two wars with the Indians, as well as, of course, in the War of Independence. On arrival, many of the new waves of immigrants were immediately plunged into battle, fighting for a country that was not yet theirs, indeed was not yet born.

The Germans of Broad Bay were described as 'the

very flower of German peasantry… sturdy of frame and strong of muscle… accustomed by the tradition of centuries to the hard life of toil and little in the way of comfort and earthly possessions'. Such was the fortitude that forged Waldoboro into being. By 1760 one settler was proud to claim 'I have in rich measure what I need, it flows into my house', although there was a contemporaneous account of piteous poverty, with families of between eight and twelve children, each with only a shirt to wear in the winter. The soil was poor and their tools were meagre, and as there initially were no ploughs, every inch of every sod had to be hoed by hand. Typhoid and smallpox had both struck at the settlers. In 1849 the lands were invaded by so many millions of grasshoppers that Waldoboro was almost laid to waste – the only way to destroy them being to catch one by hand and squeeze it to death. Parson Smith of nearby Falmouth reckoned that his poultry were doing useful service by eating at least ten thousand a day!

But in these bleak times, there was a lone and curious luxury. Despite their painfully scrimping circumstances, it was standard practice for every family to own a peacock, which served no purpose other than to add colour and brilliance to their otherwise dim and colourless lives.

The church was the cornerstone of the German congregation – the very structure of their spiritual as well as social lives, with baptisms, weddings and funerals being among the few ordered occasions for gathering together. Feasts that followed the ceremonies would be 'bountiful'. Weddings would always last for a least three days and often as long as a week. All of them would be based in this beauty of a building that would do aesthetic honour to Freiberg or Assisi.

The immigrants were preached to from the first, initially in the groves or cabins by the Medomak River. They built their first church in 1743, and in 1764 they built another by the river, with 'pews… of logs, hewn something like the old horse blocks'.

The pulpit was the 'ornament of the house… ingeniously contrived… semi circular; the front of plaited work and gracefully centered to a point below… the windows… made of sheepskin'.

Their preacher was a Dr Schaeffer, who, like our old friends Kast and Kurst, was an unscrupulous poseur to the priesthood. He was a rogue and a charlatan, 'an ignoramus and a quack' and an adulterer to boot, who cruelly capitalized on the spiritual hunger of the settlers. Among his many crimes, when posing as a doctor – surrounded by such fantastical paraphernalia as astrological instruments, as well as bottled snakes and skeletons – he would insist on regular inspections of urine, as well as bloodletting, with families being forced to pay him a week's wages for the service.

Under Schaeffer, Waldoboro was once again without spiritual guidance, with a congregation seen as 'destitute of the Ministry of the Gospel… scattered and fainting for the want of spiritual pasture'. And so it was that the Reformed Lutherans were born, those who, as well as having doctrinal differences with the old church, had been desperate to escape from the scoundrel Schaeffer, and the 'dire and destitute' spiritual state of the place.

In 1772, the Reformed Lutherans built a new church by the river, but as the traffic turned to the road, so its site was to be changed, with the settlers hauling the self-same beauty of a building that is there today, plank by plank, across the frozen Medomak River in the winter of 1792 – despite the impassioned objections of the early immigrants, with one old-timer, a Major Reiser, dragging off essential timbers at the dead of night and hiding them in the woods.

Walk into the old Meeting House in twenty-first-century America and you find yourself simply and straightway in eighteenth-century Rhineland – so perfect and complete is the illusion. Soothed by its simple beauty, intoxicated by its aroma of age, preened with the patina of its years, the spell is set.

Here then was the settlers' haven, where the preacher was 'the shield and buckler against the terror by night and the destruction that laid waste at noonday'. Such was their continuing poverty that for years shoes were a luxury worn only in winter. In summer, they would be worn only on such special occasions as Sunday worship, and even then, would be carried until the church was in sight, then taken off again after the service, once the building had disappeared from view. All the settlers dressed in linsey-woolsey, a material that they made from flax and the woof of wool, worn 'until fit for nothing but rags'.

The first baby born in the settlement had been Conrad Heyer. Extraordinarily, it is his photograph – or rather ambrotype – that stares forth from the old Meeting House walls, taken when he was 103-years old. His father died of exposure shortly before he was born, but Conrad would live through 106 years of the evolution of Waldoboro – from its earliest days, on through the town's growing prosperity based on wool, shipbuilding and lumber, when it was considered 'second to Boston in freight trade up and down the coast'. He saw the Colonial days of the New World and he fought under George Washington in the Revolutionary War. He lived through two Indian wars, as well as the War of 1812, and he was to die in 1856, within earshot of the rumblings of the Civil War, having survived under fifteen presidents. A lifelong Lutheran he sang for over seventy-five years in the Meeting House (both before and after it was moved across the river) and he could still read without spectacles when he was 100 years old. His stern visage gives truth to the claim that 'he possessed a physical constitution like that of seasoned oak'.

Many such testaments to Waldoboro's past lie in the Meeting House: a cupboard full of bibles,

The simple beauty of the Meeting House.

hymnals and sermons date from the 1730s. Beside a card inscribed 'Two-hundred-year-old Relics' there are huge hand-hewn nails used in the building of the first church across the river in 1772 and then reused here, in its rebuilding, twenty years later. A lone gravestone was brought from the earlier church, to stand forever sheltered in a box pew: 'To John Martin Gross… who passed out of time in 1768… being 90 years'. He had lived through the hardest years of hunger, poverty and Indian warfare, but saw peace in the settlement before he died.

In the cemetery an obelisk records the unhappy lot of the original settlers: 'Who emigrated to this place with the promise and expectation of finding a populous city, instead of which, they found nothing but a wilderness.' Besides are many hundreds of eighteenth- and nineteenth-century gravestones, all as white and bright as the day they first stood on the greensward.

A lone descendant of the original immigrants, Bill Little, has recently been paid to single-handedly restore each and every one. And so the Waldboro settlers are lauded and loved to this day, alongside a building which would stir nostalgia into hearts in the Old World, let alone in the New.

CONRAD HEYER
Born April 10th 1749
Died February 19th 1856
Aged 106 Years, 10 Months, 9 Ds.

A colony emigrated to this place
from Germany and landed here
November 1748
Conrad Heyer was the first child
born of European parents in
Waldoboro. - He served in the
Revolutionary war three years

MARBLEHEAD

'Marblehead… that fought so early and so freely bled.' So lamented the great French general, the Marquis de Lafayette, after hearing of the suffering inflicted on the beautiful town of Marblehead, then an outpost of England, during the War of Independence. In the eighteenth century the British lion had taunted, only to have had its tail most vehemently twisted by the people of Marblehead.

The town is one of the oldest in America. It was settled only nine years after the landing of the Pilgrim Fathers, and was established as a fishing port in 1629. Thereafter it was to flourish – with the blessing of King James II, who declared fishing to be 'an honest trade… 'twas the apostles own calling'. Such was the quantity of sea bass off its shores that in 1636 John Morton wrote that 'it seemed one might goe over their backs dri-shod'. By 1649 Marblehead was considered 'the greatest towne for fishing in New England', and by the eighteenth century it was one of the richest seafaring networks in the country, beating Boston into second place.

From Marblehead's society of interdependent seamen, shore men and middlemen, there rose to the surface a new merchant oligarchy – the 'codfish aristocracy' – who, for the most part being of English descent, took as their model the grandees of the Old World. One such magnifico was Jeremiah Lee, who, in 1768, built a splendid mansion to match his new-found eminence.

It is with a pierce of pleasure that you suddenly spot the house – sheer and sharp and seemingly of stone – rising up most unexpectedly amidst the clapboard Colonial dwellings. Although having all the appearance of grey ashlar, it is in fact built entirely of wooden boards, cut up and coated with a mixture of grey paint and sand, so as to resemble granite – an imitation of English cut stone emulating the monumentality of a mansion from the motherland.

The handsome exterior of Jeremiah Lee Mansion is merely a whisper, however, when compared to the deafening roar of old England that confronts you when you cross its threshold. Before you is a hall and stairway of vast and handsome proportions, covered with soaring stretches of hand-painted scenic wallpapers dating from 1768. In exquisite imitation of frescoes and painted panels of romantic ruins and rustic scenes, surrounded by *trompe l'oeil* frames of swirling rococo plasterwork, it strives – with admirable success – to affect the full-whack wonder of such decoration in the stately piles and palaces of Europe. Not only that, but by being painted in soothing shades of grey – *en grisaille* – it would have given the double delight of satisfying the taste for engravings and prints that was so fashionable at the time. The scenes decorating these walls were mostly taken from engravings by Pannini and Vernet; panels of trophies, again simulating plasterwork, are composed of clusters of armour, masonic emblems, architectural symbols, as well as fishing tackle and gardening tools. Such were the fanciful fads pandered to by the eighteenth-century paper stainers.

Each panel was first hand-painted in tempera – watercolour with egg-based binder – having been designed specifically, and with the utmost delicacy,

Opposite: *Jeremiah Lee Mansion. Hand-painted English scenic wallpapers dating from 1768, the like of which no longer survives in its entirety anywhere in the world.*

for these walls, with precise instructions as to where they should be hung written on the back. Many too have English excise tax stamps and the curvaceously entwined 'GR' for 'George Rex' beneath a crown. These exquisite papers were, for the most part, made from layers of old linen rags in London in the eighteenth century. Never has there been a more elegant example of making a silk purse out of a sow's ear.

The panels enhance a fine and exotically-rooted stairway; its carved balusters and dado are made from Santo Domingan mahogany, thought to have been brought back on one of Jeremiah Lee's many trading vessels. Lee, the creator of this sanctum of English swelldom at Marblehead, stands proud over the landing, painted by John Singleton Copley in 1769. Before the War of Independence, Copley lived in London, where his son grew up to become Lord Lyndhurst – the Boston-born Lord Chancellor of England.

Despite being a fourth-generation American, Jeremiah Lee embodied the very essence of the Old World in his choice of architecture, manners and dress. (In contrast, for example, to George Washington, who developed a new Colonial style.) Lee looks a mightily impressive fellow, in terms of wealth, girth and nose, he cuts as English a dash, as ever there was. With his perfumed peruke, his silk stockings, his velvet coat and a waistcoat that appears bejewelled with braid, he strikes an air of splendour by 'making a leg' – foot forward in a grandee stance. A contemporary manual on etiquette would have advised him so: 'Rise up, put off thy Hatt, extend thy Hand, make a leg.' His wig was but one of the colourful variety worn by swells, soldiers and sailors alike. There were many styles to chose from including the Brigadier, the Foxtail, the Giddy Feather Top and the Grecian Fly – made from the hair of either goats, horses or humans. Thus, proudly did Lee pose for posterity – an English grandee to the roots of his peruke.

Nevertheless, when the cry went up for Liberty! in the late 1770s, it was Lee alone out of all the affluent men of Marblehead, who flung himself full-bloodedly into the fray. Whilst his fellow grandees were loyal to the Crown – wining, dining and conniving with the British – Lee was unstinting in his support of the rebels. He gave both his mind and his money to the Revolutionary cause. In all outward appearances still the great British nobleman, yet inwardly ever ready to light the fuse of the anti-colonial cannon – what a cauldron of conflicting passions must have been boiling in that fulsome breast, at this, the great turning point in American history.

Revolutionary rumblings had been reverberating through Marblehead from as early as 1732, when iniquitous demands were made on local seamen to pay 6d a month to support the Royal Hospital in Greenwich, London. When England imposed the Stamp Act on 1 November 1765, thereby charging a tax on every piece of paper used, the town took on a sombre mood. Bells tolled, flags were hung at half-mast and Marbleheaders gathered to mutiny. 'Presses groaned, pulpits thundered… Crown officials have everywhere trembled', wrote the politician John Adams. In England, William Pitt was one of the few who spoke up in defence of the Marbleheaders, inspiring one grateful commentator to write: 'I thank thee, Pitt, for all thy glorious strife/ Against the foes of LIBERTY and life.'

Such was Marblehead's appreciation of Pitt's support that they named a vessel after him. The *Pitt Packet* had a minor but grisly role in the impending conflict, when, in 1769, it was harassed by the British who attempted to press its seamen into serving under the King. The limeys shot at the crew, only to have the favour returned – with the harpooning of an English lieutenant. The seamen were tried and released, but were later executed by a phalanx of English field gunners outside the Boston Court House.

Marbleheaders continued to fight long and hard

against the 'train of abuses and usurpations' inflicted by the Crown. So steadfastly did they stand their ground that the great English-born radical, Thomas Paine, declared that by their example, they could change the face of the nation. In the struggle, Lee, 'the worthy patriot who does not fully show himself when the state is secure and tranquil, but shines illustriously in the midst of attacks and dangers', positively *gleamed*, regularly sallying forth from his stately pile with hogshead marked 'Fish' filled with powder and guns to stockpile the local powder house. The building still stands today, circular and brick with an enchanting onion-domed slate roof.

Lee was not to live to see his endeavours rewarded however. On the night before the firing of the first shot of the American Revolution – 'the shot heard round the world' at Lexington – Lee was to catch a chill that would kill him. He had gone to Menotomy, Massachusetts, for a clandestine meeting with Samuel Adams and John Hancock (both future signatories of the Declaration of Independence). Lee and fellow Marbleheaders, Azor Orne and Elbridge Gerry (also future signatories), were warned that British soldiers were nearby 'out on some evil design'. Lee and his men were forced to hide in a cornfield and, clad only in their nightshirts, they shivered that last pre-war night away. Lee caught pneumonia and died three weeks later on 10 May.

Lee enjoyed the magnificence of his mansion for only six years; his widow and two of their six children were to live on there, with the war ravaging both their fortune and the town.

A year before the war's outbreak, George Washington had felt sufficiently moved to send money to Marblehead, for 'the relief of the distressed sad wives and children of the soldiers…' A year after its conclusion, the Maquis de Lafayette, when given a hero's reception at Marblehead, was told that it was 'misfortune not a fault' that had reduced the town to such a sorry state. 'May your losses be a hundred fold repaired by the blessings of peace' was the general's

response at a grand ball held in his honour at the Lee Mansion. How sweetly ironic must have been the scene in this self-consciously English house with the great Frenchman surrounded by so many French scenes, elegantly underlining that country's help and influence during the American Revolution. (One of the walls where the reception was held had a view of Mont Ferrat, after an engraving by Vernet, after le Vau, which hangs at the Bibliotheque Nationale in Paris.) How clearly too, it mirrored the mixed loyalties of the late-lamented Jeremiah Lee himself.

George Washington also graced these rooms, when entertained by Lee's widow in 1791. She had decorated the house with a silhouette of the American eagle at every window, all of them flying proud against flickering candles. What a splendidly-symbolic huzzah for this most English of buildings – hailing its American future.

Stand on the Old Burial Ground, high on a hill above the roofs of Marblehead, and you sense the history of the place. Beneath your feet lie the bodies of over 600 of the town's Revolutionary heroes and before you still stand the houses in which they lived. Here too, the town's domestic past is richly in evidence with a quantity of fine dark blue, grey slate and stone seventeenth-century gravestones, many of them with the winged death's head, crossbones and the hourglass –'death moves in when time runs out'. Here lie the bodies of those such as Wilmot Redd, the wife of a Marblehead fisherman, executed for witchcraft after the Salem trials of 1692 and 'Marblehead's "Black Joe". A Revolutionary Soldier. A Respected Citizen. Born 1750' and 'Mrs Miriam Grose… Decd in the 81st year of her age & left 180 children, grandchildren and great grandchildren'.

Marblehead's prosperity was not to last. The town never fully recovered from the ravages of the Revolutionary War. In 1848 its fishing industry was damaged beyond repair when most of the fleet – eleven vessels and sixty-five mariners – was lost in a hurricane off the coast of Newfoundland. In the

long-term, however, these sad fates were to be Marblehead's architectural fortune. The town has never been re-planned or rebuilt; hundreds of pre-Revolutionary buildings survive, standing on either side of steep and narrow, winding streets.

Whereas Marblehead is a notable survival, the existence of Jeremiah Lee's house is nothing short of a miracle. The building was a bank for over a hundred years – a bank of either modest means or finely-tuned architectural appreciation, since the building was to suffer none of the spoliations of plumbing, heating and electrification. The house was alarmingly auctioned off in 1909 to a man who had schemes to strip it bare but the townspeople rallied asking for a 'dime, a nimble quarter or quick dollar' and so it was saved.

Since then it has been owned by the Marblehead Historical Society, who from the first have shown great foresight in simply arresting the house's decay, and then leaving it alone. As has been written of the town, so the same may be said of Jeremiah Lee's Mansion: it has 'more of the crust of antiquity… than any place of its years in America'.

The Lee Mansion
1768

Opposite: *Jeremiah Lee's writing desk and the exquisite wallpaper made in London from linen rags.*

COLUMBUS CHAPEL

There could be no more extraordinary an example of the cross-cultivation of the Old World and the New than what is to be found off Route 322 at Boalsburg, Pennsylvania. One minute you are bowling along the highway, the next – Abracadabra – you are in Christopher Columbus's family's chapel, a candlelit holiness of ecclesiastical treasures dating from the first to the eighteenth centuries. Show me a surprise greater than this and I will eat my hat – and anything else that I happen to be wearing at the time.

Paintings hang heavy in their gilded frames on dark green walls and silk shines forth from late-medieval vestments. There are waxen and robed figures of Mary and Joseph dating from 1450, and a wooden St Margaret and the Dragon from the late-fifteenth century. All this, surrounded by a quantity of seventeenth-century furniture and family relics.

How in heaven's name has this come to be in Pennsylvania? It is thanks to a nineteenth-century soldier, architect, cowboy and a collector *par excellence* named Theodore Davis Boal. In 1894 he married a descendant of Christopher Columbus, the Franco-Spanish Mathilde Lagarde, who was to inherit her family's chapel in 1908.

And so it was to be that the interior of this little building – so central to the history of America – was hauled forth from the great Columbus Castle, Llamas Del Mouro 'Flames of the Moor', in Spain, and dispatched to the United States to make their startling appearance in Pennsylvania in 1909. Having studied architecture at the École des Beaux-Arts in Paris, Theodore Boal designed a tiny ecclesiastical building of Pennsylvania limestone in which to house this terrifyingly rare treasure.

In a place of honour in the chapel sits Christopher Columbus's own *vargueno* – a handsome, richly-gilded, fall-front sea desk – which was with him when he 'discovered' America. There is also an ornamental seventeenth-century chest hoarding such alarmingly rare books as *The History of the Death of the Glorious Margolo* of 1583. Over all a reredos of the late 1500s looms large, adorned with paintings of St Francis of Assisi and St Jerome accompanied by a monkey-like lion. Below on the altar are portraits of the Columbus family posing as saints, a fashion of the day whereby you got two pictures – one family, one religious – in one. Eighteenth-century cherubs fly on the ceiling and ornamental fifteenth-century *cartouches* adorn the walls.

Pull open some prettily painted and panelled doors – once the chapel's confessionals – and you find yourself staring at some 165,000 documents relating to the Columbus family's affairs between 1453-1902, all faded and frail and tied in string and red ribbon bundles, and with enormous contemporary labels of yellow card. The sight of their agedness makes you wince in wonder.

Most unbelievable of all though is the sight of a silver reliquary which contains pieces of the 'true Cross' – taken from the monastery of St Toribius of Liebana to Spain in 458 by St Toribius of Astorga. He was the keeper of the holy relics in Jerusalem. When the town was attacked by the Moors in the fifth century he fled to Spain where he founded a monastery in his own name. In 1817 the Bishop of Leon gave the reliquary as a holy gift to Joseph Columbus – a fellow member of the Royal Council, along with an exquisitely-written silken

The Columbus family chapel, hauled forth from the Llamas Del Mouro in Spain to Pennsylvania in 1909.

authentication, which hangs on the chapel walls. Mass is still said here every Columbus Day (9 October), overseen by a chaplain from the local Catholic fraternity, the Knights of St Columbus.

The chapel stands hard by the Boal Mansion, an architectural cabinet of curiosities in itself which, along with the little holy building, has achieved perfection with the preservation of its past. Despite having been open to the public since 1952, it is still owned, lived in and loved by the descendants of its creators. Christopher Lee, the great-grandson of Theodore Boal, is at the happy helm today. Not one centimetre of the place had been preened and polished into an soullessly inaccurate and sanitized

present. Here is no Hearst haven of the arts, nor a costumed charade 'experience'; rather, it is an entirely unassuming and unknown house, which by odd chance and circumstance has been filled with quite extraordinary objects.

The ballroom is a big surprise. Built by Theodore Boal it is heated by a charcoal stove *brassero* of *c.*1600 from the Llamas Del Mouro. Here ladies could besport themselves in front of the 'petticoat mirror', made specifically for them to see if their undergarments were in order. Handsomely tasselled and heavy with leather, Spanish bagpipes hang on the seemingly *bas-relief* wallpaper in the hall. In the parlour, the back parlour and the dining room, all the

walls are covered with *toille de jouille* of the most gentle hues. A piano that belonged to the redoubtable Dolley Madison, the first chatelaine at the White House, stands proud in the parlour. (It was here, in this Europhile house in Pennsylvania, that I learnt the origins of the word parlour: it is from the French *parler* – a room in which to talk.)

It is though, the cabinet of curiosities within this cabinet of curiosities that excites true delight. Who could not fail to be charmed by a lock of Napoleon's hair, in a magnifying-glass-topped French prisoner of war gaming box of bone and wood? It came to the family through General James de Trobriand, Mathilde Boal's uncle and one of Napoleon's top generals. His sword, with which he fought over a hundred duels, lies in the chapel. Once, when fighting as a mercenary with the Prussians he was told by a general 'You French fight for money, we Prussians fight for honour', to which he replied 'Naturally! Each man fights for what he doesn't have.'

Trobriand's pistol is here too, as well as a medal awarded to his cousin Simon Bolivar in 1821. Made of St Helena bronze, on green and red ribbons, this was *the* prototype of the *Croix de Guerre*. Cheek by jowl with this military paraphernalia is a brick from the ruins of Cape Isobella in Santo Domingo – said to be the first European settlement in the New World, founded by Columbus in 1493.

Stirringly here also are the accoutrements of war brought back from the First World War by Theodore Boal's son, Pierre: the helmet he wore in the French Heavy Cavalry in 1915, as well as his portrait as a member of the Lafayette Flying Corps in 1916. Pierre was offered all the lustre of the lands, properties and titles of the Columbus family – on condition of course that he became a Spanish citizen. He chose instead to remain an American.

Spanish bagpipes hang on the seemingly bas-relief *wallpaper in the hall of Boal Mansion.*

Then there is the treat of seeing such Americana as the so-called 'Beecher's Bibles' – the carbines used by John Brown in his revolt at Harper's Ferry, Boston in 1859 (at the start of the Civil War), secretly sent by Henry Ward Beecher and other abolitionists in crates marked 'Bibles'.

In 1916 Theodore Boal was posted with General Pershing and the US National Guard to apprehend the *bandido*, Francisco 'Pancho' Villa, after he and his men had raided the border town of, appropriately, Columbus in New Mexico. Although they failed to catch him, Theodore returned triumphant with Pancho's hat and epaulettes, which are still at Boal Mansion today. During that same jaunt, it was Theodore's idea of attaching machine guns to trucks

that foreshadowed the first armoured units in the US Army.

Theodore Davis Boal died in 1938, claiming to have 'had the honour of inheriting three fortunes and the pleasure of spending them'. He left a considerable legacy in the area: as well as beautifying the house and the chapel, he founded innumerable businesses and was responsible too, for a great shrine to the US Army's 28th Division across the highway.

He had been named after his uncle, Theodore Davis, who was largely responsible for Howard Carter and Lord Carnarvon's discovery of Tutankhamen's tomb. Davis had held the concession for all archaeological digs in the Valley of the Kings from 1902-12, and had found a cache of ancient oddments. He gave them to the Metropolitan Museum in New York, where they were to languish for nine years. It was only in 1921 that they were studied and found out to be the cast-offs from the farewell feast in Tutankamen's tomb, (although accounts vary that it was King Tut's grandmother's and grandfather's tomb). Thus it was established that the long-searched-for treasures *were* in the Valley of the Kings, and so Lord Carnarvon renewed his concession for a final year. Theodore Davis's portrait hangs in the house, as do portraits of most of the players in its cosmopolitan history.

The foundations of the Boal Mansion go back to the late 1700s, when David Boal, having just arrived from Ireland, found himself straightway commanding a company in the War of Independence 1775-83. Pioneering for cheap land, he built himself a stone cabin – on the edge of a wilderness, as this then was. It still stands as the kitchen of the Boal Mansion today. His son meanwhile, was warring in the Irish rebellion of 1798 and, forced to flee, booked a passage for his wife and children, and accompanied them onto the boat, hidden in a blanket chest – that chest too is in the front hall in Pennsylvania.

Nearby is the pretty-as-can-be, white clapboard small town of Boalsburg – named after the second David Boal – who, like his family before him was a local benefactor, playing a large part in the prosperity of the area. His son, George, laid the foundations for Penn State University and thereafter successive generations of Boals left firm footprints on the land. The fourth generation made money out West, while the fifth, Theodore, spent the lot! But how we can all revel in that profligacy today.

So next time you are tempted to turn off the American highway be prepared to be boiled in a cauldron of European fare!

Opposite: *Curiosities at Boal Mansion.*

SABBATHDAY LAKE

I can still sense the strangeness of driving for the first time towards Sabbathday Lake in New Gloucester, Maine – home of the last-surviving Shakers in America. It is the feeling that – despite having just guzzled a ham sandwich at a nearby gas station – you are being beckoned ever further back in time. It is no ordinary sensation, even with the evidence of rural America before you, to know that within minutes you will find yourself among people whose beliefs and way of life date back to mid-eighteenth-century England.

The Shakers are thought to have originated in France in 1689, when the Camisards (named after the robes that they wore), developed a faith that embraced simplicity, whilst denouncing depravity, and manifested itself literally by shaking and trembling when moved by the spirit. Exiled from France in 1706 for the extreme enthusiasm of their beliefs, they came to England where they gathered together an ever more rhapsodic following. In 1747 an English society, based on their doctrine, was founded in Manchester by John and Jane Wardley, one-time Quakers from Bolton. With their new-found 'singing and dancing, shaking and shouting, speaking with new tongues, and with all those various gifts of the Holy Spirit known in the Primitive Church', they became mockingly known as the 'Shaking Quakers'. And so the Shakers were born.

That they went to America was thanks to Ann Lee, daughter of a blacksmith of Toad Lane in Manchester. A 'grave and solemn' girl, a cutter of hatter's fur, as well as a cotton mill hand, she could neither read nor write, but, according to several scholar clergymen, when 'feeling the power of God'

she could speak fluently in seventy-two tongues. 'Strongly impressed with a sense of the deep depravity of human nature, and of the odiousness of sin', she became an ecstatic follower and eventually 'Mother' of the Shaker movement, writing that her sufferings had been so great 'that my flesh consumed upon my bones, bloody sweat pressed through the pores of my skin, and I became as helpless as an infant. And when I was brought through, and born into the spiritual kingdom, I was like an infant just born into the natural world'. So loud were her lamentations, 'labouring and crying to God… against the fleshy lusts which war against the soul', that it was because of Ann Lee that celibacy became part of the Shaker doctrine.

Shaker zeal knew no bounds and many an unholy scene was created as they interrupted church services to denounce both clergy and congregation. They, in turn, were persecuted, sometimes to the point of death. Ann Lee was set upon and clubbed and stoned by mobs in Manchester. She was imprisoned for her faith many times – once for fourteen days, in a stone cell in which she could neither stand up or lie down. Sent there to starve, legend has it that she was secretly fed on wine and water through a tobacco pipe – its stem poked through a crack in the wall by James Whittaker, who was to go with her and her brother to the New World in 1774, as one of the founding fathers of the Shaker movement.

Despite being described by one observer as mild, gentle and forbearing, the evidence of his own pen suggests otherwise. Whittaker was the fiercest of zealots, whipping the world free of all wickedness. In a letter of vitriolic farewell to his parents in

England he declared with his 'whole heart… a final close between you and me thro' time and eternity'. He denounced their 'fleshy lives and… fleshy generation… and your pleading the command of God to increase and multiply… defiling yourselves with effeminate desires… therefore you are but a stink in my nostrils'.

As leader of the sect in America, James Whittaker withheld none of his wrath. The idleness of the newly-converted farmers was 'abominable in the sight of God', while the women who lived with him were as 'idle hatchers of Cockatrice eggs and breeders of Lust and abominable filthiness'. One Reuben Rathbun was to get his revenge in 1799, however, accusing Whittaker of 'whoredom' and his fellow founders of blasphemous language – 'there was never a sailor that stepped off the sea that exceeded them'.

Many and holy, in fact, are the literary legacies left by the Shakers. They called themselves the Millennial Church or the 'United Society of Believers in Christ's Second Coming' and Ann Lee was now seen as the 'temple' in which Christ would 'appear'. She had had a vision of America: 'I saw a large tree, every leaf of which shone with such brightness as made it appear like a burning torch, representing the Church of Christ, which will yet be established in this land.' It was said that her words were delivered with such 'mighty spiritual power, accompanied with so heart-searching and soul-quickening a spirit, that it seemed to penetrate every secret of the heart'.

Aged only twenty-three, Ann Lee had left Manchester for the New World with eight followers. After two years of often violent struggle, the seeds of Shakerism had been successfully sown, first in New York State, then throughout America – from New Hampshire to Florida, from Pennsylvania to Kentucky – Shakers villages were built throughout the land.

Knowing all this as you near Sabbathday Lake gives a sense of utmost awe to be about to see where the last eight surviving Shakers, live, work and worship in the buildings that have stood there since the 1790s. Nor is it only the sense of the singularity of meeting them, but also the unsuitability of them meeting me, along with thirty pieces of ferocious camera equipment, flashing and crashing into their lives. Suddenly I was there, surrounded by some twenty, white clapboard buildings

The Meeting House – still in daily use – most starkly symbolizes the simplicity of Shakerism. It was raised on 14 June 1794. The exterior has all the clean clapboard of the Shaker style, with green shutters shading the windows. Two enormous chimneys – serving the famed Shaker stoves – were each made from 10,000 bricks, hand-hewn by the brethren. Within, the serene lines of the building quite streak into your soul. It is a room that has not been retouched since the day that it was built, with such fervent faith, over 200 years ago.

For sheer delight I write a roll call of names of those involved in the founding of the Shaker Movement in America: Hezekiah Hammond was imprisoned in 1780, for being 'unfriendly to the patriotic cause'. Then there was Eliphalet Slosson, who wrote of Ann Lee's 'prophecies, visions and revelations', and to whom she prophesized that the Shakers would set root 'in the South West', which they later did – in Kentucky, when Elisha Thomas founded Pleasant Hill in 1806. Among the first to establish Sabbathday Lake, were Ephraim and Barnabas Briggs, Josiah Holmes and the followers Nathan Farrington and his daughter Mehetabel. Abel Allen recorded the progress of the brethren in the New World, as did Amos Rathbun; other 'brothers' included Zeruah Clairk, Abijah Wooster, Isaac Cranch, Cornelius Thayer, Elizur Goodrich, Eleazar Rand, Issachar Bates, Ebenezer Cooly, Elijah Myrick, Shadrach Ireland and Freegift Wells – what names to conjure with, as they spread their message throughout the land.

But it was not only their message that spread, but

Sabbathday Lake Shaker Meeting House (1794).

also their methods. With the motto 'Put your hands to work and your hearts to God' the Shakers literally wove much of the very fabric of America, running textile mills as well as creating a basket industry producing over 70,000 baskets by 1900, it is an industry that still flourishes today. Far from fleeing from the world in holy righteousness, the utilitarian-minded Shakers were also responsible for oiling the wheels of much of modernizing life. The circular saw was a Shaker invention, as were hand-cut nails, the flat broom and metal pen nibs. They produced the first screw propeller, the first automatic spring, a sash balance that worked without strings or pulleys, and they built the first municipal water system in

Kentucky, in 1833. All this without a single patent applied for. This, they decreed, would be 'hinding the giver of the gift'. Most remarkable of all – almost too weird to write – is that the Shakers invented the first washing machine, winning the gold medal at the Centennial Exposition in 1876. One such is still doing sterling service at Sabbathday Lake today: wooden agitators attached to a metal frame stir great water-filled granite basins of some eight feet long.

From the start, the Shakers triumphed in agriculture. In the 1790s, they were the first to produce packet seeds. Shaker peddlers would plod round the states with a horse and a cart, touting the 'papers'. Dried herbs and flowers – wormwood, spikenard, catnip, bonset, mandrake, horehound and skunk cabbage – were also produced, hand over fist, in the 'Shaker way' from 1799. Sabbathday Lake still does a brisk trade in herbs today. The Shakers owned the largest herd of Durham Shorthorn cattle in America, having bought a champion bull in England – the breed are still kept at Pleasant Hill. So too are flocks of the Border Leicester sheep, as well as the Leicester Longwoods – otherwise known as 'Bakewells' – first bred by Robert Bakewell in Derbyshire in the eighteenth century, brought over from England to Kentucky before the Civil War. In Maine they still sell skeins of wool, in twenty-five colours, 'Spun from the fleece of Sabbathday Lake's own hearty flock'. In many other ways besides they have refused to withdraw from the world: they run an extensive library, a book shop, a store, as well as a museum of furniture, inventions, tin ware and 'fancy goods'.

Despite flourishing in America for a good hundred years, the Shaker community began to decline by the end of the 1800s, their numbers falling from six thousand to a mere handful. But now, at the start of the new millennium, their has been a resurgence of interest in this millenarian sect, the original 'French Millennial Prophets'. To search the internet alone is to be swept into a little tornado of time. With a click of the mouse you will find the site: 'Shaker Manuscripts On Line' containing such as 'A Holy, Sacred and Divine Roll and Book – from the Lord God of Heaven to the Inhabitants of Earth, via Philomeon Stewart 1842.' Or what about the 700-page 'Divine Book of Holy and Eternal Wisdom – Revealing The Word Of God Out Of Whose Mouth Goeth The Sharp Sword, via Paulina Bates, Instrument 1841'?

Not only has this renewed interest been in their religion. Since the 1960s there has been, of course, an ever-growing admiration for Shaker art, architecture and most particularly, their craftsmanship in the form of wooden furniture and their by-now-

The Sabbathday Lake Shakers. Sitting, left to right: Minnie Greene, R. Mildred Barker, Marie Burgess, Frances A. Carr. Standing: Elsie A. McCool, Theodore E. Johnson, Wayne Smith, Arnold Hadd. (Photograph by Ann Chwatsky; courtesy Ann Chwatsky, Rockville Centre, New York.)

world-famous oval wooden boxes. Shaker settlements too, have been restored throughout America and are now preciously preserved along with exhibitions and examples of the Shaker way of life. In 1966 Thomas Merton, one of America's most famous theologians and mystics, wrote that 'The peculiar grace of a Shaker chair is due to the fact that it was made by someone capable of believing that an angel might come and sit in it.' Today, that angel might well be Oprah Winfrey, who recently paid $220,000 for a piece of Shaker furniture. Such is the dichotomy of the Shaker legacy.

Sabbathday Lake has remained faithful to the original beliefs and practices of the Shaker brethren. In the 1980s the settlement's leader, Sister Mildred Baker, stated that she almost expected 'to be remembered as a chair or a table', despite her determination to 'emphasize the greater importance of our spiritual work which we feel has served as the little "leaven that leaveneth the whole lump".'

After 206 years, shaking has given way to the motions of bowing, clapping and stomping. Regular Sunday meetings are held, and so too are regular fast days. Shaker hymns are still sung and the sense of holiness at the Meeting House is palpable. With their aim to 'Fill a worthy place, however humble; fill it well, so as to honour God and bless the world', the Shakers of Sabbathday Lake have most stirringly succeeded.

Most suitably, it has taken an Englishman, the author John Fowles, to sum up the singular magic of the Shakers:

Something in Shaker thought and theology (not least in its holding that a Holy Trinity that has no female component cannot be holy), in its strange rituals and marvellously inventive practical life, in its richly metaphorical language and imaginative use of dancing and music, has always seemed to me to adumbrate the relation of fiction to reality.

RUGBY, TENNESSEE

High on the Cumberland Plateau in Tennessee, surrounded by mile upon mile of thick forests which suddenly split open to spellbindingly-distant views, there is a corner of a foreign field that is forever England – the very distillation of nineteenth-century English culture. The creator of this 'English Eden', as he called it, was Thomas Hughes, author of *Tom Brown's Schooldays* – the autobiographical novel of his days at Rugby School in England. In 1880 he created his own Rugby in Tennessee.

Hughes was a Queen's Counsel, a liberal statesman, a philanthropist and a social reformer, who founded the first Working Men's College in London (where he taught boxing) and who helped to set up the first trade unions and working men's co-operatives in England. But it was here, in the wilderness of the New World, that Hughes set out to create a utopian version of the English Rugby, where the younger sons of the English 'squirearchy', as well as those of the ever-increasing professional classes – the 'Will Wimbles', as he called them – could learn a decent trade.

In the Old World, where primogeniture predominated, boys brought up as swells and stultified by snobbery had but few 'socially acceptable' professions to choose from. They were expected to 'starve like Gentlemen, rather than thrive in a profession that was beneath them'. As prosperity had increased in nineteenth-century Britain, so too had this problem, with the newly-rich following the lead of the grandees. Ever more public schools were being established with all of them instilling notions of superiority in their students. 'Go through any English county', wrote the impassioned Hughes 'and you will scarcely find a family which does not own one or more cadets, of fair average abilities, good character… and strong bodies, who are entirely at a loose end, not knowing what in the world to turn their hands to… first rate human material going hopelessly to waste… drifting into weary colourless middle age'.

Hughes despaired of the British incapacity for shedding tradition, or of 'something deeper – some law underlying and governing the results of training of a particular kind… at this time and in our country it is plain that the spirit of our highest culture and the spirit of our trade do not go together.' For years he determined to fight the life-withering legacy of the old school, and where better to start afresh than in the New World? Here was to be a 'New Centre of Human Life', a 'co-operative class free society', where these 'second sons – this vast overplus of might', along with farmers and artisans, teachers and tradesmen, could work 'shoulder to shoulder, for the good of all', cultivating the land as well as the mind, with 'temperance and high Christian principles'.

Having spoken up against slavery 'by tongue and by pen' as a Union sympathizer during the Civil War, Hughes was glad to be able to help heal the breach by building on some of the 'waste places' of the southern states. *The Rugby Handbook*, published in 1884, would speak enticingly of such reconciliation: 'The War Hatchet is buried and lost past all recovery… Northerners are welcomed with open arms… No-one need for a moment entertain any shot-gun policy.'

In 1878, hearing that 75,000 acres of wilderness was for sale in Tennessee, Hughes dispatched a British barrister to inspect the plateau, who lyrically reported that: 'Nature has liberally supplied this

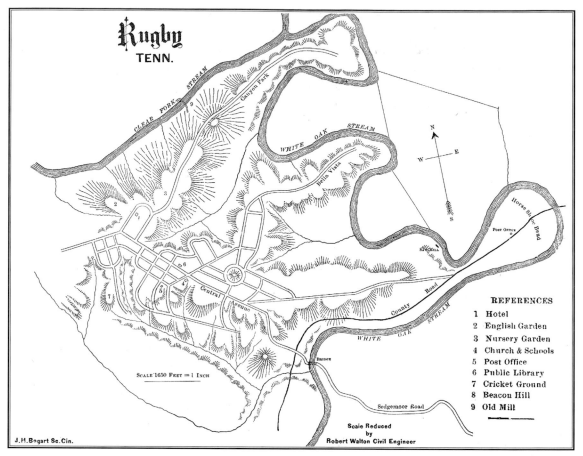

Map of Rugby, first published in the Rugby Handbook of 1884.

charming land, which only awaits the hand of intellect of man to awaken it to prodigious fertility. I rejoice to think that… your sound scheme for peopling those lovely and now lonely woodlands… will be rewarded by seeing noble results… '

Within two years these woodlands *were* peopled with a pathfinding population in an ever-growing, pretty-as-a-picture town. The houses were to be 'sightly… and good in form and proportion although' wrote Hughes 'we must act prudently and cut our coats according to our cloth'.

The cloth turned out to be handsome, but modest. Each house in Rugby has a muted ornateness and great deal of charm with 'the little rural knick-

knacks the lover of home influences is ever apt to devise'. It was said at the time, that 'few communities the size of Rugby, can show so much assistance given to nature by art'.

On 5 October 1880, the town was officially opened with Hughes at the helm. Guests from the North and the South, including the Bishop of Tennessee and the Mayor of Chattanooga, were hauled up onto the plateau by mule-drawn omnibus, along the newly-built road, softened by incessant rain into what Hughes called the 'Slough of Despond'. The Bishop held a service of blessing to the bracing accompaniment of 'All people that on earth do dwell' followed by 'Jerusalem the Golden'. Hughes summed up his vision for the place:

> Our aim and our hope is to plant on these highlands
> a community of gentlemen and ladies; not that artificial
> class which goes by those grand names, both in Europe
> and here, the joint product of feudalism and wealth, but
> a society in which the humblest members who live…
> by their labour of their own hands, will be of such strain
> and culture that they will be able to meet princes at the
> gate, without embarrassment and without self-assertion,
> should any such strange persons ever present themselves
> before the gate tower of Rugby in the New World.

A Mrs Virginia French stepped in to fuel his fervour,
with a poem that she had penned for the day:

> Long years and years the wilderness in regal beauty
>   slept
> As did the enchanted Princess, in whom the bands
>   of fairies kept
> In slumber for a century, until a princely knight
> Should come and break the bondage with his glance
>   of love and light
>
> For why! The princely knight has come, so loyal
>   and so true
> With love light from the Old World as a blessing
>   to the New
>
> Here Albion's braves, and Scotia's sons, and Erin's
>   hearts of fire
> From castle court, and cottage home, and ivy-
>   mantled spire
> We hail you all, as brothers born, we bless the
>   union true
> Of this royal pair of loves—the Old World and the
>   New.

From the first there was a steadfast determination
that a library should be established in the colony. It
would speak *volumes* as to the purpose of the place:
'Heads and hands to the fore!' the settler 'will have

to lead a peasant's life during working hours' wrote
Hughes. 'At other times, when his work is done, he
will find himself in a cultivated society, within easy
reach of all the real essentials of civilisation, beginning
with a good library'.

Thus it is that in Tennessee there is as tremendous
a surprise as is to be had anywhere in the New
World. Step inside a little red-roofed, spired and grey
clapboard building – remembering all the while that
you are in the Cumberland Mountains– and you will
think you are hallucinating. Within a split second of
breathing the bracing high altitude air of America,
you find yourself inhaling the mustiness of a
nineteenth-century English lending library, untainted
since the day it was opened, and filled with some
7,000 volumes and periodicals from Victorian
England. With all the associations of such sights and
smells, you feel as if you are going magically mad.

All about you gilded bindings glint, from
Smollet's *Peregrine Pickle* to Charles Kingsley's *Sanitary
and Social Essays* (he was a close friend and ally of
Hughes). There are works by Wordsworth, Cooper,
Pope, Tennyson, Dryden, Dickens, Macaulay, Maria
Edgeworth as well as Thomas Carlyle, Coleridge and
Chaucer and a complete set of Richard Cobden's
speeches. Then there are such lesser-known volumes
as *Moonshine Fairies*, a children's book by E. H.
Knatchbull Hugessen (Lord Brayborne) from 1875
and the flamboyantly-bound *Morals and Mottoes*;
suitably shining forth is *Noble Boys* written in 1877
by William Martin, with such tempting chapters as
'A Noble Witty London Boy' and 'Our Noblest Boy
of All – The Duke of Wellington'. Copies of the
Illustrated London News from the 1880s and 1890s
stand in stacks alongside many years of *Punch* that
have been handsomely bound in red calf.

A natural humidity, with no interference by either
heating or electricity, has ensured this extraordinary
survival. All the card indexes are still in their drawers
arranged by the first librarian, Edward Bertz, between
1881-2 – a man, it was said, who was 'sensitive to

Above: *Looking into the library at Rugby on the Cumberland Plateau.*
Opposite: *'No dream is dead that leaves an afterglow...'*

grossness and vulgarity'. It was he who arranged the cataloguing and classification systems. Bertz had always said that his work was 'not for the moment only' and the whole bang lot remains to this day.

Rugby's library was considered 'more complete and extensive than is possessed by towns numbering their inhabitants by the thousands and their years of growth by the tens' (at the time that this was written Rugby was two years old and had a population of about three hundred). Its dedication ceremony on 5 October 1882 was described as 'a ritual for the belief in the survival of Rugby'. 'Why should not this beautiful country be settled by industrious people and "blossom like a rose" by "Parthians and Medes and Elamites and the dwellers of Mesopotamia" and

beyond Jordan?' intoned one of the many speakers – with accompaniment by the newly-formed Rugby Cornet Band, with a 'noise' that was 'sometimes excruciating'.

Thomas Hughes stands proud over all, in the library's reading room, in a photograph that was presented by his 'venerable' old mother, who had battled out to Tennessee in her eighty-fourth year to join her 'beloved and loving son' in his Appalachian New Jerusalem. It must have been a far far cry from her former life at Park Walk in Chelsea, London, where she had entertained such friends as Tennyson and Leslie Stephens (father of Virginia Woolf). She seemed game, though, to embrace the frontier spirit: 'As for chairs' she wrote, 'I care not a straw for

what… I sit on, nor what tables I eat off.' Neither did she care for carpets or curtains, but insisted only on 'thoroughly good beds!'

Known as 'Madame Hughes', as befitted her matriarchal role at Rugby, she died seven years to the day that the colony had opened – a 'grand old gentlewoman… she was drawn to her grave by her faithful old white horse… led by her sorrowing gardener'.

Madame Hughes's house – Uffington – stands to this day. Stored in its attic are school desks of the 1880s, used by the boys of Arnold's School, named after Dr Arnold, the famed headmaster of Rugby School in England. Thomas Hughes's house – Kingston Lisle – survives also. He lived here for two months of the year and spent the rest in England. It was here that, with wincing pleasure, I saw primroses in the garden. They had been brought from England, over a hundred years ago, and still flower annually, as do lilies of the valley and Michaelmas daisies.

Alas, Hughes's utopian dreams were soon to dim. After having endured a shaky start, with the settlers shivering through Tennessee's worst winter for twenty-five years, typhoid struck in the following summer of 1881. The promised 'genial temperature' had not materialized; neither had the assurance of easily-cultivated soil 'on which droves of hogs abound, fattening inexpensively on luxuriant fruits of the beech, oak, chestnut and hickory'. A planned spur line of the Cincinnati and Southern Railroad never appeared; instead every visitor had to tackle three hours of muddy and tortuously winding roads from the nearest station – 'in postures that would have done honour to a cheap circus acrobat'. The closest town was, and still is, some seventy-miles away.

The settlers struggled on, with some successes, for twenty years. A drug company was developed, as was a dairy. They established the Rugby Printing Works and built up the Rugby Stone Quarries Company. The 'live and energetic' *Gazette* was published every Thursday.

Some English habits were to die hard in this 'other Eden'. Although saloons and 'the traffic in intoxicating liquors' were absolutely prohibited, Rugby's Tabard Inn (named after the inn in Chaucer's *The Canterbury Tales,* in Southwark, London), served afternoon teas and held concerts every evening, as well as croquet matches for the 'refined society' who patronized 'this gem in its sphere'. Some Rugbeians even claimed that the Lawn Tennis Club, was 'almost as famous and well known as the Coliseum in Rome'.

Ironically, though, it was the ineptitude of the 'Will Wimbles', who, having sown the original seeds for the colony in Hughes's mind, were to considerably contribute to its demise. From the start there had been negative nonsense from the young 'gentlemen', who with their loafing, lounging and grumbling, undermined Hughes and all his beliefs. One of them penned a poem, objecting to such bodies as The Rugby Total Abstinence Society:

> *Bass, Alsop, Ian, Cooper and Guinness,*
> *Divine inspirations of man!*
> *Were the ocean's expanse not between us*
> *How soon would I taste ye again!*
>
> *My whistle I also might moisten*
> *In tumblers of Soda—and more!*
> *Might turn from this bachelor folly,*
> *And be cheered by the Sally of yore.*

In part though, it was the class system of the Old World – which Hughes had set out to clear away – that was to clog this experiment in the New. Sarah Kellogg Walton, the first child born in the town, wrote that 'perhaps the real reason for the failure of Rugby was the fact that the colony started at the top, bent upon enjoying the social and intellectual pleasures before laying a foundation for economic prosperity through industry and self denial'.

Foolishness too, cast a few shadows. It was said that rather than listen to the advice of the local farmer, the settlers chose to heed an agricultural teacher, who had, until recently, been a butler in London. Disaster struck too when a venture for canning tomatoes collapsed; the labels, ordered from London, were printed with the price in shillings and pence.

By 1900 many of the settlers had left the colony. But Rugby was never to die; rather it was to live on as a modest Tennessee mountain town – a surreal English survival in its Appalachian midst.

In 1964, a sixteen-year-old boy, Brian Stagg, stumbled upon Rugby and, captured by its magic, he later set about reviving and restoring the place. After his death in 1976, his sister, Barbara, and her husband, John Gilliat, took over, giving Rugby a renewed kiss of life. Once again there is a 'Harrow Road Café' – originally founded in 1881 by two enterprising young Englishmen who did 'a roaring trade' serving up such Old World delicacies as 'capital Welsh rarebit'. (As for the New World 'Squash Cobbler', how I yearn to be digging into my giant second helping as I write these words.)

The general store – the Rugby Commissary of 1880 – has been rebuilt. It was so-named by Hughes 'to indicate our own wishes and intentions as a commissary is especially a public institution'. Today on this Tennessee mountain top, you can buy such treats as Dundee marmalade, lemon curd, English toffee, shortbread and Cadbury's chocolate.

Opposite the library, on the edge of this enchanting town, an old English ship's bell still peals out over the forest, from the belfry on Christ Church Episcopal. Repainted in its original pinks, this Carpenter-Gothic building, designed by Cornelius Onderdonk and opened in 1880, is built of virgin pine, walnut and poplar – the trees that then covered the plateau. These forests, it was claimed, offered opportunities for studying geology, botany, entomology, zoology and in fact all the '"ologies" few other places can more abundantly give'. A student of specimens, it was said, 'can… collect a very rich cabinet'. Inside the church is a harmonium reed organ made by Ralph Alison and Sons of 108-9 Wardour Street, Soho, London in 1849. There are a multitude of such details to stop you short in your tracks: cut into the base of the church's alms tray, for example, is the dedication 'For the Love of Tom Brown'.

Above the altar a stained-glass window commemorates the founder's mother, Madame Hughes, 1797-1887, and Mary Blacklock, 1791-1885 – the mother of Rugby's first reverend, Joseph Blacklock. He bought her here from Yorkshire, along with his wife and seven children. Two photographs show the two factions that founded the colony: Uncle George Barry, a labourer (every settler went by the name of Aunt or Uncle) and Uncle Samuel George Wilson, one of the original 'second sons', who would brag that he was the happiest member of the colony, as he never shaved and never married. Both men lived on here into the 1930s.

Before Thomas Hughes died in 1896, he wrote, 'I cannot help feeling and believing good seed was sown when Rugby was founded… and some day the reapers, whoever they may be, will come along with joy bearing heavy sheaves with them.'

And so it has come to be, with the charm of the place being enhanced and embraced once again. As the Tennessee poet, Lois Walker Johnson, wrote on seeing Rugby for the first time:

I saw a little church, steep roofed and bright,
Its narrow benches waiting, row upon row,
And thought I'd like to send a word to Hughes:
No dream is dead that leaves an afterglow.

SEAMEN'S BETHEL

In New Bedford, Massachusetts, currents of the Old World course through the New – skeins of that past that will be forever interwoven into the fabric of New England. Before the American Revolution, the fortunes of such towns as New Bedford were founded and fuelled by the English. Mournful witness of this can be seen in the town's Seamen's Bethel of 1831, hung heavy with marble cenotaphs.

> *Parker Smith. A Native of England…*
> *He his adopted country loved*
> *And saw with pride its banner wave,*
> *And faithful to its cause he proved,*
> *And from this Bethel found a grave.*

As well as settling the first colony in the New World, at Jamestown in Virginia, Captain John Smith had another string to his bow – or rather, a mighty rope to his harpoon – for it was he who is credited with making the first whaling expedition to New England in 1614. Two years earlier Samuel Purchas had written in *Pilgrimes* of the English in the New World, pursuing this, 'the greatest chase which nature yieldeth'. Whaling was an industry that was to wax prosperous in New Bedford for three centuries: 'When the wharves were swarmed with ships and barks, whose hundreds of masts fringed the sky-line like the bayonets of a great army marshalled in battle array', whereupon they would set sail in search of the spermaceti whale, which according to Thomas Jefferson was 'an active, fierce animal, requiring vast address and boldness in the fisherman'.

Relations between New Bedford and London ebbed and flowed from the start. There was the usual, and well-founded, fury at the whaling taxes, which, according to Sir William Blackstone, made up 'A tenth branch of the king's ordinary revenue'. A dead whale 'when either thrown ashore or caught near the coast' was deemed a royal whale. Edmund Burke was fierce in his defence and admiration of whaling, asking Parliament: 'What in the world is equal to it?'

Huge and handsome profits were made from the products of whaling, such as soap and candles, which were shipped across the Atlantic by the ton. It was whale oil from New England that first lit up the streetlamps of London. John Adams wrote to William Pitt persuading him of its excellence:

> *the fat of the spermaceti whale gives the clearest and most beautiful flame of any substance that is known in nature, and we are surprised that you prefer darkness, and consequent burglaries, and murders on your streets… The lamps around Grosvenor Square… and in Downing Street, too, I supposed, are dim by midnight, and extinguished by two o'clock; whereas our oil would burn bright till nine o'clock in the morning.*

These were but some of the reasons for New Bedford's prosperity, a town Herman Melville was to describe in *Moby Dick* (1851) as 'perhaps the dearest place to live in in all New England'. Where else, in all America, he asked

> *will you find more patrician-like parks and gardens more opulent… Whence came they? How planted upon this once craggy scoria of a country? Go and gaze upon the iron emblematical harpoons round yonder lofty mansion and your question will be answered. Yes, all these brave houses and flowery gardens came from the Atlantic, Pacific, and Indian oceans. One and all they were*

harpooned and dragged hither from the bottom of the sea Many were the architectural gems built for the seamen as well as for the swells. The towered and clapboard building of the Seamen's Bethel still stands on Johnny Cake Hill, as pure and simple as the day it was dedicated as a non-denominational Christian church on 2 May 1832, save, that is, for a fantastical pulpit, shaped like a ship's prow, that now shoots forth above the pews.

This is the Whalemen's Chapel of Melville's *Moby Dick*. When John Huston made the film of the book in 1956, with Gregory Peck, he was refusing to work in America after having been accused of communist sympathies. The interior of the chapel therefore had to be meticulously recreated on a film set in England, but with one charmful difference, in that in place of the box pulpit, there was, as Melville had decreed there should be, the prow of a ship:

> *for the pulpit is ever God's foremost part, all the rest comes in its rear. From thence it is the storm of God's quick wrath is first decried, and the bow must bear the earliest brunt. From thence it is the God of breezes fair or foul is first invoked for favourable winds. Yes, the world's a ship on its passage out, and not a voyage complete; and the pulpit is its prow.*

People flocked to New Bedford to see the wonder, only to discover that it did not exist. And so, in 1961, the prow pulpit, originally created in England, was built in the Seamen's Bethel. Sadly not recreated at New Bedford is the bow's 'perpendicular side ladder, like those used in mounting a ship from boat at sea… with a handsome pair of red worsted man-ropes'.

Halting at this, the chaplain, who had been a whaleman in his youth, would 'cast a look upwards, and then, with a true sailorlike but still reverential dexterity, hand over hand, and mount the steps as if ascending the main-top of his vessel'.

In the pew in which Melville sat to describe the Whalemen's Chapel you can gaze, as he did, at the Bethel's cenotaphs. Most moving of all, is the inscription to Daniel Burns, who died aged twenty-six:

> *We laid him in his watery bed,*
> *Beneath the mountain billow:*
> *No Mother, Sister placed his head,*
> *Upon his foaming pillow:*
> *But here the sorrowing bosom finds,*
> *The token of our kindred minds.*

Poor Charles Petty died nine hours after being bitten by a shark, while 'John Glover of London, Aged 22 years' was lost overboard'.

'What despair in those immovable inscriptions!' wrote Melville

> *What deadly voids and unbidden infidelities in the lines that seem to gnaw upon all Faith, and refuse resurrections to the beings who have placelessly perished without a grave.*

Among the Bethel's congregation he could see several women

> *in whose unhealing hearts the sight of those bleak tablets sympathetically caused the old wounds to bleed afresh.*

Shipwrecks and sharks were not the only hazard for the mariners; piracy was also rampant on the high seas. One scoundrel of particular malevolence was a Captain Ned Low, who captured two whaling sloops near the Rhode Island shore in 1723. Ripping open one master's stomach – whilst the poor fellow was still alive – he took out his heart, had it roasted, and made the ship's mate eat it. The other master's ears were then cut off, which he was forced to eat, after they had been roasted and seasoned with salt and pepper.

Even without such edifying encounters, the lives of these mariners set them apart from other men. Born with the fever of the sea in their veins, theirs was an extraordinarily hazardous existence. On the vast whalers – described as 'floating hells', although

with their sails aloft they appeared as the very clouds of heaven – these great ships would often be away for over three years. In the case of one Charles W. Morgan of 1841, the captain's new young bride went too – for three years and six months.

'There is death in this business of whaling' wrote Melville, 'a speechlessly quick chaotic bundling of man into eternity.'

Having harpooned the whale from their tiny row boats, the men might then be hauled through the water at terrifying speed for several hours by the 'giants of the deep' – driven mad with the agony of the spear. Once killed, the bulk of the leviathan would have to be hauled aboard by men balanced on a skeletal-slender wooden scaffold. The junk piece alone – the whale's forehead – might weigh over ten tons. 'Toes are scarce among blubber room whalemen' wrote Melville. The cutting spade was razor sharp and the spadesmen's feet were shoeless. Every whaleman was a David to those Goliaths of the deep – 'the motion of whose vast bodies can in peaceful calm trouble the ocean till it boil' – so wrote Sir William Davenant in the seventeenth century. No wonder such terror made this conflict tremendous.

The Englishman, Frederick Apthorp Paley, a Victorian classical scholar, as well as an expert on Gothic architecture and the earth worm (a combination that, to my mind, gives considerable credence to this description of the whale), vividly described the magnificence of the whalemen's quarry: 'The aorta of a whale is larger in the bore than the main pipe of the water-works at London Bridge, and the water roaring in its passage through that pipe is inferior in impetus and velocity to the blood gushing from the whale's heart.'

Despite our abhorrence of such slaughter today,

whaling was then thought of as a 'princely sport' – a battle 'with the largest and most powerful creature known on this globe with all the mystery, glamour and romance of whaling that fed the flames of boyish imagination and desire.'

Before the voyages, it was a matter of superstitious certainty to the mariners of New Bedford that they should gather in the salt box – the meeting room beneath the body of the chapel, so-called because the salt box aboard ship lay beneath the main deck. There the whale meat was preserved, as they hoped their lives would be.

With photographs of successive Bethel chaplains staring out from the walls and with the simple wooden seats, whose backs can be swung so as to be able to place yourself on either side, the New Bedford salt box has all the unsullied savour of its legacy with the sea. A marble bust of the Revd Enoch Mudge stares solemnly over all. Mudge was the first chaplain, immortalized by Melville as Father Mapple 'in the winter of a healthy old age… merging into a second flowering youth, for among all the fissures of his wrinkles, there shone certain mild gleams of a newly developing bloom – the spring verdure peeping forth even beneath February's snow'.

Upstairs in the chapel he would address his congregation as 'Shipmates', and would then order their scattered number to condense: 'Starboard gangway, there! Side away to larboard – larboard gangway to starboard! Midships!' From the pulpit, he would offer a prayer 'so deeply devout that he seemed to be kneeling at the bottom of the sea'.

To the crowd's cheers of 'Greasy Luck!' to the top-hatted captain, the great ships would depart on their 'distant journeys to quasi-legendary lands where strange folk lived… the "Queerquegs" that the ships often bought home… They would watch the vessels leaving… they would see them return… but between the departure and return, in watery realms far, far beyond the horizon, what brave glory there must be!'

Opposite: *The Seamen's Bethel. The photograph is taken from the pew in which Herman Melville sat to gain inspiration for* Moby Dick.

Within the chapel all was calm. Without, the streets of New Bedford were turbulent with, according to Melville, an ever-brewing social storm:

Mediterranean mariners will sometimes jostle with affrighted ladies. Regent Street is not unknown to Lascars and Malays, and all at Bombay, in the Apollo Green, live Yankees have often scared the natives. But New Bedford beats all Water Street and Wapping. In these last-mentioned haunts you see only sailors; but in New Bedford actual cannibals stand chatting at street corners, savages outright, many of whom yet carry on their bones unholy flesh. It makes a stranger stare… Feegeeans, Tongatabooarrs, Erromanggoans, Pannangians, and Brighggians… wild specimens of the whaling-craft which, unheeded, reel about the streets.

Alongside the Seamen's Bethel on the cobbled street stands the Mariners' Home, originally a 1780s clapboard Colonial house, that was hauled by oxen, lock, stock and barrel, across the town in 1851, to become a seafarers' refuge. It had been bequeathed by a Quaker, Sarah Rotch Arnold, a woman, it was said, 'of exquisite delicacy and modesty, which like a veil enveloped the rare gifts and graces it could not hide'. It was once her father's house, built on the site of her grandfather's home which had been burnt to the ground by the British – torching the town that was lighting London – during the Revolutionary War.

The Seamen's Bethel and the Mariners' Home, a spirit-lifting pair, were created under the auspices of the New Bedford Port Society (in the case of the Mariners' Home, the Ladies' Branch), and they are under that same seemingly God-sent guardianship today. The Mariners' Home still offers sanctuary – charging $10 a night if you have the money, otherwise it is free.

The Port Society was originally founded 'For the moral improvement of seamen' – when bars and brothels abounded a block away. It now ensures that both the buildings and the customs are preserved – customs that salute the past and present of New Bedford in a scarcely credible-in-their-excellence way.

Every year, special services are held at the Seamen's Bethel. One, 'The Four Chaplains', commemorates the deaths of the four priests who gave their life jackets to others on the troopship *Dorchester* in February 1943; a survivor who saw the chaplains praying with their arms linked, as the ship went down, still comes to speak at the service. Then there is the fishermen's Thanksgiving – 'The Harvest of the Sea', held in November. At the Fisherman's Memorial Service, held every year since 1867, a ship's harmonium is put onto a tiny red wheelbarrow and pushed forth from the Bethel. Accompanied by a procession of parishioners – led by a young boy carrying a wreath, and a priest at the rear – it is taken down to the port. After a service held by the waterside, the names of those lost at sea in the preceding year are read out, each to a single toll of a bell. The wreath is then cast upon the waters. This organ, wheeled on the same barrow, was used in the original services on board the world-wandering whaling ships.

And so, as was written a year after the last whaling ship left New Bedford for the high seas in 1925, 'the proud masses of canvas fade away on the horizon'. Nowhere in the Old World is the majesty and mythology of the whale, which has held its mighty sway over the imagination of man since time immemorial, so deeply embedded and embodied, as in this small port on the eastern shores of the New.

McSORLEY'S OLD ALE HOUSE

Mc Sorley's Old Ale House on 7th Street in Manhattan is so extraordinary that even the best of Irish blarney could not do it justice. It was founded in 1851, and from that day to this every inch of the place has remained unchanged, save, that is, for a multitude of mementoes – rich encrustations of Irish and American history, that have been added over the years. I doubt whether there is another such treasure-trove of a nineteenth-century tavern surviving in Ireland, in the Old World, let alone in Manhattan, in the New. Ireland may be marching into modernity, but not so McSorley's.

A mere peer through the door and you feel straightway smothered in the patina of the place, suffused with the life and lore of Irish America. It was established by John McSorley as 'The Old House at Home' – modelled on his memories of an Irish tavern of the early 1800s. And so it still stands today. With the motto 'Good ale, raw onions and no ladies', McSorley's flourished from the first.

Giant golden numbers, '145', proclaim the years of the tavern's triumphant survival: the '5' gleaming, the '1' and '4' both thick with grime. All about you the walls are covered from floor to ceiling with keepsakes from those years. McSorley's has never had a cash register, instead three cups stand ready for nickels, dimes and quarters, on the huge and handsome mahogany bar – ever welcoming to 'twenty elbows' – installed ten years before the American Civil War. Wooden tables and chairs 'sandpapered velvety through accommodations of humanity', call you in from all corners. One of the most moving of all McSorley's glories hangs over your head: a gas lamp onto which are hooked a collection of turkey wishbones – the shape of each one enlarged twofold with dust and dirt – hung there by the 'boys' leaving for the front in the First World War. If they were lucky enough to return, they reclaimed their bone. Eighteen wishbones remain.

Old John McSorley's head gleams forth on the bar's tap heads, rendered shiny bald with use. According to Norbert Griffin in his *McSorley's Old Ale House, Forgotten by Time in its Flight*, he was 'an honest hard-working son of Ireland… a gentle man who made his ale house a gentle refuge that was more a *home* for the Irish immigrant, than his cheerless lodging, where he could become for a while, a member of a congenial family'.

From the day the Ale House opened no women were allowed through its doors. They were barred by the 'holier than holier' rule that 'no members of the weaker sex be allowed within the bar's thoroughly masculine precincts… where the working man, after a day's labour could gather with his companions over a glass of October's Brown Ale, unencumbered or distracted by the frivolities of Eve's daughters'. There was, though, one notable exception – a certain 'Mother Fresh Roasted', a peanut peddler, who was given special dispensation. She claimed that her husband had perished from a lizard bite in Cuba during the Spanish-American War, and so grateful was she for the favours of John McSorley's ale that she embroidered him an American flag, which still takes pride of place on the walls today.

If any other female attempted to breach this

With the motto Good ale, raw onions and no ladies' McSorley's flourished from the first.

bastion, however, John McSorley would gently insist that she left without delay, escorting her forthwith to the door with the words: 'Madam, please don't provoke me. Make haste and get yourself off the premises, or I'll be obliged to forget that you are a lady.'

When John's son, Bill, inherited the tavern, the reception given to women was even more robust. At the first sight of a would-be female tippler, he would savagely jerk on a bell above the bar. To an accompanying chorus of yells from the patrons, she would be forced to flee.

'All surliness and no affability', Bill McSorley was a man 'who vigorously minded his own business' and claimed to drink nothing but tap water and tea. His father's policy remained gospel: free drinks to all at the end of each evening. This, despite a legendary

meanness that inspired such jokes as: 'Hey Bill, there ain't no pockets in a shroud!' If the tavern was getting too rowdy or crowded, whatever the hour, Bill would simply close, grumbling that he was 'getting too much confounded trade'. There were behavioural standards to be met, or it was banishment from the bar, 'a punishment almost to heavy to bear'.

Ladies were eventually to storm these bastions, though, after a court case brought by two 'Syracuse housewives'. Elaine Everett was the first to cross the threshold in August 1970. Again the bell was rung, this time in welcome. 'It is enough to make men drink,' wrote the *New York Times*, although it was not expected that 'the saloon would start looking like the audience at a Wednesday matinee'.

Rather, McSorley's was, and still is, a raffish and bohemian bar with a host of grand literary and artistic associations, frequented by the big noises in sport, politics and the arts, as well as Mao black-suited designers – who stand hugger-mugger with the Irish regulars.

With sporting history, as with everything else at McSorley's, to read the walls is to spin hither and thither through time. Stand and study the signed photographs of regulars Jackie Gleason, Joe Coburn and James Dempsey, and the poignant and instantly-recognisable rear view of Babe Ruth, who, when the picture was taken, had been retired for years and was dying of cancer. Here, he stands alone, facing many thousands of cheering fans at a Yankee Stadium benefit in his honour. Then there is the print of the bare-knuckle fight of 1849 between Yankee Sullivan and Tom Hyer at Still Pond Heights, Maryland – overseen by top-hatted judges.

Between 1912-30 the artist, John Sloan, worked a series of paintings on McSorley's Old Ale House and its clientele, which are to be found in art galleries all over America. He and his 'dear friend' W. B. Yeats, were regulars here, slaking their thirst and relishing the 'poetry' of the place. Hippolyte Havel, the anarchist, was also a regular; he was held in highest regard by reactionary Bill McSorley, who always called him 'Hippo'. Havel even penned a too-poor-to-write-here poem on the place, while the patron, on the other hand, made his own excellent contribution to the walls, ending with the words:

When St Peter sees him coming he will leave the
*   gates ajar*
For he knows he's had hell on earth, has the man
*   behind the bar.*

In Bill McSorley's time there were eighteen cats in the bar, which must have added considerably to the colour and cosiness of this Irish enclave. When it was time for him to feed his feline friends he would bang loudly on a tin pan – however busy the bar – and all eighteen of the creatures, grown enormous on bull's

liver, would lope heavily forth, from all sides of the saloon. There are cats there to this day, although sadly only two (Stinky and Scratch) – always most picturesquely draped over the mantelpiece, the tables and the chairs, or otherwise toasting themselves by the pot-bellied stove. But two is too many for the Board of Health, who have decreed that the cats should leave the premises by eleven in the morning. Regrettably, says Mathew Mahon, the tavern's current owner, 'they can not tell the time'.

Trawling the walls of McSorley's where a pin could not be pricked between the mementoes, you are swept into the lore of the Irish and of their adopted country. Alongside photos of the 'All-Irish Hockey Champions 1904-13', prints of 'the Irish who served under Washington' stare proudly forth. There are newspapers from the era of the Civil War, as well as a pair of convict shackles from a Confederate prison in Georgia – tried on, and wrestled off, by the great Houdini.

There is a contemporary account of the Irish Rebellion of 1916, as well as one of the Siege of Limerick and the 1848 trial of the 'Young Irish' accused of treason against Queen Victoria. When asked by the judge if they had anything to say, one replied: 'This is our first offence but not our last. If you will be easy on us this once, we promise on our words as gentlemen to do better next time. Sure we won't be fools and get caught'. One was to become prime minister of Australia, another the Governor of Montana and the remainder ended up in either the American or Australian governments.

A framed copy of the *London Gazette* of 22 June 1815 announces the start of the Battle of Waterloo, and in the same paper and making surreal reading in a Manhattan drinking saloon, is a message from the Duke of Wellington to Earl Bathurst giving news of the death of one Major Sir William Ponsonby, described as 'an ornament to his profession'. Faded and frail, the oldest oddity in the place is a page from the *New York Morning Post* of 1783 warning readers of the perils of 'insulting the colours of any foreign nation' after a vessel had been seized in New York harbour and its colours destroyed 'in a righteous and disorderly manner'. Most up-to-date of all is a framed, coloured photograph of Socks, the Clintons's cat, signed by the president himself.

These are walls that reverberate with history. President McKinley, who was of Irish descent, was assassinated by an anarchist in Buffalo in 1901 and his funeral is described in detail here: 'Broadway's silent tribute lasted a full five minutes'. Beneath his portrait are the words 'Goodbye all, goodbye all. It's God's way. His will be done' – signed by the deceased! The images of Presidents McKinley, Garfield and Lincoln are together in an oak frame, put up by old John McSorley in 1902, along with a vituperatively-inscribed brass label: 'They Assassinated These Good Men, The Skulking Dogs'. Martin Luther King and the Kennedys have since been added to the unhappy group.

But it is the engraving of President James A. Garfield's deathbed scene that looms most grimly large, positively demanding that you find out more. An embittered attorney, incensed at not being made ambassador to France, had set out to kill Garfield. Having arranged for a hansom cab to collect him and take him to gaol after the deed was done, he shot the president at Washington station. One bullet grazed Garfield and the other lodged itself in his body but seemed to pose no immediate danger. It was only then though, that the real trouble began for the president. Successive doctors poked deep into the hole with unsterilized fingers, gouging false trails, and with one even puncturing his liver. Alexander Graham Bell, the Scottish inventor, was called in with his new invention – the induction balancing electrical device, or metal detector – to find the slug. Bell declared it to be buried so deep that they would have to operate. Digging deep and finding nothing, they realized that it had been the bed springs rather than the bullet that they had been

aiming for. Massively cut about and infected beyond any hope of recovery, the wretched Garfield died, after only 200 days in office. Great must have been the outrage throughout the country at the president's plight, inspiring those such as John McSorley to commemorate the sorry event.

In the back-room bar, hung high on the wall is the welcoming message 'BE GOOD OR BE GONE'– hailing those who attended the Bible school classes and prayer meetings that were once held here. The words 'BIBLE HOUSE' are writ clear merely feet away from a painting of a languorous nude looking at a parrot.

When John McSorley died, his desolate son, determined that his father's legacy should live on, ensured that each and every precariously-hung frame was nailed hard and fast to the walls. And so they have safely remained. Bill McSorley commissioned a portrait of the old gentleman from a Cooper Union student; it now hangs reverently above the fireplace in the back-room bar. As a mark of respect, he decreed that his father's face should be permanently aglow with a hooded light bulb, which still shines throughout the day on his bewiskered features.

The Cooper Union was established in 1859 and was the first organization to offer free education to working-class children and women. Its founder, philanthropist Peter Cooper was a regular at McSorley's. 'Philosophizing with the working men', he became a close friend of old John. He was held in such high esteem that he was allocated a table and chair of his own, made more comfortable with what must have sounded alarming at the time, a vulcanized-rubber cushion. This had been invented by Cooper's friend, Charles Goodyear, who died penniless, but whose name will be forever remembered in the Goodyear Tyre and Rubber Company. When Cooper died in 1883 his chair was draped in black.

Sitting at Peter Cooper's table, it is worth dwelling on the achievements on this great son of

The back-room bar with a portrait of its founder old John McSorley permanently aglow.

To read the walls of McSorley's is to spin hither and thither through time.

America. As well as founding free education, Cooper designed the first passenger locomotive in the country – 'knocked together with musket barrels'; he was largely responsible for laying the first transatlantic cable; he masterminded methods of bringing fresh water to New York City; his iron foundry was one of the biggest in America and his inventions included an automatically-rocking musical cradle, an endlessly-moving chain to haul boats through the then all-important Erie Canal, he made a vast fortune producing the United States's best glue – he even invented jelly! One singular failure was his aeroplane of 1833, which exploded into fragments before take off. But perhaps most remarkable of all,

he made an automatic washing machine for his mother, when he was still a little boy.

Manhattan mourned on the day that he died in 1883 when 'one after another the flags stole half way down the mast on the public buildings… An American of his time, he was also, in no unimportant sense, an American of all time' wrote his biographer, Edward Mack. Cooper's funeral was symbolic in its simplicity: with 'only four carriages… under the leafless trees… with the moisture made by the morning rain dropping like tears upon the place beneath where lay all that was most mortal of Peter Cooper, the friend of the working man.'

McSorley's had been the perfect setting for this

colossus to chinwag with students and workers, quaffing ale from a pewter mug, on which his name had been engraved with an ice pick. His life was written into song, by Guy Gaylord Clark, Dean of the Cooper Union Art School. Richly illustrated its eleven verses hang in great columns on the walls above Cooper's table. It starts:

> *A mechanic from Manhattan and a good one too,*
> *Grew up hale and hearty on McSorley's brew.*
> *Made his money mostly just a'makin glue,*
> *Sorts stuck together, pardner, me an' you.*
> *Here we are, never far, from Peter Cooper's table at*
> *   McSorley's Bar.*

And ends:

> *Peter's disposition was mostly sweet,*
> *He had no education but he would stand treat,*
> *He put up Cooper Union, where the great all meet.*
> *An 'took his life preserver to the judgement seat.*
> *Here we are, never far, from Peter Cooper's table at*
> *   McSorley's Bar.*

As befits the wise ways of McSorley's, Peter Cooper's chair is safely preserved, perching aloft, out of harm's way, on a mountain of mementoes above the bar. Not only did the chair embrace the long-haired and whiskered Cooper, but Abraham Lincoln also sank between its arms.

Lincoln, 'the gaunt giant from the West', had originally been nominated for the presidency by Cooper, and he always believed that the speech he made at the Union had made him president. Newspaper clippings telling of Lincoln's assassination decorate McSorley's walls, alongside a 'Wanted' poster for John Wilkes Booth. In an astonishingly surreal chain of events, Lincoln was to die in the very same boarding-house bed that Wilkes Booth had slept in the night before the assassination. A theatrical poster on McSorley's walls announces the appearance of John Wilkes Booth's brother, Edwin – an actor and theatre-owner. Edwin and his younger brother, Junius Brutus Booth Jnr, trod the boards together all over America. But after the assassination of the president a curse seemed to descend on the family. Two of Wilkes Booth's sisters were to die of melancholia, Edwin's theatre burnt to the ground; his son died, his daughter's fiancé went mad and his wife died 'a raving maniac'. Shortly afterwards, Junius's son lost his mind and committed suicide after killing his wife. Edwin died in 1893 weary 'of the hell of misery to which we have been doomed'. As his funeral was taking place, Ford's Theatre in Washington – the scene of Lincoln's assassination – collapsed killing over twenty people.

Playbills abound throughout McSorley's. One is for Mark Twain's *The Prince and the Pauper*, while another, a fraction less tempting, is for a one-act comedy, *The Cup of Tea*. Of great pride to the place, is *McSorley's Inflation* – a 'slum comedy', written in honour of the tavern, by Harrigan and Hart, the Gilbert and Sullivan of America.

Prohibition seems to have done little to stem the flow of ale at McSorley's, with 'Near Beer' being 'produced mysteriously' in a row of washtubs in the cellar by a retired brewer named Barney Kelly. According to Joseph Mitchell, in his book, *McSorley's Wonderful Saloon* (1938), Near Beer was 'raw and extraordinarily emphatic'. The *Boston Sunday Globe* described it as 'foamless and bitter, as black as coal and just as opaque', even suggesting that anthracite was the main ingredient! 'But', it went on, 'the taste after the third mouth was of no consequence. The potion had worked its magic by then.'

By 1956, McSorley's was being threatened with the wrecker's ball, but, as is written on the walls: 'A cry went up from the multitude. Editorials were written and prayers were said by the devout and the shrine was spared.'

And so McSorley's continues. There have been five owners, all of them Irish or of Irish descent, and all have been passionate to preserve the place whilst at the same time leaving marks of their day upon its walls, or more recently on the ceiling as there is now little room left elsewhere.

Daniel O'Connell took over from the founder's family: 'a rookie cop from Manhattan's east side… with engrossing charm', he was said to be 'an inexhaustible fount of whimsical and rib-tickling anecdotes'. It was then that – wonder of wonders – O'Connell's daughter, the 'gracious Mrs Kirwan', took over this female-free establishment. She always 'held aloof' though 'from entering into life at McSorley's'. Her son eventually sold the tavern to Mathew Mahon whose Irish tones ring out there today.

I leave the last words with Norbert Griffen, who penned these immortal lines in 1934:

As consistent and eternal as the pyramids, the sphinx and life itself, McSorley's Old Ale House has, with Gaelic fatalism, so out of step with the rugged Irish realism that founded it, shrugged its plastered shoulders when the angel of death visited its proprietors and said 'That life' and continued dispensing ale to all comers – women excepted.

SHIRLEY PLANTATION

If there was ever an example of the Old World lurking within the New, it is to be found with Shirley Plantation, on the James River in Virginia: a chaste Queen-Anne brick box of the early 1700s, English to the base of its foundations, yet radiantly attired with that architectural symbol of American democracy – the columned porch. Beautiful yet bewildering to behold, Shirley Plantation is the very embodiment of both English and American eighteenth-century architecture.

By 1616 the land surrounding the house was already prosperously producing tobacco. Today it sprouts cotton – always so surprising in the summer, with its glossy green leaves and its thousands of white and pink trumpet flowers. In 1653 the estate was granted to Colonel Edward Hill – a 'feisty, two-fisted swashbuckling Englishman' – for 'personal adventure'. It is an adventure that has since been enjoyed by eleven generations of his family, three of them alive today, headed by one of the most endearing sweethearts of all, Charles Hill-Carter II, who, with a laugh a second and a nineteen-to-the-dozen stream of Southern talk, keenly expounds on every aspect of his beloved Shirley.

In 1723 the estate was inherited by Colonel Hill's great-granddaughter, Elizabeth, described as 'a good humoured little fairy', who made a sensationally satisfactory move for the place when she married John Carter, son of one of the richest and most powerful men in Virginia – the second generation Englishman, Robert 'King' Carter. Together the Hill-Carters built the house that still stands on the James River today. John Carter's grandfather came from Hertfordshire and both he and his father had been educated in England. Elizabeth Hill was the great-granddaughter of an Englishman, so their house was bound to hark back to the homeland. The New-World finery of the porch was later added to its Old World body by their son, Charles.

The very font of Shirley Plantation's prosperity was the James River, which, when the house was built, was a highway to both commercial and social success. The front of the house therefore had to face the great waterway, standing proud on the greensward rolling down to the water's edge. Over all, a pineapple, a symbol of Colonial hospitality, rears into the sky. It was a symbol too of the immense wealth of the place, showing that this most delectable and costly of fruits – newly-imported from the West Indies – could be devoured within these walls.

The founder of the great fortune, Robert 'King' Carter gazes forth, periwigged and proud, from his portrait in the hallway. A man of immense power, when he died he left some thirty thousand acres– stretching from the Chesapeake Bay to the Allegheny Mountains – forty-five plantations, all growing the 'noxious weed', as James I called tobacco, which would be shipped overseas in his own fleet of ships.

A political star by the time he was only thirty-three-years old, King Carter was eventually to hold every important political office in the Colony. He became Speaker of the House, as well as acting Governor of the Colony, to name but two lofty appointments. A man of no mean moment and an Englishman through and through (his father hailed from Watford) – he was hauling America into being.

Radiantly attired with a columned porch and topped with a pineapple, Shirley Plantation House (1723) and owner, Charles Hill-Carter II.

He ate English trifle and drank English cider, once washing down 'a whole squirrel… plentifully with cyder and six glasses of wine'.

Despite his somewhat luxuriant velvet-clad appearance in his portrait, King Carter always demanded that his garments be both plain and practical. 'It is not fine cloaths or gay outsight' he wrote, 'but prudence, learning and knowledge and wisdom and virtue that make a valuable man.' Everything from his boots, shoes and stockings, ruffles, hats, sword belts, coats and trousers to the house's china, pewter and silver had to be of the first quality and either English or Irish.

Many of King Carter's treasures still shine away on Shirley's Chippendale and Hepplewhite sideboards and tables today. Richly embellished, crested and engraved by eighteenth-century London silversmiths, there is enough English silver at Shirley to fill a strong room. Teapots and tea caddies, as well as tankards and candlesticks, adorn the house, having been safely hidden in a well during the Civil War. One particular treasure is a heavy tray of 1716, made from Britannia Standard – an almost pure silver decreed by William and Mary so as to deter English silversmiths from melting down coins of the realm.

What too, about the books? A 1576 edition of

'The Magna Carta' and *The Collection of Debates in The House of Commons*, dating from 1725, for example are just what you would expect to come upon in a Virginia Plantation! Altogether the family collected well over a thousand books, dating from between the sixteenth and twentieth centuries, as well as some twelve thousand letters, manuscripts and papers. With the written word alone at Shirley, the Old World blossoms in the New.

That everything survives to this day is thanks to the hero of 20 December 1975: when the house was saved from a great fire by a Hill-Carter, who kept the flames at bay with a lone hose whilst standing on the portico roof in a position so precarious that the fire brigade could not get to him. The books were subsequently kept from further deterioration by being stored in commercial freezers, becoming, in the words of Charles Hill-Carter III, 'cooked and frozen tomes'. Eventually they were bought back to Shirley and allowed to dry out. Now for the most part, they are safe and sound in Colonial Williamsburg Foundation's Library.

England hails you at every turn through the house. There are lead Tudor roses in the broken arch above the dining-room door in the hall beneath the only matching funeral hatchments in America. Four picturesque scenes of England hang in the dining room, which, according to their labels, were sold to the Carters in 1749 by Elizabeth Bakewell of Cornwall Street, London. King Carter had insisted that his son, John, should follow in his scholastic footsteps to London, thereby greatly influencing his design of the house.

John's portrait hangs at Shirley in a gallery of family members poetically described as 'A family council from the nation's dawn'. Here he is captured, languorously lording it in London, posing for the fashionable portrait painter, Sir Godfrey Kneller – who also painted Charles II, James II, King William, Queen Ann and George I. John is portrayed as the noblest of Old World grandees. With a weird warping

of time his face lives on bearing a startling resemblance to the current occupier, Charles Hill-Carter III, while Hill-Carter II has all the features of the 'King' himself.

Between 1720-50, when many of the Carter ladies were painted, a delightful deceit was practised by the English artist, John Wollaston. During the lean winter months he would paint a quantity of flattering bodies without heads. When spring came, armed with these enticing forms, he would then proceed at speed around all his sitters. They could then choose a beguiling body for themselves and in a trice, their head would be on it! Hence we see the somewhat slender Ann Carter, the mother of fifteen children.

It was Ann's husband, Charles, who decided that Shirley should be dressed with the finery of a columned porch, as if joyfully huzzahing the emergence of America's independence, making this most English of houses a beautiful beacon of American architecture. Having fathered twenty-three children (eight from his first wife and fifteen from our slender-waisted friend), Charles felt the need to enlarge and aggrandize the place. This he did with full-bodied flair, clothing the walls with panelling and fancy woodwork, and installing a colossal square-rigged hanging staircase – heavy (or rather floatingly light) with the influence of Christopher Wren – which, with no visible means of support, is the only such stairway in America.

Most charming of all, Charles installed hot and cold water, not in a bathroom and not even with a washbasin. Nor was this innovation for the kitchen, but rather, spouting forth from brass faucets in the dining room. Since the house's fine china was forever being smashed by those who worked for him, he devised this novel arrangement whereby the plates could be washed straight from the dining table.

In 1834, Hill-Carter installed another technological triumph to join forces with the hot and cold water taps. He devised a central heating system, with a wood burning stove, that would dispatch hot air via

iron ducts through delightfully-decorative wheel-like brass vents into all the rooms. It is an early example of Old World taste and New World technology, that is still in perfect working order today.

Over the fireplace in the dining room, Charles Carter had placed an oak log (a symbol of longevity) carved with twenty-five acorns (the symbols of perseverance). But by a twist of irony they are virtually no more: twenty-two of them were gouged from their cups by Charles's sons. Four remained for two hundred years. 'We were very proud of those and showed them off to all who came' says Hill-Carter, 'I think too often though, as our older son Charles got in one day and cut out three and was working on the fourth, when his mother caught him.' Charles Hill-Carter III later wrote that he pleaded precedent: 'My father accepted my argument and proceeded to warm my rear just to be historically accurate.' Now a lone acorn remains, proclaiming the perseverance of the place.

On every window pane, etched into the history of the house, are the initials of every bride married at Shirley since 1748, (a family tradition that is still maintained, the last initials being those of Harriet Carter in 1995). Here, in 1793 Ann Carter (one of the twenty-three children) and 'Light Horse Harry' Lee were married. Their son, Robert E. Lee, was to become the 'Hero General of the Revolutionary War and the First Gentleman of Virginia… he who lost a war but won immortality'. It was said that you had to see him to believe that so fine a man could exist. When the Civil War was over his horse had been made 'half bald' by so many people reaching out to grab a part of the great man for themselves. His soldiers, their 'eyes smouldering', had pleaded 'Lets keep our anger alive. Lets be grim and unconvinced and wear our bitterness like a medal. You can be our

leader in this.' But Lee replied: 'Abandon your animosities and make your sons American.'

Robert E. Lee's childhood bed – now a small sofa – is still at Shirley. Robert attended a school set up for the Carter children. According to his mother he took on the somewhat highfalutin airs of his Carter cousins, 'but nothing that a hickory switch would not take out of him'. The schoolhouse – once the laundry – was one of the many eighteenth-century 'dependencies' in the grounds to the back of the house – rare little brick beauties on whom the day-to-day running of Shirley once depended. Stables too stand amidst this most pleasing group of mellow Flemish-Bond brick buildings. The round and shingle-roofed dovecote – the 'living larder' – is as pretty as a picture, (Hill-Carter's grandfather hid here during the Civil War, when on a secret visit to his mother). Then there is the ice house, which would have been filled for the year with great blocks of ice cut from the James River in winter. The barn is still filled with such items of nineteenth-century machinery as the 'three mule plow' and 'middle busters' – used to break up the earth. The smokehouse – topped with a great bell for emergencies – was where dozens of hogs would be hung after slaughter. Hill-Carter loathed the task although 'combat training really taught you how to kill a hog'.

So popular was pork at Shirley that it has been estimated that between 1840-60 over two hogs per person were eaten each year. If the job was done properly there would be meat until the following fall. (Fall is an English word, first recorded in the homeland in 1545, and taken to America by the first settlers. It survived in the New World but died in the nineteenth century in the Old.)

During the Civil War the land that forms the forecourt of the house was used as a hospital for the enemy wounded, with Union soldiers lying on the lawns after the six-day Battle of Malvern Hill. Thanks to their solicitous care of the soldiers, the Carters were spared Northern harassment for the

One-foot high American soldier dog-irons at Shirley.

rest of the war. Even when the legendary brute, General 'Beast' Butler, was posted on the opposite river bank, the house and the family were protected from any harm.

Today, Shirley's original boxwood garden is being recreated on this land. When the first European settlers arrived in America, gardens had been, perforce, simply for food. But by the eighteenth century, the grandees of the New World were harking back to the aristocratic gardens of the Old, to the formal seventeenth-century layout that they

remembered. Such was the garden designed at Shirley, which survived until the Civil War when it fell into wrack and ruin. Now, at the dawn of the twenty-first century, the seeds of an English seventeenth-century garden have once again been sown in Virginia.

Shirley is mightiness in miniature. You feel as if you could pick it up in the palm of your hand, smothering it with admiring kisses, whilst wondering all the while at its quite captivating combination of the Old World and the New.

CHRIST CHURCH

As if Shirley Plantation was not an admirable enough Old World architectural legacy to leave to America, the Carter family left another equally rare treasure in the form of Christ Church, in Lancaster County, Virginia. Built in the early 1730s, it was commissioned by that 'public figure exemplary' our old friend Robert 'King' Carter, who was also commander-in-chief of the Lancaster and Northumberland Militias in the Revolutionary War, and, according to the Latin inscription on his ornate tabletop tomb at Christ Church: 'Speaker of The House and Treasurer of the Colony, under the most serene Sovereigns William, Ann and George I and George II.' His descendants included three signatories of the Declaration of Independence, two presidents, General Robert E. Lee, a Chief Justice of the Supreme Court and several Episcopalian bishops. We also read on his tomb, that, 'Provided with extensive wealth worthily acquired, he erected at his own expense this sacred building as a great monument of devoted duty towards God.'

From the first, there were hymns of praise for Christ Church. It has been described as the finest church in the United States – 'an artistic marvel... in its sophistication, its beauty of materials, its assured use of decorative detail and its subtlety of line and proportion'. Others have kept up the swell – with one architectural critic proclaiming, 'It is of all extant buildings by far the most evocative of the great but vanished world of eighteenth-century Virginia. Its lonely majesty perfectly preserved... it is the very embodiment of glories departed.' What too about the elegy from a Virginian historian, delighting that Christ Church 'remains as it came from the hands of its builders and it has never been out of possession of those of the faith of its founders. The simplicity and perfection of its design teaches us an architectural grace that is permanent.'

It is indeed an exemplar of Georgian grace, with an elegance so subtle that you are hoodwinked into admiring the building for its sublime simplicity. With every new look, however, you realize that here are forces of genius at work. Vast pedimented and pilastered doorways stand well over half the height of the cruciform body of the building. Its steeply-pitched and seemingly-simple roofs have eaves that suddenly and sharply splay, almost Chinese-like, at variance with the rest of the building. Ox-eye windows take up almost all the space that is left above the doorways; the rest of the brickwork – in three soft colours, all from Carter's own kiln – is pierced by twelve enormous clear glass compass-head windows, which, with their decorative keystones, are, like the doorways, over half the height of walls.

Step through these three-foot-thick walls – treading on Purbeck paving stones from Dorset – and you are quite overawed by the delicate severity that confronts you. The sheer expanse of the curves of the groin-vaulted plastered ceiling sweep over sharp stretches of great box pews on either side of the aisle. Straight ahead is a pedimented and pilastered wooden reredos, mirroring the form of the doorway through which you have just passed. Before you is only wood, white plaster and the stone beneath your feet. Over all, the handsomest of three-decker pulpits flies forth.

The lowest level was for the clerk, where he would 'raise the tunes' with a tuning fork – there being no luxury of music in the early Colonial country churches. Behind him and one step up, stood

Walk up the aisle of Purbeck stone from Dorset and be quite overawed by the delicate severity of Christ Church, Virginia.

the reader, while perched on high – and reached by a curved staircase – is the cock loft hexagonal pulpit for the preacher, crowned by a domed sounding board and topped with a fancy finial – all seemingly suspended over the crossing of the church. Here is the perfect eighteenth-century post-Reformation church – 'A large room in which as many people as possible could hear the preacher in comfort, a room that was full of light and clarity and common sense' – in this case, a large room of very considerable beauty.

It was a room too, with few distractions, except to marvel at the glass windows. The high pews were designed so as to prevent any peering at, or being

peered at, by the rest of the congregation. The men would sit on one side, the women on the other. The bigger, grander Carter pew in the chancel was originally complete with the extra precaution for privacy of a railing of brass rods with damask curtains on all sides except that of the pulpit. According to Bishop Meade, who went to Christ Church in 1850, this was 'in order... to prevent the indulgence of curiosity when standing'. There are tiny tack holes around the Carter pew, suggesting that upholstery too once softened the spartan spot.

Bishop Meade wrote of preaching 'the words of eternal life from the high and lofty pulpit, which seemed as it were to be hung in the air'. It was 'peculiarly delightful' he wrote 'to raise the voice in such utterances in a house whose sacred form and beautiful arches seemed to give force and music to the feeblest tongue beyond any other building in which I ever performed or heard the hallowed services of the sanctuary… The form and proportion of the house are also most excellent, and make a deep impression on the eye and mind of the beholder.'

The architect of Christ Church is unknown, although scholars are certain that it was created 'with an English background' – or at the very least from an English pattern book. There are suggestions too that it was designed by an architect who had worked under Christopher Wren – when he was rebuilding London after the Great Fire – who then bore the fruits of those labours to Virginia. Some even claimed that Christopher Wren himself designed this building (although he died seven years before it was proposed), and that 'in its provincial simplicity it is Wren stripped to the essence'.

Whatever the truth, Christ Church reveals the refined taste of the eighteenth-century Virginian, as he built the New World upon the foundations of the Old. Here was a building of noble beauty, in which the Carter family could gather. It was to be a gift, 'provided always the chancel be preserved for my family as the present chancel is'. King Carter built it to replace the earlier church of 1669 where his father had been buried. Thus we find the gravestone of John Carter, native of Watford, who died in 1669, along with those of four of his five wives, who 'sucksessively… dyed before him'. The last outlived him and returned to England.

In the aisle is the stone to his father's indentured servant, David Miles, who died in 1674: *Chodie mihi cras nil*' – 'Today for me. Tomorrow for you.'

Becoming a minister in the New World was no easy task, in that no man could do so without being ordained by the Bishop of London, in London. There were no bishops in the Colonies to take his place and despite fervent pleading from the colonists there was never to be one. 'Never mind their souls' spouted the English ecclesiastical authorities, 'let them plant tobacco and look to England for their religion…' Suitably, ministers in the New World were paid in tobacco, which, if the crop was good, could amount to twice the wage of their Old World counterparts – although invariably they were given the poorest grade weed. Lucky indeed was the preacher of 'a good sweet-scented parish'!

The Virginians were, in fact, the only colonists who did not beg London for a bishop. Instead they relished the control of their churches via the Vestry – the body of authority controlling the 'Colonist's Church of England' which minded the morals and manners of the congregation. Funerals must have been occasions to watch over, since some wills specified that no strong drink be provided, neither should there be 'vainglory displayed'; ammunition, on the other hand, could be fired! There being no bishop, no colonist could be confirmed, although King Carter ordered communion silver as early as 1720, for which he paid 'two hogshead of tobacco'.

Theologically, however, the colonists were held in a vice-like grip, with the Church of England decreeing that it was the only denomination allowed. But there were to be dismal days ahead for the Church of England in Virginia. In the aftermath of the War of Independence most church buildings were either confiscated or sold and their furniture dispersed, else they were left to wrack and ruin. But because King Carter had commissioned and entirely paid for Christ Church himself it was declared part of his private estate and thereby saved from this desecration.

Thereafter, the fortunes of Christ Church waxed and waned. In 1836, it was leased for ninety-nine years to the Episcopalian Congregation, who, despite earnest efforts, were unable to manage the magnitude of the task of keeping the great building alive, and after the Civil War the building was abandoned to

The handsome three-decker mahogany pulpit at Christ Church.

decay. One local man, Ammon G. Dunton, remembered his father's descriptions of the place between 1875-80, when the doors had dropped off their hinges and 'animals would wander in and out of the church at will. On many occasions during his youth... especially after a thunderstorm, his father would send him over to Christ Church to drive out the cattle'.

By 1884, the Revd Derby wrote in *The Northern Neck News* that 'This ancient and time honoured building... has become a place for plunder and vandalism.' He lamented that for years 'impious hands... fiends in human form' had been perpetrating acts 'too shocking to relate'. Heaven alone knows what they were, as he did feel able to tell of 'a fine party of young men at this sacred spot' who 'in a drunken carousel, with whiskey and crackers went through a mock celebration of our Lord's Supper'.

Thereon, serious but piecemeal attempts were made to save Christ Church from collapse with slipping and sliding success, until finally in 1958 the building was saved by the bell with the setting up of the Foundation for Historic Christ Church.

We are beholden to King Carter – the only man in Virginia to build a church 'at his own cost and charges'. Thanks to Christ Church being owned by his family, whatever neglect there was simply ensured that the perfection of the place was pickled, rather than plundered; it has been spared from destruction, and spared too, from the misguidingly-modernizing hands of the nineteenth and twentieth century. So we have this singular survival, with the magically unspoiled sight and sense of the power and the pride of early eighteenth-century colonial life.

King Carter died before his building was finished. His son, John, was to take over, writing in 1734 that: 'There is none in the country to be compared to it... but the expense occasioned thereby has been considerable.' Nearly three hundred years later we can safely say that it was money exceedingly well spent.

THE SEELBACH HOTEL

There is a glorious glut of German taste to be found deep in the sod, beneath the Seelbach Hotel in Louisville, Kentucky, a hotel that when it was built in 1905 was described as 'representing the triumph of immigrant brothers Louis and Otto Seelbach and the culmination of their own version of the American Dream'.

Echoes of Germany though, were to resound around these walls, when the brothers created their fantastical Rathskeller in 1907 – a beauty of a beer hall, run to ground in a basement in Kentucky. With its gleaming tiles heaving up in hefty relief, displaying great villagescapes of Bavaria, this vaulted chamber seems to be spellbound by the fatherland.

Your first sight of the Seelbach is a sumptuous one: a thumping great beaux-arts Baroque building hauling itself up into the sky in Bowling Green stone and Harvard brick. 'No city in the country' wrote one enraptured critic in the early 1900s, 'can boast of a better, handsomer, or more magnificently equipped hotel... built by men of splendid taste.'

It was the innovations of the New World that inspired the great and grand hotels of the Old. Although the first swell hotel in the United States was designed by a British architect, Benjamin Latrobe, when he built the City Hotel in New York in 1795, it was the Tremont House Hotel in Boston of 1828 – acclaimed as 'One of the triumphs of American genius'– that laid the foundations for the era of 'The Grand American Hotel', which, with the superiority of its technology – elevators, electric lighting, plumbing and gas – was to inspire its European counterpart. As the Grand Hotel burgeoned across the Atlantic so then the American hotels were built on an unrivalled scale. As the nineteenth-century English writer, Augustus Sala, commented: 'The American hotel is to an English hotel, as an elephant is to a periwinkle.'

The Seelbach Hotel was – and still is – one such mammoth melting pot of architecture and the arts, as well as a triumph of technology. Described as 'The only fireproof building in the city and modern in all respects' the German brothers embellished their hotel with layer upon layer of European decoration. Craftsmen were brought over from the homeland (nearby Germantown is still peopled by their descendants). Marbles were laid from Italy, Switzerland and Vermont. The hardwoods were European, bronzes were sent from France and the linen was bought from Ireland. The Venetian-Renaissance style reigned in the main dining room; the English Renaissance in the ladies' private dining room; the Spanish Renaissance in the bar. French damask covered the walls of the ladies' parlour – 'an exquisite example of Louis XVI' – while the ladies' elliptical reception room was 'executed in the style of Marie Antoinette, with all... delicacy and sweetness'. The gentlemen's private dining room was hung with Italian leather, while the gentlemen's café – 'majestic in its proportions' – was described as 'a replica of a room in Hampton Court, one of England's most famous country seats'.

As is right and proper, it is America that embraces you as you enter the main lobby, where you find yourself surrounded by murals, framed in marble, of Kentucky's great pioneering days. Daniel Boone looms large – he who braved 'the howling wilderness, the habitation of savages and wild beasts', between 1769-83, when he wrote of Kentucky 'rising from obscurity to shine with splendour… with cities laid, that in all probability, will equal the glory of the greatest upon the earth'.

When the Seelbach opened to the tune of $1 million in 1905, it caused a sensation as 25,000 people 'fought for hours' to cram into the building for a 'public inspection'. Women fainted and were borne home in private carriages – 'compliments of Louis Seelbach'.

Charles Dickens was flung out on his ear from the brothers' first hotel in Louisville, with the scene being most delicately described in a brochure from 1900:

> The manager of the house belonged to the class of Southerners who think themselves superior to any accident of avocation and, with the elegance of manner appertaining to that class, he waited on Mr Dickens, intending to show him the hospitality for which Kentucky then, as now, was famous. Having explained his purpose and his relation to the guest, he was met with the chilling response 'When I want you, I will send for you'… Well, in Louisville and, especially in The Seelbach, Gentlemen did not dismiss the manager of the house as a servant. The insulted man immediately had Mr Dickens' bags placed on the sidewalk and told him to follow them.

Looking up Dickens's account of his stay in Kentucky I read with delight, 'The city presenting no objects of sufficient interest to detain us on our way… we resolved to proceed the next day by another steamboat' – not, though, without resisting the jibe that Louisville's 'improvements' seemed to intimate that the city had been overbuilt in the ardour of 'going ahead and was suffering under the consequent upon such forcing of its powers'!

Dickens was not the only literary lion to be disgraced in a Seelbach establishment. F. Scott Fitzgerald was to pass drunkenly out on the ballroom floor when he came here as a young soldier on leave in 1918.

The splendours of the Seelbach were described in *The Great Gatsby* when Daisy Fay, the most popular girl in Louisville – who dressed in white and had a little white roadster – 'married Tom Buchanan of Chicago, with more pomp and circumstance than Louisville ever knew before. He came down with a hundred people in four private cars, and hired a whole floor of the Seelbach Hotel, and the day before the wedding he gave her a string of pearls valued at three hundred thousand pounds.'

Such, still, is the Seelbach's grandeur, inviting a sumptuousness into which Tom Buchanan would happily sink today. The hotel fell on hard times in the sixties and early seventies with 'The Legend of Louisville' being forced finally to close in 1975. Three years later, a modern-day hero hove into view when this great urban monolith was saved from oblivion by the actor Roger Davis (who starred in, of all suitable shows, *The Little House on The Prairie*!).

Once again your step takes on a swagger, as you saunter into the Seelbach. Here you can walk in the shadows of such figures as Howard Taft, Woodrow Wilson, Franklin D. Roosevelt and Harry S. Truman – indeed virtually every president has been graced by the Seelbach, including Clinton. Edward G. Robinson too, was a guest, along with a string of names that sum up show-business America: George Raft, Alan Ladd, Roy Rogers, Gene Autry, Victor Mature – all of them rollicking down to the Rathskeller – the *piece de resistance* of the place. These are the 'veritable catacombs of Gambrinus', the legendary king who was said to have invented beer, where, according to old German tradition, 'the fairies besport themselves and revel in the fragrant beer'.

In the nineteenth century, Germany was making a heady impact, both brewing and building throughout America with such tongue-tempting names as Stifel and Winklemeyer, as well as Fieuerbacher and Schlosstein, both hailing from St

Louis. Breweries flourished in New Jersey and New York, in Pennsylvania, Minnesota and Massachusetts. The Muhlbach brothers were established in Kansas City and the Krugs in Omaha, Nebraska. Many were the handsome saloons, restaurants and Rathskellers. For example in the 1890s, in the Hotel Goetz at Frankenmuth, Michigan, the lumberman's saloon was built with highest aesthetic aspirations. Stained glass and mahogany embellished the bar, as well as a fancy tin ceiling and inlaid tiles. It resisted the temptation of becoming a TV sports bar until the late 1990s. But even with this dastardly development it can still boast of eighteen handsome Tiffany chandeliers.

Such German landmarks are to be found throughout America. In Indianapolis, Das Deutsche Haus-Athenaeum of 1894 allows you not only to imbibe, but also to embrace the whole gamut of German life, with a theatre, a beer garden, a Rathskeller as well as a ballroom and gym, which all survive intact today. It was built by the Turnvereins, followers of the father of gymnastics or 'Turnvater' – Friedrich Ludwig Jahn – who embraced the tenet of 'sound body sound mind' for all round development. Here, the Rathskeller is Teutonic to the tips of Mephistopheles' finger – who stands by the fireplace, pointing at Faust. Decorated with such delights as hearty hands holding dumbbells, foaming tankards, a splayed fan of playing cards and a stained glass window of a single bagel, this is as German as the many mottoes on the walls. If further proof of Germanic sympathies were needed, the steadily-selling book *Fifty Years of Unrelenting German Aspirations in Indianapolis 1848-1898*, amply testifies to the spirit of the place.

As with Indianapolis, so too with Louisville: 'A glass of amber translucent lager, brewed in a palace like this, is fit for Gambrinus or any other God.' At the Seelbach Rathskeller you have the added bonus

Mitred pelican bishops stand guard in the vaults of the Seelbach Hotel's Rathskeller (1907).

of being blessed by bishops – ninety-six mitred pelicans – each one standing beneath its own Gothic canopy: together they form the capitals of the thumping great pillars that support the vaulted room.

In Germany, the pelican is a symbol of good fortune and hospitality; so here they all are; with their legs wide apart, so as to make room for their enormous webbed feet. This conglomeration of ceramics was made at the Rookwood Pottery in Cincinnati – a grand family establishment that died when the last Rookwood died, taking all the secrets of the ceramic recipes with him. The Rathskeller is the lone surviving room of the work. Subtlety shining above the bar, a leather ceiling is tautly stretched over its vaulted forms – all elaborately decorated with signs of the zodiac and writhing with foliage and fruit. As peculiar as it is to come upon, the subterranean chamber is made even more bewildering by being one of the first air-conditioned rooms in the world. It was built in a bubble, constructed so as to allow space for a daily dose of forty tons of steam-produced refrigerated air to pass along pipes behind the walls. Icy breezes would then waft through the ornate iron ventilators.

During Prohibition there had been many a scandalous slaking of thirst in this richly-encrusted room, when the Attorney General, the chief of police and the mayor of Louisville could all be found quaffing away with Al Capone, along with bootleggers from all over America. Max Allen, who works there today, can remember it all as a child – when his father was a barman here – and with eyes aflame he will tell it all, hell for leather, with countless colourful tales of those times. Louisville was then at the hub of railroad connections, so here would congregate the big-noise gangsters, coming from north, south, east and west to do business with the moonshiners at the Seelbach. One such bootlegger was George Rhumus from Cincinnati, who went to

night school to learn to become a pharmacist so as to claim the 200 gallons of whiskey a month allowed for medical work. One by one, he bought all the corner saloons in the town and turned them into drug stores, each time ordering his quota of spirits. By the end of Prohibition he had amassed almost a million gallons of bourbon. 'They took him to court but he beat them and walked free' cheers Max 'he was one of my heroes.'

Another, more genteel customer, was a Miss Marcella, who was later to become the first woman distiller in Kentucky. During Prohibition, she would come to the Rathskeller bar, although it was illegal for women to do so; looking 'very dignified and respectable' she revealed that she kept her whiskey in the safety deposit box in the bank 'Left alone we would take our nip, nobody ever raided the bank'.

To lighten up these grim days, such stars as Glen Miller and Tommy Dorsey and his band would play away in the Seelbach's shining vaults. Max can remember his father keeping him from school, so as to help mix talcum powder with cornmeal 'to throw on the floor, so that the ladies could dance'.

Such was the rebellion against Prohibition that had put some 300,000 people out of work in Louisville – a city of 2,000 small distilleries, fifty-seven cooper shops, twenty bottling houses and thirty-four breweries. 'Old King Alcohol is dethroned in the South' said a skit in the *American Magazine*, as early as 1908, 'I see that the prohy-bitionists are gettin' a strangle hold on me old friend an' bosom companion… He's like th' Jook iv Orleens in Paris. Some iv th' old fam'lies receive him quietly in their homes an' bow lower to him than they iver did whin he was on th' throne.'

Throughout it all, the Rathskeller has remained intact – even staying dry when the rest of Louisville was under water in a flood of 1937 – blessed as it were, by the pelican bishops!

ANHEUSER-BUSCH
BREWERY

Come join in a stein, old friend of mine,
For life is a dreary travail;
And the rust of care and the dust of despair
We'll drown in a homely revel...

Then fill up the bowl! There's a merry soul
In this cup the gods have sent thee
No malice or rue in its amber dew,
But Hope, and a sweet nepenthe.

So begins a slender and exquisitely-engraved volume published by the Anheuser-Busch Brewing Association in 1889. A triumphal angel blows the word 'Prosit' from her trumpet above the book's captivating title:

Light Hearts, Happy Hours,
An Autobiography Of A Child
That Uncle Sam Is Justly Proud Of.
Some Account Of A Triumphal
March From Humble Obscurity In
The Wild West To Glorious Supremacy
In All The World's Centres.
A Symphony In Hops And Malt.

Under the motto 'Whoso bloweth not his own horn, the same shall not be blowed' the reader is invited to admire the beauty of Anheuser-Busch's brewery in St Louis, Missouri – 'the most magnificent structure devoted to manufacturing purposes to be found in the United States... which were it followed by manufacturers in other lines, would prove a great blessing to mankind' – words that still ring rousingly true today when you see its gargantuan magnificence before you. Anheuser-Busch, founded by German émigrés in 1891, must surely be the most beautiful brewery in the world.

During the nineteenth century, brew houses great and small were built throughout America. In 1879, Jefferson declared beer to be America's national drink:

The ruling nations of today drink malt liquor. The strong hardy German drinks beer. The tough stubborn Briton drinks ale and beer, and the American is beginning to drink beer more than anything else. Germany and Britain are conquerors, physically and mentally... the qualities that make them conquerors are attributed to the strengthening properties of their national drink... The least pernicious of all beverages, however used is beer.

Beer was regarded by Thomas Jefferson and others as a temperance drink, in contrast, to whiskey 'which kills one third of our citizens'. Beer had, in fact, flowed quite freely in the United States from the days of the earliest European settlers. One of the Pilgrim Fathers wrote of being forced to anchor at Plymouth, 'our victuals being much spent, especially our beere'. When establishing Philadelphia in the 1680s, William Penn made sure to build a 'beautiful little brick and shuttered brew house', and in the early 1700s, Governor James Oglethorpe enticed new settlers to Georgia with the promise of forty-four gallons of beer each. The Massachusetts legislature even passed an act advancing the manufacture of 'strong beer, ale and other malt liquors as an important means of preserving the health of the citizens of this commonwealth'. Both

Thomas Jefferson and George Washington had home breweries. Perhaps most symbolic of all, the American national anthem, 'The Star-Spangled Banner', is sung to the tune of the eighteenth-century English drinking song, 'To Anacreon in Heaven', composed by John Stafford Smith, a member of the Anacreonic Society in London.

As German migration to America increased, so too did the habit from the fatherland of producing the finest beers, with it being claimed by the end of the nineteenth century that '...the popularization of beer during the past twenty years in the New World, had been greater than it was during the last twenty centuries in the Old'.

At the head of this brewing brigade, marching magnificently forth was the German firm of Anheuser-Busch. Its founder, Eberhard Anheuser, was a native of Kreuznach in Rheinish Prussia, who emigrated to America in 1842 and established his Bavarian brewery up the Mississippi at St Louis ten years later. He was a man, it was said, who was 'capable of far-seeing and far-reaching endeavors... he builded upon rocks and laid deep and broad foundations'. In 1864 he was joined in business by his son-in-law, Adolphus Busch, the second son of twenty-two children from Kastel in Germany, who had come to America in 1857. When only twenty-two years old he met and married Lily Anheuser, and her father enticed him to join the firm.

Thus Anheuser-Busch was born. Soon the Germans of America were beating those of the fatherland at their own game. At the Paris Exposition of 1878 Anheuser-Busch won first prize over hundreds of rivals from Bavaria, Austria and Britain. It was said that 'all Paris was seeking to quaff the American nectar'. The American Dream, applied with German doggedness, was to make Anheuser-Busch the biggest and most successful brewery in the world, producing over forty-five alcoholic beverages, including Budweiser – first advertised in 1876 as 'The Favorite of the Fair Sex', and Old Burgundy –

claimed 'to equal and surpass in beneficial qualities the best French Red Wines'. The brewery was responsible too for a quantity of innovations including pioneering the pasteurization and bottling of beer in America. It also had its own railroad on which the first refrigerated land cars were used. Indeed, Anheuser-Busch goes from strength-to-strength today. It is both comforting and curious to find that this vast concern is run by a descendant of Adolphus Busch – August Busch III, the great great nephew of Adolphus – that 'Baron of the Beer Industry, the Knight of St Louis, the toast of the Gilded Age'.

The Gormenghastian brewery at St Louis is a citadel to this success. It was designed by the architect E. Jungenfeld in 1891, who was most cruelly cut down in his prime, aged only forty-four years old, after finishing the main brew house. Seldom did such nineteenth-century industrial buildings live up to the powerful promises of their architects, which on paper appeared as tremendous temples to their trade – cities of cathedral-like factories, amid belching satanic mills. Never, I thought, have such schemes been realized in bricks and mortar, until I saw the pulsating palace of Anheuser-Busch!

Monoliths of monstrous beauty rear up to a seeming city of a skyline, with ramparts and castellations, columned chimneys and towers – flaming red brick amid swirls of pure white steam. It is like walking into an idealized utopia of nineteenth-century industrialization, but one that is thunderingly alive.

The buildings were admired from the first as 'one of the wonderful realities of a wonderful age'. In 1883 *The Western Brewer* described them as 'stately palaces of industry, erected in pursuance of one grand architectural plan, not a heterogeneous mass of bricks and mortar built haphazard, as is so frequently the case with many large manufacturing establishments... [architects of the new millennium should take note] The tall chimneys and cupolas, rise... to great

An idealized Utopia of nineteenth-century industrialisation: Anheuser-Busch brewery, St Louis, Missouri.

heights… like the superb needle of the Duomo in Florence… The great volumes of escaping steam seem like a breath of a healthy giant blown from a vigorous lung engine.' 'This great brewery' concluded *The Western Brewer*, 'will probably be standing centuries hence.'

And so it is, with golden knobs on – or rather eagles (the company's trademark since 1872) made out of terracotta, stone and iron. Golden eagles appear all over the building, flying forth from the walls and perching on every prominence – one rears twenty-feet high. In this vast empire, the streets too

belong to the brewery, and here also the eagle stands proud – on lampposts and rubbish bins, on gateposts and even embedded into pavement grills and manhole covers – 'the familiar eagle that everywhere greets the St Louisan as an old home friend'.

On the brewery's main gateposts there are elephants, trunks aloft, hailing hope from the days of Prohibition when Anheuser-Busch became the nation's largest producers of yeast. The elephant was chosen to symbolize the strength of the yeast that was made. During those bleak days for the brewing industry, the company produced such non-alcoholic delicacies as Buschtee, as well as Bevo – named after *Pevo*, the Bohemian for beer – which was made to seem particularly desirable when recommended by Bevo's Reynard the Fox, the wisest animal of the forest. Reynard appears again in stone, four times life-size, on all four corners of the Bevo Bottling Plant (1919), enjoying the simple pleasures of Missouri life – a chicken drumstick in one paw, a stein of Bevo in the other. He also appears resplendent in a Gothic frieze throughout the lobby.

As with all the buildings of Anheuser-Busch, the exterior glowers whilst the interior glitters. The main brew house looms over all with its Gwelfic battlements slicing into the sky. Outside it is handsome in its heaviness; inside it is gossamer light, with floor upon floor of white-painted ornamental ironwork, kept aloft by gilded columns. Most flyaway of all are the chandeliers of writhing wrought-iron hop vines, bought from the Belgian Pavilion at the Chicago World Fair of 1893. Still in use are the vast burnished-copper steam brew kettles, each filled with enough hops and wort for 400 barrels of beer.

In case you should forget the cultural and national foundations on which the firm was built, there are two immense tiled tableaux to remind you. On one sits Germania, on a canopied throne, life-sized, with plated bosoms and stomach to the fore. She holds a furled German flag, as the spires of Cologne cathedral soar to one side of her and the waters of the Rhine flow to the other. The owl of Minerva perches, quill in beak, and the works of Goethe, Schiller and Kant rest against a bust of Martin Luther. On the other America sits, with flag aloft, holding a wreath over a bust of Columbus; an oval of George Washington rests at her feet together with a sheaf of wheat from the Great Plain states, a copy of the Declaration of Independence and a scroll bearing the words: 'Abolition of Slavery'. All is spilled over by the cornucopia of plenty: barrels of beer are piled by the quayside at Brooklyn Bridge and the Capitol Building stands proud over all.

Such is the shock of finding such beauty in a brewery, that you quite take in your stride the discovery of Anheuser-Busch's flamboyant nineteenth-century stables, the Equine Palace of 1885, still in brilliant working order in the middle of St Louis today. Adolphus Busch had arranged that the Equine Palace be given 'liberal and tasty ornamentation… [with] the same care of decoration that would be ordinarily bestowed upon a costly dwelling'. According to *Light Hearts, Happy Hours* the stables were made beautiful, 'not because of a desire for ostentation… but rather in the hope that it will carry a lesson… that there is no good reason why an animal as cleanly, as orderly, and as free from destructive disposition as a horse, should not be housed as comfortably and with as much regard for sightliness as a human being'.

A new note of dash and dignity was added to the Palace, when, on the stroke of midnight on 7 April 1933 – the very minute that beer could be imbibed once again after Prohibition – August Busch gave his father a celebratory gift of a team of Clydesdale horses and a four-ton wagon.

The wagon is still hauled by a team of the huge horses who are handsomely housed in the splendidly appointed circular stables – highly-ornate mahogany and stained-glass surroundings, lit overall by a gargantuan brass chandelier bought from the French Pavilion at the Chicago World Fair. Some twelve feet in diameter, it has sixty bulbs writhed about with shining swags of hops and hop leaves, rising and falling from a circular band of splayed-winged eagles. The stalls are of the fanciest wrought-iron scroll work, and are steam heated. This is a building that in both scale and style is ideally suited to its occupants, who each weigh more than a ton. (Anheuser-Busch

Opposite: *The main brew house with hop vine chandeliers and burnished copper steam brew kettles, each capable of producing 400 barrels of beer.*

have made a film that set me shouting out with delight, continuing with that fine tradition of advertising that rates as art, of the Clydesdales playing football in Wyoming!)

Thanks to the wise wardenship of Eberhard's descendants, the great buildings of Anheuser-Busch have been cherished and protected, whilst at the same time they have never been robbed of the pounding purpose for which they were originally built – to give pleasure to the eye as well to as the stomach!

Architects the world over should be forced to go to Missouri to see for themselves how an industrial assembly of buildings can actually beautify and add immeasurable charm to a city, and, furthermore how it continues to do so, with the considerable majesty of the old structures being given new and admirable architectural additions – one of the great towers is only two years old.

As was written in 1891, this is architecture that by its excellent example should 'carry the name and fame of St Louis among all the English and Latin speaking races in the New as well as the Old World'.

The Magnificent New Private Stable of Adolphus Busch. Esq.

An Equine Palace — All Horse lovers should visit.

GRACANICA,
ILLINOIS

At Third Lake, in Illinois, some fifty miles north of Chicago, surrounded on all sides by suburbia – the smiling symbol of the American Dream – you come upon a building that positively *howls* of medieval Europe – a vast monastery built at the end of the twentieth century.

If nigh on impossibly strange to imagine, a stone Serbian cathedral – a larger than life replica of Gracanica monastery near Pristina in Kosovo (dating from 1321) – has been built amid the landscaped executive homes of Illinois. This is the 'Monastery of the Most Holy Mother of God', built as the spiritual centre of the 'Free Serbs of America' – as they were called when they arrived in the New World – fleeing first the Ottoman Empire and then communism. With such turbulence continuing in the homeland, Metropolitan Irney, Bishop of the Serbian Orthodox Diocese of all America and Canada, set about recreating the building, that above all others, symbolizes the Serbian spirit. It was the Battle for Christian Kosovo, against the Turks in 1389 that first brewed up the troubles that have not ceased boiling to this day. Here though, their church was to rise into the free American sky.

The groundbreaking ceremony took place on Independence Day in 1980, when a wooden post was set into the spot where the altar would be 'to drive away all evil spirits with their assaults and tricks'. A year to the day later, the foundations were blessed when, it was said, 'the spiritual excitement was truly great', with the Bishop, followed by the clergy and choir processioning around the trenches – already outlining the body of the building – sprinkling holy water and intoning prayers to 'Christ the cornerstone and foundation of the church'. The following year the bells were blessed 'to be compared to trumpets from the Old Testament... that their sound would expel every power of Satan, every ruse and assault by the enemies upon all of the faithful who hear...' Celebrations lasted late into the night, with the hope and prayers that 'God grant the bells from our Free Gracanica be the sounds of freedom, reminding us of the silenced sounds of the older Gracanica in Serbian Kosovo.' So we are told in a great bilingual book recording the celebrations.

The original Gracanica was built by King Milutin, a monarch with many strings to his bow – a much-married murderer, lecher and 'savage debauchee', he was also responsible for founding thirty-seven orthodox monasteries, as well as establishing six Catholic sees. Fearing that his son might try to usurp him, he ordered (unsuccessfully) that his eyes be gouged out. What bitter irony that the Turks, who desecrated the monasteries over the next centuries, were to gouge out the eyes of all the icons that they could reach.

At the celebrations and consecration of the Illinois monastery in 1984, the holy sacraments were bestowed on the building as they would be given to a man: the church was christened with holy water and the holy chrism of red wine, oil and balsam. Bishop Basil censed, Bishop Peter sprinkled and Bishop Irney anointed, blessing the altar and then the body of the building to the east, west, north and south – in the sign of the Cross. Holy relics – the bones of the holy martyrs Cyriacus and Mother Julita

– were poured over with wax-mastic – a blend of myrrh, aloe, white incense, crushed mastic, wax 'and other fragrant ingredients', as decreed by the Seventh Ecumenical Council in the year 787. Having covered their rich vestments with robes of white linen – in imitation of Christ's shroud – the bishops then tore them into shreds to give to the people – all this, in middle America, alongside the I.94 North-to-Wisconsin highway, and just a few miles from the 'Great America Theme Park'.

After consecration, Gracanica was allowed to 'settle' for twelve full years, before a most tremendous transformation was wrought.

Open the wooden doors, carved with the Serbian monasteries and chapels of Yugoslavia, standing forth in thickset relief. The church is dedicated to 'The Most Holy Mother of God', and one of the first frescoes that you see on entering the building is of the kneeling Metropolitan Irney, who, with a tiny Gracanica in his hands, is offering it as a gift to the Virgin Mary.

Step inside and the shock is so great that you simply stagger beneath the force of the thousands of figures about you, of walls coated with iconography telling (the icon is considered to be the written word) the tale of Christianity and of Serbia's upholding of the faith. Here, in the Byzantine style, is the universe, with heaven on high, then paradise, then earth. Christ Panocrator guards all from the top of the central dome. Only the holy are represented on high, progressing from the Annunciation to the Koimesis (the Death of the Virgin). Below, Serbian saints gather, halos hugger mugger. Tiny devils are painted riding pigs over cliffs. These are the demons Christ allowed to enter Hades as swine, rather than go into a state of permanent non-existence. Most marvellous of all is St Antonio Nehigho – a scarlet angel on a scarlet horse arched over by a rainbow, who is trampling a green devil representing the end of the world. Beneath him courses a flame-ridden torrent, filled with buildings – all white and Byzantine

in form – being swept to their doom.

Most symbolic of all, in this most evocative of spots, is the fourteenth-century Battle of Kosovo, still raging on the walls. Serbia was the beleaguered bastion of Christianity between Islam and the West. To save both itself and Europe it launched into battle against the Ottomans. Tsar Lazar was hopelessly outnumbered by the Turkish forces, led by Sultan Murad II. It was said that the Sultan 'had so many men that a horseman could not ride from one wing of his army to the other in a fortnight'. The plain at Kosovo was described as 'a mass of steel; horse stood against horse, man against man; the spears formed a thick forest; the banners obscured the sun, and there was no space for a drop of water to fall between them'.

On the eve before the battle, varying legends have it that either Saint Elijah, a grey falcon, or an angel offered Lazar the choice of a heavenly or an earthly kingdom – he would be victorious if he chose the last. Knowing that death was his reward, Lazar chose heaven. His son, St Stefan, described his father's troops: 'these were… men who shone like glistening stars, like fields embellished with dazzling flowers… who shone as though they were adorned in golden raiment and precious stones. There were so many choice horses with golden saddles and the knights who rode them were all wondrous and fair.' They included the nine sons-in-law of Tsar Lazar, who were slaughtered to the last man. And so Kosovo became the nation's invisible temple: the Serbian Jerusalem, with Gracanica at its soul.

In Gracanica, Illinois – with its wealth of frescos emulating this holiest of buildings in the homeland – every inch of the iconography was executed by one man over two years, a Russian-American Orthodox priest who obdurately remains too modest to be named. Not only has he created what appears as a giant illuminated manuscript on the walls – if it did not seem sacrilegious I would be pleased to write 'a great comic of the cosmos', so suitable is the analogy

The ceiling of Gracanica Monastery in Illinois.

– but he has also gathered into his holy fray Serbs of bespectacled modern times. Immortalized here are: Sebastian Dobovich, from San Francisco – the first American-born Serbian priest and also a gold rush pastor. Then there is Barnoda Nastich, who was born in Gary, Indiana, after which his family moved back to Serbia where he was eventually to become a bishop, railing against communism. He was imprisoned for eleven years in 1947 and there were innumerable attempts to assassinate him, with the government even arranging train crashes to kill him.

What poignant paradox that, as Gracanica in Illinois shines solidly and securely forth, so the source of its inspiration, Gracanica in Kosovo – rebuilt several times after being destroyed by the Turks and Arnauts – today stands cracked through and in peril after being shaken by the shelling and bombing of the recent wars.

The Serbian spirit, embroiled in such strife and bloodshed in the homeland, seems here, thanks to the spirit of America, to be purged of all ill, whilst loosing none of its raw passion, energy and power. Here there are two powerful forces at work: the Serbian zeal of the Old World coupled with the zest of the New – so intrinsic to America. Together in Illinois they have produced a vast cathedral in the 'Kosmet' style that evolved at Nerezi, near Skopje in 1164.

And so, in Illinois, we have come full circle –

from a modest German meeting house in Maine, built in 1764, to a great Serbian cathedral in the mid west, finished in 1998.

Two-hundred-and-fifty years ago the Germans in Maine created a sense of the homeland with their Meeting House which survives untouched to this day. So at the beginning of the new millennium, the Serbs have built the very foundations of their faith into the fabric of America – thereby ensuring that what happened 600 years ago in Kosovo is part and parcel of the Old World *and* the New.

The exterior of Illinois's 'Monastery of the Most Holy Mother of God', a replica of the fourteenth-century Serbian cathedral in Kosovo.

This has been an exploration of European survivals in America, but an exploration too of America itself and of how it has preserved the European spirit in its midst. This is sublimely summed up in Gracanica, when, in this twentieth-century 'medieval' building surrounded by 1990s suburbia you see the black-robed and bearded Serbian monks, side by side with anoraked Serbian students, as well as Sister Angelina in medieval attire, all of them chanting – as they do for many hours a day every day – in plainsong dating from the 900s – sounds that seem to come from the very soul of Serbia.

AMERICA PRESERVED

HONOLULU HOUSE

Little is more evocative of the Old New World than still-thriving small-town America. Midway between Detroit and Chicago, along Interstate 94, lies one of the most satisfying small towns of them all – Marshall in Michigan.

But first, as part of a grand architectural tour of the United States, marvel at the colossi of Detroit, with its jaggedly-colourful Art-Deco Guardian Building of 1929, as well as the palatial Fisher Building of 1928, with its marble, mosaic-coated and chandeliered arcade. In the Institute of Art, Diego Rivera's murals of industrial Detroit in the 1930s will knock you for six, with stylized workers and machines toiling away in frenzied unison. As for the Fox Theatre of 1928, no more exotic building could be found in America (save that is, for its exact replica in St Louis, Missouri!). Gigantic and gilded, in a combination of Chinese, Hindoo and Arabic styles, they have been described by critics desperate to define them as both 'Cambodian Gothic' and 'Siamese Byzantine'. Here Frank Sinatra and Bing Crosby, as well as Dean Martin and Jerry Lewis entertained amidst a plaster menagerie of some thousands of golden creatures, elephants and butterflies, parrots, peacocks and monkeys, all decorating a building, the crazed flamboyance and scale of which can only be seen in such movies as *Metropolis*.

With your architectural taste buds set a-tingling by Detroit, head west – through the university town of Ann Arbor, the handsome and cosmopolitan 'Harvard of the West' – to Marshall. The town lies at the fork of the Kalamazoo River and Rice Creek. Founded in 1830, it was built by land speculators from the east. As its elegance grew, so too did its aspirations; promoting itself as the 'future state seat of Government' it developed a dashing beauty. Thankfully, in 1847, Lansing was chosen instead as the state capital. Thus Marshall has retained all its original charm, proudly preserved, yet vibrantly alive with the challenge to keep it so.

Within seconds of leaving the interstate, suddenly and without warning you find yourself in the midst of an architect's dream, surrounded by utopian-like scenes of every style, set down upon greenswards surrounded by gardens with white picket fences and a wealth of great trees – all run through, incidentally, with a multitude of fat black squirrels. Gleaming white Greek-Revival columns stand side by side with spiked, gabled Gothic villas. Italianate towers jostle with the bulging turrets of the Queen-Anne style; the Romanesque Revival and the Federal styles stand proud beside the ever-extraordinary octagon form. Built in brick and clapboard, stone and shingle, with many painted in every colour under the sun, one fine building follows another. It is like driving through the pages of a giant pattern book of American architecture, brought to lively life. For here is no self-conscious tourist trap – thereby trouncing the true spirit of the place – but rather a bustling and proper town with a main street. In 1991 no fewer than 867 of its fine buildings were designated as part of a National Historic Landmark District – the largest number of all America's small towns. As if this was not enough Marshall can boast of a house the like of which exists nowhere else in the world.

A singular sight by any standards it is the Honolulu House of 1860 that was designed both inside and out by William Buck in 1860, in the Gothic, Italianate and Polynesian styles for Abner Pratt, Justice of the Supreme Court of Michigan and

The Honolulu House (1860) in the Gothic, Italianate and Polynesian styles, a reminder of the South Seas in Marshall, Michigan.

native of Marshall, who, having been made US Consul to the Sandwich Islands (now Hawaii) in 1857, wanted to remind himself of the architecture of the South Seas. Not only did Pratt build the Honolulu House, but he had it painted throughout with murals of tropical scenes, he crammed it full of curiosities from Japan, China and the Sandwich Islands and surrounded it with a Hawaiian garden, filled with plants such as breadfruit. To complement his house, Abner Pratt ate tropical food and wore tropical garb. In 1863 he died of pneumonia caught, it was said, whilst dressed for the tropics in Michigan's inclement weather.

In 1883, the house was sold to Martin Wagner who commissioned F. A. Grace to paint the rooms with fanciful forays of his own. Whilst many of the

original murals were painted out, many were not, and all the ceilings and dados were given as extravagant a treatment as it was possible to paint; over 120 colours were used in the south parlour alone, and over 200 were painted throughout the house. Grace created a riot of patterns and architectural illusions, often most beguilingly 'affixed' with *faux*-brass nails. All the old ceiling roses were whirled into the overall design.

So as not to war with his predecessor's primitive exotica, Grace created a primitive classicism laced through with a highly-stylized exotica of his own. Most remarkable of all is the front hall with its elaborate *faux*-stone pilasters and panels further embellished with 'marble' panels all 'screwed' though with enormous 'brass nails'. A spiral staircase sweeps up to the tower, where, out of sight until the top landing, there is a mural of a conservatory filled with cacti and other lush vegetation. Between 1975–84 every inch of the paintwork in the house was meticulously restored.

Martin Wagner was one of the patent medicine men of Marshall, who gave the town its notorious claim to fame throughout the nineteenth and early twentieth centuries. Dr Oliver Cromwell Comstock Jnr was the first, selling his Ague Pills in 1838. Produced to relieve the malarial fever brought on by the mosquitoes that plagued Michigan's early settlers, the pills were laced through with quinine, and therefore seemed to succeed in doing their job. Thereafter though, the innumerable quack remedies of Marshall's medicine men were shamefully deceiving. Patent medicine – available without a doctor's prescription – allowed such people as Hiram A. Peterman and his wife Salome Amie Slout to prosper on the gullibility of thousands. Along with Dr Henry Sharpsteen, they produced Peterman's Nerve Pills as a remedy for '…paralysis, chronic rheumatism… also to rescue the brain from the early stages of insanity'. Their 'Astoria', produced as a panacea for ailments of the head, was claimed to relieve headaches and grow hair on bald pates, whilst 'smelling wonderful'. Dr Sharpsteen's Lavender Ointment was advertised as a cure for sixty-five ailments, including diphtheria and bee stings, scarlet fever, frostbite, 'feet that sweat' and 'gunshot wounds'.

From the late 1800s, Sharpsteen's son, Verne, put Marshall on the map with his Patent Medicine Show, which ran for fifty years. (Buster Keaton's parents were part of his ensemble.) He played to opera houses – a happy feature of small towns all over America to this day – and held great outdoor assemblies, performing such miracles as suspending his wife between two chairs and putting great stones on her stomach which he would then bash to fragments with a hammer. With the audience warmed to feverish appreciation, he would then sell such remedies as 'Hindoo Oil', said to banish tapeworms. With

flourishing showmanship he would show off formaldehyded examples of the expelled creatures, retrieved from satisfied customers. One, from a Michigan farmer, was 160- foot long.

Gullibility was hard to kill, with the medicine men of Marshall on the case as late as the 1920s, with Hazen Horton advertising 'Ox-o' to restore 'lost manhood': a salve of capsicum and menthol, it created hot and cold sensations. Along with your sample came the notice that 'If you experience any warmth in the organ you should loose no time in ordering a full course of treatments'. Horton was inundated with orders.

Remedies to restore virility were legion in Marshall. 'Dr Joy's Electrical Devices' included a belt that administered shocks. Dismissed from the Medical School of University of Michigan for associating with such quackery, Dr Joy sold the manufacturing rights to our old friend Martin Wagner, who set to work with a vengeance to prove the efficacy of his newly-named 'Voltaic Belt'. It was, he claimed 'The Grandest Discovery of the Nineteenth Century' that would cure everything from venereal disease to impotence. The advertisements showed that within the 'Thirty Days Trial' you would be transformed from a stooped weakling into an upright, hearty and, of course, virile man – complete, furthermore, with waving mustachios.

Business boomed. Thus Wagner made a fortune that enabled him to buy and richly decorate the Honolulu House. It was a luck, however, that was not to last. Wagner died, insolvent, from a heart attack in 1891. His son killed himself playing Russian roulette in 1897, and his daughter attempted suicide by swallowing needles and pins. She recovered but died during an operation to save her after she had swallowed napkins and handkerchiefs.

Out of this mire of roguery there was one major medical breakthrough: 'Stuart's Dyspepsia Tablets', made by Frank Stuart in the late 1890s. The Alka-Seltzer company offered to buy his formula, but

A riot of patterns and architectural illusions: the 1883 ceilings of the Honolulu House.

wanted to add fizz. Stuart would not agree, so Alka-Seltzer adapted it for themselves, and to this day the claims made in Marshall in the 1890s still hold true the world over: 'Eat what you want, when you want it… take Stuart's Dyspepsia Tablets and forget all about stomach troubles'.

That Marshall survives in such an unspoiled state is mainly due to one man, Harold Brooks, whose father founded the Brooks Rupture Appliance Company in the 1890s, and who for some sixty years saved the town from unsympathetic modernization. From 1912 – long before such notions as 'historic preservation' were afoot – until the late 1970s, if a building was in danger of misuse or demolition, Brooks would buy it and hold onto it until a sensitive purchaser could be found. Otherwise Brooks would have it converted by his own architect, Howard F. Young from Kalamazoo. When he thought the plans for a new post office unsightly, he paid for Young to design a Greek Revival building, and for the sandstone to build it – quarried from the Kalamazoo River. He converted the old livery stables – by then a run-down gas station – into a handsome brick and pedimented town hall. He sold land to the Michigan Bell telephone company on the condition that he approved the designs for their new office building. He also commissioned Young to design a great white-columned fountain, based on the Temple of Love at Versailles. Brooks was also almost single-handedly responsible for the building of Marshall's Methodist church. And, as if all this was not enough, he commissioned the landscape architect, Jens Jensen, to beautify the town and then paid for a member of Jensen's staff to stay on for two years supervising the gardens and planting of Marshall's trees. When one resident wanted to cut down a mature walnut to sell for wood, Brooks paid him to leave it standing. He gave annual prizes for the best-kept garden, best lawn and best-kept house.

In 1951, when the Honolulu House was threatened with demolition (to replace it, with of all things, a gas station,) it was of course Harold Brooks who saved the day. He bought the building in an agreement with the Calhoun County Historical Society that they pay him $1,000 a year interest free until it was theirs. Eleven years later he sold it to them for a sum that barely covered his expenses, on condition that they renamed themselves the 'Marshall Historical Society'. Thus was born the body that has continued to cherish this perfect town, organizing house and garden tours and even tree tours throughout the year.

So much can be learnt about America's past from this small town alone. During the early-nineteenth century, for example, Marshall was an all-important east-west stop on the stagecoach line. When, in 1844, the first 'iron horse' locomotive steamed into town it was the stagecoach proprietor, Zenas Tillotson, who was perched atop its tender yelling to the engineer to 'Whip 'er up!' The town thrived as a railroad centre for years. In 1863 America's first railroad union was born here: the Brotherhood of the Footboard

was founded by Jared 'Yankee' Thompson and such locals as Linus Keith and Uriah Stevens.

In 1834, the foundations of Michigan's public-school system were laid in Marshall by John D. Pierce and Isaac Crary, (Crary married Bellona, Judge Abner Pratt's daughter). The withered stump of the oak tree under which they worked on their schemes was carved into a memorial life-size sculpture of the pair in 1980. A 'Historic Marker' shows the spot where it grew.

Most surprising of all Marshall's sagas though, is the Adam Crosswhite affair which was said to have largely contributed to the iniquitous Fugitive Slave Law of 1850, and subsequently to the outbreak of the Civil War.

Adam Crosswhite was the son of a slave and a slave master in Kentucky, who, when only a child, was given to his half-sister as her servant. At the age of forty-five, and married with several children, he heard that there were plans afoot to split his family up; and so they escaped north to Michigan and settled happily in Marshall. In 1846 Francis Troutman, grandson of the employees from whom Crosswhite had fled, came to carry him back to Kentucky. Outraged, the citizens swore to save him; and so they did. With medicine man Oliver Cromwell Comstock Jnr in their midst, several hundred people surrounded Crosswhite's house, and prevented the abduction. George Ingersoll then saw the family to safety through a route on the Underground Railroad – a secret organization set up to help slaves escape to Canada where slavery was illegal. (Railroad terms were used so as to disguise its activities; the slaves were 'freight', the routes were 'lines'. Its self-proclaimed president was Levi Coffin.) In this area of Michigan it was run by Erastus Hussey, who was responsible for arranging the escape of over 1500 slaves.

Troutman took this case of 'Northern outrage' to the Kentucky courts. The men of Marshall were prosecuted and, sorry to say, lost the case. They were

The highly-stylized exotica of the front hall at Honolulu House.

ordered to pay $1,900, thought to be the value of the slaves. Furthermore, Henry Clay of Kentucky took the case to the Senate, which led to the passing of an even more stringent Fugitive Slave Law, in 1850, strengthening the rights of slave owners.

Described as 'the most damnable law that ever received the sanction of the American Congress', it was said by Civil War veteran and Michigan Congressman, Washington Gardiner, to be 'the law that was the straw that broke the camel's back'. For many years after the conflict, a bootblack called Ben Crosswhite – son of Adam – would be asked what role he had played in the Civil War. The answer would be: 'I was de cause of de war'.

Having absorbed the history of Marshall, and thereby so much of the history of America, you should sally forth to Schuler's Restaurant which is crammed to overflowing morning, noon and night.

Within its dark wooden interior, designed in 1909 so as to frame enormous tinted photographs of the town, there is a wealth of gilded Gothic lettering marching round the top of every wall and across the many ceiling beams. Sit there surrounded by scenes of old Marshall and read your way through the wise words of 'celebrated men', with such presidential pontifications as 'Fear is the tax that conscience pays to guilt' by Zachary Taylor, or else Grover Cleveland's 'If honour be your clothing, it will last a lifetime'. Abraham Lincoln was responsible for 'I have never met or heard of anyone who could out-smart honesty', whereas Andrew Jackson wrote that 'One man with courage makes a majority'.

You may find many a historic town tweaked up to the tourist nines the world over, but few have the combination of beauty and work-a-day buzz of Marshall in Michigan.

CASTLE TUCKER

Castle Tucker commands a singular presence on a meadowed hill, high over the town and estuary of Wiscasset in Maine. Originally built in 1807 as a chaste classical villa on frontierland, it was given a fancy glass gown in the 1860s with window panes covering its entire first floor and three great arches below.

Judge Silas Lee was responsible for its first surprise appearance in the then edge-of-the-wilderness America, standing above the 'hovels' of the early settlers scattered beneath it. Lee had studied at Harvard with the great architect Charles Bullfinch, who, no doubt, influenced Lee's building of no fewer than three classical piles in and around Wiscasset. It was said that he had 'a passion for building which he indulged beyond his wants or his means… which kept him embarrassed in his finances'. After the War of 1812 he and his wife collapsed into penury and he died of spotted fever two years later.

For years the house stood empty, looming over the town in a state of rotting, ivy-clasped decay. According to the *Lincoln Intelligencer* of 1829, it had been constructed 'on so expensive a scale, no one offered himself as a tenant; if anyone had the occasion to pass it after nightfall, it was *auribus erectis*, with a breathless silence and a light and hasty step'.

After Silas Lee, Castle Tucker was owned by a series of similarly rousingly-named Americans, among whom were Abiel Wood, Barnabas Sullivan, Seth Hawthorne, Ebenezer Hilton and Dr Moses Shaw, who, when he died in 1847, was to leave his four children only '$8.75… three buffalo robes and a bearskin'.

In 1858, the house was set on a surprising new course, considering its sparse classicism, with a new owner in the form of the cultivated Richard Holbrook Tucker – sea captain and part owner of a fleet of cotton trading ships. It was Captain Tucker who decorated the house with dazzling discretion in a taste of the times that was at once both lush and dignified. As well as building a new facade, which he later almost covered with glass, he filled 'Castle Tucker' to the gunnels with his nineteenth-century American seafaring treasures.

And so the house has remained, unchanged to this day, with first, Tucker's daughter, then his granddaughter, both called Jane – managing to hang on to it all, come hell or high water, over the years.

It is such houses as this that excite the sense of wonder at the survival of the humdrum, of how, after a hundred years, the ordinary can become rare. The first thing that you see when you walk through its doors are nineteenth-century 'fire salvage bags' – Father Christmas-like sacks into which you would cram your most precious belongings for a quick getaway in case of a fire – one of the many Captain Tucker devices to be found here. Leather fire buckets still stand at the ready as does the 'Automatic Fireman' – an escape ladder that would fall from the windows.

Throughout the house every room is hung with nineteenth-century wallpaper, that, in its luminosity seems to bring the house alive – hallelujahing from the past in glowing oxide tones of gold, copper and bronze, grey and green, blue, pink and mauve. Paintings and prints hang heavy throughout, with such gems as 'The Prodigal Son Revelling with Harlots' – a print by Robert Sayer of Fleet Street, London, dated 1791; then there is 'Leonardo da Vinci Dying in the Arms of Francis I'; and what about 'The Divorce of Queen Caroline in the House of Lords

in 1820'. Making you laugh as well as cry is the print 'Execution Militaire' of a poodle trying to defend its master from a firing squad ordered by Napoleon I, which hangs alongside exquisite prints revealing the architectural grandeur of Potsdam in the early 1800s. With such objects as these you are straightway imbued with the atmosphere of Castle Tucker – a late nineteenth-century cultivated taste, laced through with the American seafaring spirit.

How pleasurable, for example, to come upon the patent for the invention of the hovercraft – or rather the 'round Surf Boat'– devised by Richard Tucker, but from which he never made a dime. Described as 'shaped like a saucer… the interior forming a reservoir for compressing air… It can be driven five or six miles an hour by one man and carries twenty as fast as one. She is of great strength and buoyancy… And it is thought will be a complete success'. Tucker's hovercraft was launched in Wiscasset Harbor in 1879, but no more was ever heard of this 'pneumatic propulsion of vessel at sea'.

For the last thirty-five years, Captain Tucker's granddaughter, Jane, a scholarly sweetheart of a woman, has been putting in order many thousands of papers found at Castle Tucker. There are 12,736 of them on ship-related matters, invoices and receipts for the house that include 5,628 letters both to and from the Tucker family to and from all the captains of Richard Tucker's ships. Those letters from Richard are written 'with a goose quill… all flowing with scarcely a scratch out… in meticulous small writing… with humor and colorful language'.

His accounts of his voyages set your senses a-shivering: 'We then experienced a tremendous gale from the north west and being in a light set of ballast were in danger of upsetting. I never saw the wind blow so

hard before or since… All hands were on deck and hung in suspense, every moment expecting the ballast to shift and the ship to go down.'

Between 1841-47 the 'long Yankee-faced' Captain, who 'never used ardent spirits except medicinally' made fifteen journeys to Europe as master of the *Alliance* on the Charleston and Savannah to Liverpool or Le Havre route. According to Jane, he apparently 'bought heavily in Liverpool in the 1840s'. In the house's billiard room there is a watercolour depicting the *Alliance* at Liverpool. On the desk below are the mail boxes from the *Alliance* and the *Othello*, through which so many of those thousands of letters would have passed. All around, the bookcases are stuffed, the tables and shelves are laden, and the walls are hung heavy with trophies of Tucker seafaring and family life: a lava bowl from Fiji, a quadrant modelled on Haley's; a sponge on the desk for copying letters – you moistened your letter, pressed it down and hey presto! – you had a replica, albeit the wrong way round. Setting sail over all is a model of the steamer the *South Carolina*, a propeller steamship with the hull of a sailing ship, it was another of Tucker's sadly unsuccessful vessel designs. This was not, however, for want of a splendid send-off. Before its maiden voyage on 10 February 1852 a delectable feast of thirty-three courses was held including, according to the framed lace and silken menu at Castle Tucker today, 'gelatine de dinde truffe decor' as well as 'crustade of rice à la financier' and blancmange.

Two ennobling white marble busts of Walter Scott and Benjamin Franklin lord it from on high on the bookcases, together with a stuffed white Arctic owl of the 1870s 'hit over the head with a shovel by the hired man' and given immortality when stuffed by Jane's father. Books by Browning, Grossmith, Milton, Sydney Smith, Longfellow and Mrs Gaskell fill the shelves, as well as such less tempting works as *Woman and Her Diseases* and *Dana's Muck Manual*.

Captain Tucker had hated the boredom of the high seas, but after being given 200 books by a man

Opposite: *The billiard room at Castle Tucker, Wiscasset, Maine (1858); it is the luminosity of the nineteenth-century wallpaper that seems to bring the house alive.*

in Savannah he became an avid reader and never looked back. There are of course works a-plenty here for mariners, dating back to the 1700s, their bindings gleamingly treated in neat's-foot oil. With just one of these handsome volumes alone, you could be guided through the seas of the world.

In the parlour everything is still assembled as it was by Richard Tucker himself, after he had bought all the furniture for the house in Boston in 1858. Furthermore nothing has faded. To settle yourself in the medallion-backed sofa in this room is to be bewitched into believing that you have been hurled back in time. Reach for a book – below the bust of Dickens – and encourage the illusion with such vigorous volumes as *Our Deportment and Seminary Souvenirs* by the Revd Bernard O'Reilly.

Out in the piazza, with its great glass windows, you come upon a treat the like of which can only be found in such survivals as Castle Tucker: a cabinet of curiosities filled with random delights. Captain Tucker's ticket to the Tsar's coronation of 1850 lies side by side with his sun spectacles of a dense royal blue hue. Jane has just discovered and added his brilliant yellow ones for fog! Then there is a weathered bag of coins, marked with the pound sign – the profits of a sea voyage that Tucker thought more prudent to keep by his side rather than trust to the Bank of England in the unsettled Europe of 1848.

Here too, in this Maine cabinet, is a coin in which the American dollar has its origins. The Spanish silver coin the *ocho reales* was the only currency accepted world-wide until the nineteenth century. Much used in America after the Revolutionary War it was then adopted as the basis of the new country's monetary system. In the words of John Quincy Adams in 1821: 'We found ourselves with four English words: Pound, Shilling, Pence and Farthing. But these words were as Babel.' In no two states did they represent the same

Castle Tucker's cabinet of curiosities of random delights.

Jane Tucker in the kitchen at Castle Tucker with her Hoosier Kitchen Cabinet (1920) and kitchen sink (1858).

value. 'We took the Spanish piece of eight, that had always been the most popular coin among us, and gave it a new name "Dollar".'

As Captain Tucker's inventions continued to flourish and fail, poverty loomed by the 1880s. Mrs Tucker tried ever harder to make ends meet, by translating, writing, and even publishing a song – 'At the Tryst', but all to little avail. She died in 1922 leaving her daughter Jane to take over, living in the house for some forty years with Annie Donnell – originally 'the hired girl' in the 1890s – who was to become her only companion. Together they valiantly kept Castle Tucker from collapse: raising squab, running a dairy farm, taking in boarders, haying the fields and ironing sheets. If the curious came to see the house,

Jane would charge them twenty-five cents but then would give it to the Red Cross!

Eventually, Jane says, 'my aunt's body gave out, her companion's head gave out; they made a poor pair'. Gradually retreating into the kitchen, they slept in one room, leaving the rest of the house untouched. As her aunt ailed in the 1950s, her niece – who would inherit the house with her sister – saw where her responsibilities lay ('the unmarried one always gets the summons') and she left her job in Arabia to move to nearby Boston in order to be able to carry out her duty. When the old lady died in 1964, Jane discovered some dozens of trunks stuffed full of remnants of life in the house, as well as a pair of loaded pistols. One trunk contained nothing but petticoats, another was

The Hoosier Kitchen Cabinet 'Want List'.

full of hairbrushes, hook and eye buttons and combs, while others held only fans and shawls.

Despite living in the kitchen, the two old ladies changed nothing. They were kept warm day and night by an Empire Crawford Royal Stove – a bulgingly ornate range of 1905 (a local farmer had remembered saving his premature baby's life in the plate warmer of the same model). They continued using the sink that the forty-two-year-old Richard Tucker had ordered to be made for his sixteen-year-old bride-to-be by local rowing-boat builder, Mr Colby, and that same sink still sets sail into the simple room today.

Most marvellous of all is the Hoosier Kitchen Cabinet – made in Indiana in 1920. 'A kitchen within a kitchen', it has a built-in flour bin sifter as well as a built-in sugar bin and dispenser. Most entrancing of all, and so frail in their cardboard survival, are the 'Turntable Menus… copyright 1915 of Mrs Christina Frederick'. You first turn the dial to the meat you want as the basis of your fare. The other windows then recommend which soups, vegetables and puddings should be chosen for a healthy balance, with the advice: 'choose only one from each group… one watery vegetable, one starchy vegetable… the body contains three elements, that are required daily'. Hyphens between ingredients suggest alternatives and there is a numbered code for dressings. The 'Want List' is adorned with clock-like hands which rotate to mark your needs, along with a smaller hand for oven timing. Not only is it all intact and in working order, but also, in their brown paper bag are the original screws – 'Necessary trimmings for the Hoosier Cabinet Top' – should it ever need mending. None have been used.

As 'Aunt Jane' and Annie lived on in this room, the rest of the house lived on alone. Until 1972, that is, when Jane Tucker moved in here for good. Since then she has been meticulously tending and recording every centimetre of Castle Tucker so as to be able to hand it over, safe and sound, to the Society for the Preservation of New England Antiquities.

Thanks to Jane Tucker's wise guidance this house has been steered safely off into the future, to enlighten generations to come.

R. H. TUCKER.
Surf-Boat.

No. 215,843. Patented May 27, 1879.

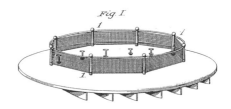

THE NEW YORK YACHT CLUB

'To look up is to learn to love architecture.' Nowhere can my maxim be more exhilaratingly applied than in New York. And where could the spirits more obviously soar than in Manhattan, with such seemingly-endless and obvious beauties as the Chrysler Building, shiningly slicing its way into the sky! For me, looking up at its eagles, over 1000-foot up, is to stroll down memory lane, for I am inordinately proud to be able to claim to have crawled along one of their necks when making a film in the 1990s – following in the footsteps of the great architectural photographer, Margaret Bourke-White, who did the same when taking pictures of Manhattan's skyline in the 1930s.

There are many such pinnacles of architectural perfection in New York which, from their rooftops down to the pavements, provide as rich an aesthetic feast as could be found the world over – often with dishes too rich to digest! One façade in particular would be hard to stomach – the ornately protruding New York Yacht Club at 37 West 44th Street, built in 1899 by the stellar swells John Jacob Astor, William Vanderbilt and J. Pierpont Morgan.

If capitalism can ever be said to have produced heroes, then the American titans of the Gilded Age most richly deserve that title. During the unprecedented growth of American industry and commerce, the 'Robber Barons' as they became known, burgeoned and blossomed with magnificent architectural manifestations of their wealth. They built themselves castles, palaces and mansions and, of course, they enjoyed those most luxuriant of homes away from home – their clubs. Manhattan alone is still thickset with their grandeur – all of them in proud, and I fear often pompous, use today. Built as great citadels for the turn-of-the-century kings of commerce, the clubs are still thrivingly alive, wearing their aspirations on their architectural sleeves with superior splendour.

The University Club, for instance, built by McKim, Meade and White in 1900, is both Gothic and classical, with each outweighing the other in extravagance. With one step through its doors the roar of the New World is left behind and you are engulfed by the architecture of the Old. The Harvard Club of 1902, also by McKim, Mead and White, cuts a sombre and dignified dash with a vast triple-height Harvard Hall of wood and stone. Making you want to scream out loud with surprise – something that would be as welcome here as a tambourine-playing clown with a performing poodle – is the head of a stuffed elephant, on high, with its trunk sticking forth, straight and horizontal, some six feet from his face.

Most grandiloquent of all club exteriors – no bombastic boast – is the New York Yacht Club, a building that bursts forth with French finery, designed in what was known at the time as the Modern-French style – first seen with such buildings as Charles Garnier's Paris Opera House of 1862-74. 'Regarding decoration', wrote Garnier, 'there is no guide... the decorative art has such independence and freedom that it is impossible to submit it to fixed rules.' Slammed by the critics as 'cartouche architecture' for its inordinate degree of swags and garlands, it was nevertheless to smother the buildings of New York. A Chicago architect, George Maher, found it wildly unsuitable: 'It destroys the Americanism in the Americans… Before they know it, they will be talking French and shrugging their shoulders.'

In a further downpour of disdain, the *Architectural Review* of 1897 virulently declared that the Modern-French style was 'abnormal' and 'dropsical'; it was invading the field of architecture 'like the bubonic plague'. But architects were not to be intimidated and with the New York Yacht Club they cocked the most flamboyant snook of all.

Whitney Warren, who, with Charles Wetmore designed this extravaganza, had studied at the École des Beaux Arts in Paris. For him such voluptuousness was the architectural answer, most especially when it was being built for such opulent lives. They designed stone seaweed to drip and stone dolphins to splash beneath its windows; fruit and chain festooned, stone-glazed sterns of *jaghts* protrude out into the street, seemingly sailing away into the hallowed haven of the club. (*Jaghts* – from which the word yacht was derived – were the handsome seventeenth-century vessels used on the Dutch canals, the ships that first suggested the idea of sailing for pleasure in America.) Inside you can settle cosily into the padded leather seats of the sterns and watch the dramatically-different world going by in the street below.

As if this was not decoration enough, Warren and Wetmore went further creating an enormous keystone above the front door of Neptune, with ropes, anchors and shells – all carved in Indiana limestone. According to the American Museum of Natural History in New York, they are the most accurate architectural representations of shells in the world!

Staggering under the weight of such ornamentation – and assuming you manage to get up the glorified gangplank of the marble stairway – you will be brought to your knees as you enter the club's model room by the sight of its quite terrifyingly-tremendous fireplace. As big as a house, and made from 47 tons of Caen stone, here, once again, contemporary critics found a want of restraint: 'The riot of swags and spinach, icicles and exotic vegetation, that is in progress… take one's breath away. Surely this is not architectural design' spouted the *Architectural Review*. By its sheer swaggery, though, it was suited to the swells who toasted their toes before it with club members including such figures as Whitney and Roosevelt. There are over 1500 models, and half models, of the members' yachts in the club and hundreds of them sailing forth from the walls about this great room. Grotesque dolphins, with chandeliers dripping from their mouths, support a balcony – complete with a musicians' galley – that surrounds three sides of the room, lit over all by a ceiling of stained glass.

James Gordon Bennett was another of the club's swells – indeed it was he who paid for the painting of the first trans-atlantic yacht race that is inset into the overmantel. This had taken place in 1866, and it was won by the yacht *Henrietta*, with Gordon Bennett at the helm, along with the poet Longfellow's son Charles, who went along for the ride!

Bennett was the commodore of the New York Yacht Club for many years. It was said that he was 'born with a silver spoon in his mouth, a spoon which he lived to see turn into gold'. He was stupendously rich, having inherited the *New York Herald* from his father, a Scotsman from Banff, who from the first indulged his son with 'pocket money enough to meet every desire'. When only sixteen-years old Bennett had built the 77 ton schooner, *Rebecca*. And so it was that as the youngest skipper in America he became a member of the New York Yacht Club and literally sailed into the highest stratospheres of society.

Owning a yacht was part and parcel of the pleasures of fashionable living in New York in the 1880s, and Bennett was to apply himself vigorously to such

Opposite: The New York Yacht Club's terrifyingly tremendous fireplace made from 47 tons of Caen stone (1899).

pursuits throughout his life, building enough craft to amount to a fleet. His *Namouna* of 1882 was described as 'an English mansion afloat' having panelled walls of cherry wood, chestnut, oak, maple and teak and ornate furniture on oriental rugs. Its bathrooms had wash tubs beneath trap doors. There was also, wonder of wonders, a padded stall in which an Alderney cow was kept to provide the swells with fresh milk and cream. There was an electric fan to keep her cool and a machine to milk her.

Despite costing as much a $140,000 a year to keep afloat, the *Namouna* was but merely a skiff compared to the grandeur of Bennett's steamship *Lysistrata* – built in Dumbarton in Scotland in 1900. Of a splendour at the time unequalled in the world, she was 314 feet of concentrated luxury with vast reception rooms, a Turkish bath and the usual and comfortable quarters for a cow.

Bennett was famed for his autocratic ways. He forbade gambling on board the *Lysistrata* and his guests' luggage would be regularly searched for cards. If a pack was discovered, Bennett would take out the four aces, tear them in half and the pack would then be returned to its owner.

An inviolate rule was that no one with a beard was allowed on the ship. Even the deck hands 'had been scraped clean of their hirsute ornaments'. Once, Bennett sent for a *New York Herald* employee, the roving reporter James Creelman. He arrived but armed as he was with a 'fine brown beard', was not allowed aboard. Enraged and resolutely refusing to shave, he followed the *Lysistrata* from port to port as far as Fiume in Italy, but was repeatedly barred from boarding. He eventually departed without seeing his boss who had sent for him in the first place.

But one employee was to get the better of him. Bennett was convinced that dogs were the true tellers of character and had a pack of Pomeranians, peeks and cocker spaniels ready to sense out the quality of the caller. The Irish correspondent of his newspaper, having had been summoned to see Bennett, sensed

New York Yacht Club by Warren & Wetmore, 1899.

(© Avery Library, Columbia University)

trouble, and knowing of the canine critics, prepared his ground by putting a slice of raw liver in his topper. The dogs frolicked in ecstasy about him and so his job was saved!

Despite these curious curbs, revelry reigned on the *Lysistrata*. In Amsterdam Bennett invited a theatrical troupe to entertain his guests and was so delighted by their performance that they were borne out to sea and not returned until they had been through their *entire* repertoire. The ship had 'mistresses' in abundance to entertain the commodore – with three permanently on call, each with an elaborately decked out apartment and with all their needs tended to by the hundred-strong crew.

One of Bennett's regular and riotous sports would be to whip the tablecloths from under diner's dinners in restaurants. If, magician-like, nothing broke, so much the better. If there was chaos, he relished handing out hefty compensation.

Gordon Bennett! It is no wonder that his name has become synonymous with surprise.

It was Bennett who sent one of his favourite correspondents, Henry Morton Stanley, to find Dr David Livingstone in 1869. Had Bennett 'considered seriously the great expense... of this little journey' asked Stanley wondering at 'the cool order of sending one to central Africa to search for a man whom I, in common with most other men, believed to be dead?' 'Well I will tell you what to do,' Bennett had replied, 'draw a thousand pounds now, and when you have gone through that, draw another thousand, and when that is spent, draw another thousand, and when you have finished that, draw another thousand, and so on, BUT FIND LIVINGSTONE!'

Two years later, in 1871, Stanley triumphed in doing exactly that. Later he was to send Livingstone a further year's supplies at the *Herald's* expense. 'Your kindness made my frame thrill' Livingstone wrote to Bennett, 'let the richest blessings descend from the highest on you and yours!'

On 1 January 1877 calamity struck with a scandal. On New Year's Day in New York it was the festive custom to 'open houses with flowing punch bowls' and Bennett caroused through them all. Very much the worse for wear, he called at the home of an eminently-distinguished surgeon to whose daughter – 'of unusual beauty' – he was paying court. Forgetting himself, he peed into the fireplace in front of his intended. 'It was conduct unbecoming a gentleman – or anyone else.'

Her outraged brother beat Bennett black-and-blue with a cow hide on Park Avenue before challenging him to a duel at Slaughter's Gap in Delaware. They both shot wide, but Bennett's life in America was finished by his disgrace. He lived out most of his days on his yacht and abroad – often wearing armour in fear of the ever-vengeful brother. He eventually went bankrupt, having spent every last cent of his $40-million fortune.

Lamentably he left no funds for his last flamboy-ant foray into immortality. He had commissioned the architect Stamford White to design a towering mausoleum in the form of an owl which, with eyes alight, would stand overlooking the Hudson River in Upper Manhattan. In it, hanging from chains, would be the suspended coffin of James Gordon Bennett.

If the gains of the Robber Barons were on a monumental scale, then so too were their gifts to others. Andrew Carnegie, for example, built 2,811 free public libraries in every conceivable architectural style all over the world all of which we can relish today. And it was the banker, businessman and collector, J. Pierpont Morgan, who, 'without the least ostentation, as if he was merely giving away a cigar', donated the land on which the New York Yacht Club was built. A titan of a man, a heady mix of commerce and culture, he created a collection of paintings, books, manuscripts and letters – from Dürer to Degas, from the Gutenberg Bible to Gilbert and Sullivan – that has few equals. Today, it is all housed in the exquisite Pierpont Morgan Library – another building by McKim, Mead and White. Everything that Morgan bought, he had bought with a passion – 'for the instruction and pleasure of the American people', dreaming that in his assembling of the very best of the Old World, no one need ever leave the New World again.

As for the man though, it was said that Morgan's splendour 'shone most magnificently at sea'. Whilst his home life was modest and his marriage was unhappy, his nautical life was flamboyant in the extreme and replete with women. He was a depressive and the sea seemed to sweep all his gloom away. His steam yachts *Corsairs I, II* and *III* became his second homes and under the cover of 'The Corsair Club' many high jinks occurred here with his friends.

The yachts were also ideally isolated settings for big business deals. During the first great railroad dispute, in 1885, Morgan kept the protagonists prisoners on his boat – sailing up and down the Hudson

River, until they came to an agreement. The result-ing treaty between the Pennsylvania Railroad and the New York Central companies became known as the 'Corsair Compact'.

As if to constantly – and cruelly – remind Morgan of his human frailty, he had to bear a humil-iating burden throughout most of his life, and one that was forever to the fore: an enormous and grotesquely disfiguring nose, which, like a purple cauliflower sprouted forth from his face. Keeping his pecker up with such pronouncements that it 'was part of the American business structure' it nevertheless was an undermining embarrassment that created countless sorry scenes. Once he was asked to take tea with a lady in Manhattan: she had warned her chil-dren to on no account look at, or say a word about the nose. So intensely was she willing them that she quite forgot herself, and leaning forward said: 'Do you like one nose or two in your tea Mr Morgan?' And when John W. 'Bet A Million' Gates – famed for his wagers on anything from raindrops to racehorses – called him 'a ruby visaged magnate', Morgan had him blackballed from the Yacht Club.

In 1858 a certain William Corrie was expelled from the club, when, whilst flying the burgee of the Yacht Club, he transported 300 slaves in his yacht from West Africa. To the last man the swells con-demned him for 'being engaged in traffic repugnant to humanity and to the moral sense of the members', and never were they to mention his name again.

By the turn of the nineteenth century such swells of American capitalism had overtaken their European counterparts in both wealth and splen-dour. This was perfectly encapsulated by the New York Yacht Club – a foghorn variant of its quieter cousins across the seas.

MOHONK MOUNTAIN HOUSE

'In the eyes of the American' wrote the great Tom Paine 'nature appears to him in magnitude. The mighty objects he beholds act upon his mind by enlarging it, and he partakes of the greatness he contemplates.' Such is the effect on your sensibilities when first seeing Mohonk – an Elysian enclave of some thousands of acres, embosoming the green waters of Mohonk Lake in the Shawangunk range of mountains of Upstate New York. Seemingly as majestic as the mountains themselves is the Mohonk Mountain House – a fantastical eighth-of-a-mile long rustic palace that was built as a 'hospitable inn' between 1879-1910 by identical Quaker twins, Albert and Alfred Smiley, and is still run on Quaker principals by their descendants today. Judging by its droves of devotees, here is living proof that much of America thrives on old-fashioned ways.

Mohonk – the Indian word for 'lake in the sky' – seems like an enchanted kingdom when you come upon it. The Mountain House looms as large as you imagine a building could be, in a setting that was described by a visiting nineteenth-century clergyman as 'one of those rare places where the creative power seems to have rehearsed for every form of grandeur and gentleness'.

From first setting eyes on the landscape in 1869, the Smiley twins were captivated; only seventy miles as the crow flies from New York City, here they were 'surrounded by romantic natural features absolutely unknown to the outside world' in an 'atmosphere almost intoxicating in its strength and purity'. As said the great scientist and geologist Arnold Guyot (after whom three mountains were named): 'Few spots on our continent unite so much beauty of scenery, both grand and lovely, within so small a compass, to be enjoyed with so much ease.'

Albert Smiley bought the land immediately with his frugally-fought-for-savings; after borrowing the balance and $300 from his wife the domain was his. 'I spent every dollar I had' he wrote 'and in order to pay for it I started a business which, above all things in the world, I had a distaste for and no experience of... I had no more thought of hotel keeping than going to the moon.' The first forty people to come to Mohonk were friends and thereafter the Smileys would ask people that they knew to stay, as well as paying guests.

There already existed a somewhat colourful tavern by Mohonk Lake – a 'small rude structure' owned by John Festus Stokes, whose way of keeping his drunken customers in order was simply to chain them to the trees! If you wanted to wash, 'the lake was handy' and for sustenance a chicken would be caught, killed and cooked in front of your eyes. One day, when there were no fowl to be found, Stokes's 'good nature' prevailed, with him roasting his pet peacock for the guest, who declared it 'the toughest morsel that he had ever tackled'.

The Smileys' establishment was, and has continued to be, of a very different order. It set out to entice the 'cultivated class of people... without molestation from the fast and rougher elements of society'. This was a sublime setting, 'where man should be nourished by nature and nature be nurtured by man'. And so the 'Mohonk Spirit' was born, which continues to thrive to this day.

A fantastical eighth-of-a-mile long rustic palace. Mohonk Mountain House, New York State (1879-1910).

Over the years I have learned to dearly love the place, knowing it is where I can see such etchings as 'Sheep on the Sussex Downs' or otherwise a print of 'Christiana and her daughters in the Valley of Death'; knowing too, that in this most gentle of atmospheres there will be either a concert or a reading in the great mahogany parlour in the evening, and for those who wish it, that there will be prayers in the family parlour each morning.

There are 151 fireplaces at Mohonk, all roaring away in the public rooms in winter; while those in your bedrooms are ready with logs. All this, surrounded by a magnificently-savage landscape. Never, ever, will I forget looking out on to the lake one evening when the only sounds were the plop of a fish in the water and the barking of a deer in the woods. Suddenly, and simultaneously 'Onwards Christian Soldiers' and Mozart's 'Exultate Jubilate' sang out into the air. One, from the hymns in the great parlour, the other a soprano rehearsing for an evening's performance – no mean American moment!

Temperance was unquestioned at Mohonk from the first. One nineteenth-century visitor delighted in the spring being 'the only bar within three miles of Mohonk' whilst declaring the view as 'scenery wrought into every form of wildness and grace... as only poetry exalted to worship can fitly rehearse'. There is still no bar, although your stomach can now

Overlooking Mohonk Lake.

be settled with either beer or fine wines. Card play-ing was forbidden, and in place of 'dancing and tip-pling' Mohonk offered 'something more desirable… a library of good standard works'. Daily services, with hymns on Sunday, have been held at the Mountain House since 1879. Albert Smiley had always hoped that in generations to come 'the all-omnipotent Creator, whose tender compassion notices a sparrow's fall, may be fitly reverenced by hotel and guests'. And so it has proved to be.

The Smileys have controlled and cultivated this land for over 120 years; not only that, but by setting out from the start to protect the place from dastardly development they have ensured that the many miles of surrounding mountains and farmlands are pro-tected in perpetuity. All around the Mountain House, vast rocks lie in petrified chaos, presenting a paradise of the picturesque, whilst following all their fissures and folds is some of the first 'aesthetic forestry' in America.

Nature walks were, and still are, organized here, as well as boating, fishing and riding. Few pleasures could be greater than leading your horse from the old wooden stables at Mohonk, then setting off past the corral of carriage mules, out into the woods. Surrounded by rocks the size of town halls, suddenly a view might break through, laying before you many hundreds of miles of either the Hudson Valley or the

Catskill Mountains. 'I think that I never had larger ideas of beauty, grandeur, and magnificence' wrote another nineteenth-century cleric. 'What a pencil I need, what canvas, and what colours, to do justice to such a scene and then I would need an angel's hand to guide the pencil.'

By 1907 Albert Smiley was to write that he had 'treated this property... as a landscape artist does his canvas'. He created sixty miles of trails, with over a hundred little thatched cedar gazebos – to lure you out of doors – scattered hither and thither about the land, many of them perched on precipitous prominences either over the lake or the valleys beyond 'where the horizon is crowded with piled up walls of azure'. Linked by wooden railings and bridges over deep dark ravines, you can progress from one to the other, with the continuous – and always supremely satisfied – expectation of a finely formed view. Here at Mohonk you have a survival of nineteenth-century landscape art, unaltered to this day.

Albert Smiley was to write that 'It would be deplorable if this house should ever acquire the mercenary spirit and make the accumulation of money without higher ulterior aims the goal of its ambition.' With the Quaker tradition for pacifism, wishing to arbitrate rather than dictate, he organized the 'Lake Mohonk Conferences on International Arbitration' in the Mountain House in 1895; the conferences continued to be held here for another twenty-one years with Mohonk being described as 'a citadel morally embattled and fearless to the foe'. In the sleekly-panelled parlour some of America's most distinguished statesmen and philanthropists would gather to pioneer for peace, with luminaries such as the great writer Edward Everett Hale passionately declaring in 1895, that they should urge 'first, second, last and always a "permanent tribunal" that is the thing... which must be rubbed into the public mind!'. Then there was the great Elihu Root, Secretary of State under Roosevelt in 1915 and winner of the Nobel peace prize in 1912. That year Root

Henry Benjamin Whipple, Bishop of Minnesota: 'Apostle to the Indians' and 'Tall Mohonker'.

nominated Albert Smiley himself for the prize, but sadly he was to die only months later. The Mohonk conferences laid the foundations for the International Court of Justice in the Hague but, sorry to say, these great men did indeed have their heads in the clouds since down below, in the real world, as these idealists were planning for peace, the European powers were preparing for the First World War.

Regulars to Mohonk are known as 'Mohonkers', while those who have made a particular mark on the place or on their country are known by the elevating title of 'Tall Mohonkers'. Their portraits hang thick along one corridor; a more worthy bunch of men – and one woman – could scarcely be found the world over. Most were ardent and active participants in the conferences for 'The Friends of The Indians' – held here for over thirty years. With the aid of the experts who are still gathered together in this gallery of fame, and with the Quaker dictum 'There is that of God in everyone', Albert Smiley determined to do what he could to protect the rights of the Native American.

One, Tall Mohonker, Henry Benjamin Whipple – the Bishop of Minnesota – was regarded as an expert on the 'Indian Question'. Described as 'having the air of a noble savage' he made so many 'extensive tours into the wilderness' that the Indians gave him the name of 'Straight Tongue', while his fellow would-be reformers referred to him as the 'Apostle to the Indians'.

The face of Hugh Lennox Scott stares fiercely forth from the walls. He was considered an authority on the Plains Indians and wrote a book on Indian sign language. Although he had initially fought against the Sioux, the Nez Percé and the Cheyenne, he was to gain the trust and friendship of some Native Americans, eventually commanding a cavalry unit of the Apache, Comanche and Kiowa tribes. Later, as Governor of the Philippines, he abolished slavery and the slave trade.

The elegantly-clad Revd Theodore Cuyler, author of twenty-two books and some four thousand devotional articles, became known as the 'Mohonk Episcopus' after being the Mountain House's resident minister for over thirty years. In 1872 'a commotion occurred in Presbyterian circles' when he invited Sarah Frances (a woman and a Quaker woman at that!) to speak in his church. She is the only female on these walls. Then there is the noble-looking naturalist, John Burroughs, who stands on a Mohonk prominence with his long white beard

Every object that has outgrown its life in the Mountain House has been preserved in the Barn Museum. Left to right: horse collar, 1890s; cash register – for items up to $9.99, 1900s; copper 'space heater', 1920s; barber's chair converted to a shoe-shine stand, 1910; glass-windowed post office boxes, 1890s; 'Magic Andees' stove, 1900s; wheelchair.

floating in the breeze. He wrote that he often came to the Shawangunk Mountains 'to find myself, as it is so easy to get lost in the world'.

In this great array of natural forms, the Mountain House is a startling eruption – so vast that with each window lit up at night it looks like a town in the midst of a wilderness. By day, however, it merges into the landscape, albeit by virtue of its immense size and at-odds-with-each-other structures – one grafted on to the other, over the years, by such architects as Napoleon LeBrun in the 1880s and James Ware at the turn of the century. The dining room, described by the great architectural writer Ada Louise Huxtable as vast enough to 'float the *Mauretania*', is two storeys of welcoming wood, with fancy ornamental brackets atop tree-tall columns. With a chef on hand to make limitless varieties of omelettes, as well as such delicacies as waffles, pancakes and French toast – served with caramelized walnuts and strawberries, maple syrup and cream, a ship the size of the *Mauretania* would be satisfied with this great sea of food.

Every object, no matter how insignificant, that has outgrown its life in the Mountain House has been preserved in its barn. This has now become full and fascinating enough to be an extraordinary museum in its own right containing everything from shoeshine chairs to an entire barber's shop,

from the Mountain House's original post office with its bevelled-glass-windowed boxes to the hand-hauled Otis hydraulic elevator of 1893. Said to be 'easy on the stomach', it was so slow that a standing joke would be for the elevator boy to say: 'Third floor sir? I am sorry but this is the Thursday trip to the fourth'! The old bellman's board hangs on the wall. Wrecked rocking chairs are piled high by the hundred alongside harnesses, farm machinery, stoves, carriages and heaven alone knows what else. There is a wooden chair which, by pumping away on its footrest allows you to swing some twenty feet into the air; it is one of the many that used to hang on giant rustic frames about the place, it creakingly evokes the early days of Mohonk.

Mohonk has continued to blaze trails of excellence. In 1963 The Mohonk Trust was founded to infuse people with the 'ecological ethic' on their many thousands of acres. In 1986 it was declared a National Historic Landmark – an honour that was laden with the praise that 'it keeps alive the nineteenth-century vision that tells us that untrammelled nature has important things to teach us'.

Not only have generations of 'indefatigable and inexhaustible' Smileys preserved the great past of Mohonk, they have so successfully seeped it into the present that this nineteenth-century monolith will take to the new millennium like a duck to water.

TREMONT NAIL
FACTORY

Step through the doors of the Tremont Nail Factory in Wareham, Massachusetts and you are plunged straightway into the clamouring dawn of the Industrial Revolution. Row upon row of nineteenth-century machines – whose designs, in some cases, date back to the late 1700s – are clatteringly churning out nails by the thousand. Leather belts, powered by overhead shafts are being hauled through the great wooden roof trusses – sights and sounds to knock senseless with delight the scholar of industrial archaeology: an authentic factory still in production today, amid surroundings that would scarcely be credible in the Old World, let alone in the New.

The Tremont Nail Factory was founded in 1819 by brothers Isaac and Jared Pratt, when they built the original factory on the site of a cotton mill operated by the Revd Noble Everett, that had been shelled and partially burned by the British in the War of 1812. The soothingly swept-over-with-shingle buildings that stand there today date from 1848. Wooden window frames, painted dark red, are the only interruptions to its great shingle stretches. A bellcote perches proud over all with the bell just visible through quatrefoil cut outs that 'has called to work and to rest four generations of loyal workers'. Spiking into the sky, the weather vane proclaims the purpose of the place with elegantly tapered cut nails, which from the earliest colonial days built the very fabric of America.

From the start the 'nayle' had been essential to the development of the New World. As early as 1623 they were deemed as important as clothes, food and weapons, and were shipped in quantity from England to Virginia. So sought after were they, that in 1645, the House of Burgesses of Virginia had to pass a law to prohibit the burning down of buildings to filch their nails to build another. In Delaware in 1691, however, the Supervisors of Kent County ordered that the courthouse *should* be reduced to cinders to 'get the nails'.

For the most part though, nails were imported from England – a trade that was, of course, trounced by the Revolutionary War. So from 1776 onwards the American 'nailers' had to sharpen up their business in earnest, since they were still producing the hand wrought nail – a job considered so laboursome, that in the South slaves and children were put to the task.

And so perforce the automatic nail-making machine was created, to chomp its way through plate sheets by the million. Even Thomas Jefferson was an early owner of such a machine, regarding its role as vital to the growth of the young nation: 'I am myself a nail maker' he proudly proclaimed, 'my new trade of nail making is to me in this country what an additional title of nobility or the ensigns of a new order are in Europe'.

The cut nail was, therefore, an American invention, stealing a march on the famed Industrial Revolution in the motherland; indeed, when Samuel Wood from Pennsylvania tried to introduce the machine in England, rioting mobs were to destroy it.

For America though, it was pivotal to patriotic pride. Many were the heroes, who nurtured its progress. Ebenezer Fitch had applied for a licence as early as 1722 to operate a nail 'slitting' mill. In 1775,

The Tremont Nail Factory, Wareham, Massachusetts.
Opposite: *Row upon row of nail cutting machines dating back to the 1700s.*

Jeremiah Wilkinson was the first to cut slivers of metal by mechanical means. Jesse Reed took out a patent in the 1790s. But it is thought that it was Nathaniel Read who produced the first fully-fledged nail-cutting machine in 1797, that 'feeds itself and cuts the heads and nails without any manual labour', producing 10,000 nails a day. Shubal Wilder, a nail maker from Newcastle, Pennsylvania, wrote of the fever that followed its introduction, with the 'hunt for nailers' throughout the states.

It was thanks to the cut nail, along with the United States' abundance of wood, that homes could be built for the country's frenzied population growth – from 5 million to over 76 million during the nineteenth century alone. The log cabin was thought of only as a temporary home, while its successor, the 'frame structure', was too elaborate to be built at

speed. So it was that in 1830, in Chicago, a new, simple and unskilled method of building to cope with the boom was born. Known as 'balloon framing', the process used cut timber and nails alone, instead of complicated interlocking hand-hewn joints, allowing buildings to leap up in their millions. Horace Greeley, founder of *The New York Tribune* and famed for his advice 'Go West Young Man' (it was in fact written by John Soule, his Indiana editor) wrote of the balloon frame that 'there is hardly better evidence of the American spirit'. He thought it 'the most important contribution to our domestic architecture' whereby 'a single man, and a boy can put up a house, such as formally, for its raising, required the combined force of a village'. He described the log cabin as 'making a fair hog pen'. And so the West was won. Timber and nail marched in tandem with the

ever expanding nation.

Here at Wareham then, is the machinery that built America. Thanks to such as the Tremont Nail Company's 'Valiant' mechanical workhorses, one factory alone could produce up to 50 million nails to sell to the West.

Cut nails by the thousand are still being sliced out by the cutting jaws of the grand old machines today, largely to make square-cut and speciality nails for building restoration and reconstruction projects. They are also pressed into service to produce the wooden masonry nail. Colossal beams loom in and out of the light overhead, crisscrossed with leather and canvas belts, loudly whirring their way around immense wheels. A furnace roars. The noise is deafening – thunderingly thumping up the past. The machines are still hand fed, with the strips of nail plate placed on wooden-handled nippers and either 'flipped over' or 'wiggled' through – over and under, or left to right – so as to dovetail their tapering forms. The 'pans' beneath the cutting machine are then filled to over-

Opposite: *The foreman's office, Tremont Nail Factory.*

flowing with the silvery slivers – extraordinarily enough the nails are still graded and named according to the quantity in weight you could buy in pounds sterling. Thus a 'twopenny' is a one-inch nail, the 'fourpenny' is one-and-a-half inches long, the 'sixpenny' measures two inches, and so on.

If you are astonished out of your wits by the factory floor, then be prepared to be knocked out cold by the foreman's office. It is a room where, according to Tremont nailer Tony Hanson, you find 'a lot of stuff that has been hanging here since the beginning of time but never used'. Walk though the door – controlled by strings and weights – and marvel at the vast vice, or boring hole machine, with its elephantine boring bits – taps that look like a giant's screwdrivers. A chain that seems large enough to tether the whole factory in a hurricane lies on the floor and all around and about there is monstrous machinery, thick with the grease and dust of their age. The foreman's chair sits proud, lording it over this remarkable domain.

There can be no better example of the past pulsating its way into the present than the Tremont Nail Factory in Massachusetts!

NEW ORLEANS
GARDEN DISTRICT

If you have ever doubted the sympathy of the suburb then go the Garden District in New Orleans and see how the seeds of the idea were first sown and how radiantly they bloomed.

The Garden District was built on the outskirts of the city from the 1830s – in part as an elegant bastion against yellow fever known as 'Bronze John'. The Shangri-la of suburbia, it is one of the oldest suburbs in America and the most happily homogenous and harmonious of them all. Furthermore it still stands true to its original layout. According to Frederick Starr, academic, Russian expert, jazz trumpeter and the historian who first introduced me to the Garden District, this one small area 'prefigured the process of urban expansion and absorption that has occurred throughout the United States in the twentieth century'. A heavy cross indeed for so delicate a place to bear!

The approach to the suburb alone bodes well as you find yourself on the oldest operating streetcar line in the land. Established in 1835 it has been in clattering service ever since, running along the middle of the broad St Charles Avenue. The dark green cars were renewed in the 1920s when some of the 'Perley Thomas Arch Roof 900 Series' were brought in from North Carolina.

Ten steps into this enclave and you are enfolded by both its natural and man-made beauty. In *Life on the Mississippi* Mark Twain described the Garden District as 'reproachless… these mansions, painted snow white… stand in the centre of large grounds that rise, garlanded with roses, out of the midst of swelling masses of shining green foliage and many

coloured blossoms. No houses could well be in better harmony with their surroundings or more pleasing to the eye'. The same can still be said today with one chastely classical building after another, this is a positive reverie in restraint.

It was a restraint exercised by the men who were the very bones of the growing body of America. Before the railroads were laid all imports and exports for Western expansion poured through the port of New Orleans. With King Cotton reigning supreme in the deep South, the mighty Mississippi delivered up the crop to New Orleans, from whence it was sent on its prosperous way to Liverpool, and thereon to the mills of Lancashire. It is remarkable to therefore realize that this most sultry of suburbs – where each house stands in its white finery like a stately Southern belle – was almost entirely built by Northerners, some of whom were English, Scottish or Irish born. These were the fortune-seekers, finders, and losers whose entrepreneurial drive helped to establish the West.

Thanks to the peculiarity of New Orleans still largely operating under the Napoleonic civil code of law, instigated in 1803 – with as bold and as beautiful a classical courthouse as can be found anywhere in America – its notaries public have been obliged to make detailed records of every legal transaction. Thus, much is known of the Garden District and its occupants.

Leap into their lives in Prytania Street, the first that you come to and as good a street as any in these sixty-six blocks in which to feel the flavour of the place. Before you – as with the whole of the Garden

One of the biggest and the best in the Garden District: Walter Robinson House (1859).

District – lies a celestial townscape of temple after temple amid lush vegetation, stretching off into the distance. One datura has over a hundred trumpet blooms. Here, classicism – the clarion call of the new-found democracy of the New World – combines with an adaptation of the locally-raised Creole cottage with its distinctive pillared porches. It is by far the wisest style for these Southern climes, with porches and balconies built to catch each blessed breeze. Supported by pillars of iron and wood, there are enough columns in the Garden District to keep you counting until the cows come home!

At 2423 Prytania there is a cottage that embraces the Doric order, with columns marching along to support a full-width-of-the-house porch, sweeping round in a semi-circular colonnade to the side. It was built by grocer, John Adams – a man, it was said, with 'puritanical principals of sterling integrity, determination of purpose and indomitable energy'. He was born in New Jersey, raised in frontierland Ohio, and made his fortune in New Orleans in spices, sugar and salt. Then there is the Ionic- and Corinthian-columned pile at 2507, built by Joseph Maddox of Vermont on the success of his *Daily Crescent* newspaper. Today its richly-gilded and statued parlour is as splendid as it ever was, with barely room to swing a mouse, let alone a cat.

The Old World is forever built into the Garden District: the slates on the roofs are from Wales whilst the pavements are of stone from England. Both slate and stone were brought back as ballast on the return journeys of the cotton ships – such was the boom that even ballast created a fortune.

At 2221 Prytania the rewards of cotton broking enabled Robert Grinnan to build a richly-columned house. He was an Englishman newly-arrived from London when he commissioned the eminent New Orleans architect, Henry Howard, to design this building. This though was the era of boom-bust, with its roller coaster of riches plunging every so often into dire poverty, and Grinnan was forced to sell his house

after only two years. Henry Howard suffered dreadful misfortunes too: he was unable to support his wife and children, one son was killed in a shoot-out and Howard himself died in poverty despite being one of the most sought-after designers in the District.

Henry Lonsdale was another who ricocheted from rags to riches, back again to rags and on to further riches – only to die in wretched poverty after having had to sell his cast-iron galleried house at 2521 Prytania. Jute sacks had been his first success, packaging up all and sundry for the West. After being ruined in a financial panic, he crawled his way back to fortune with coffee trading. Born to English parents, he was to become the undisputed caffeine king of the American West. Then there is London-born Thomas Gilmour, a successful cotton broker who built a cast-iron, columned Italianate villa at 2520 Prytania in 1853. Whilst at 3000, Henry Hansell, another Englishman, made enough money selling saddles to the West to build his five-bay columned house.

In this classical townscape stand two lone exceptions whose surprise appearance positively pierce their way into your view: a fantastical Gothic gateway designed for grocer Michael Hans, at 2928 Prytania, as well as a rather severe Gothic house, built for the insurance broker, Charles Briggs, at 2605.

It is, in fact surprising that the Gothic style did not take more of a grip on the Garden District. By the 1820s Sir Walter Scott's Gothic Waverly novels had taken both New Orleans and the South by storm. Mark Twain even accused Sir Walter of being 'in great measure responsible for the War', having had 'so large a hand in making Southern character'. He derided Scott's 'enchantments' that 'sets the world in love with dreams and phantoms, with decayed and swinish forms of religion… with silliness and emptiness, sham grandeurs, sham gauds, and sham chivalries of a brainless and worthless long-vanished society'.

To Twain, Scott's writings 'did measureless harm, more real and lasting than any other individual that ever wrote. Most of the world has now outlived good

As startling a social document as it is an aesthetic surprise, Zuber's 'Scenic America' wallpaper of 1834 covers the walls of the dining room in the Walter Robinson House.

part of these harms… but in our old South they flourish pretty forcefully still… But for the Sir Walter disease, the character of the Southerner… would be wholly modern, in place of modern medieval mixed… It was Sir Walter that made every gentleman in the South a major or a Colonel or a General or a judge… and it was he who made these gentlemen value these decorations'. It was Scott, too, he wrote, who created 'rank and caste' in the South and 'pride and pleasure' in them too.

It could be said that the spirit of Sir Walter Scott lives on in America's Southern states today, with extraordinarily old-fashioned mannerisms still pre-

vailing. (By way of an extra oddity – Southerners consume great quantities of 'chitterlings', the small intestines of pigs, eaten in England throughout the Middle Ages!)

Architecturally Scott fared better, however, leaving a Gothic legacy throughout America, if not in New Orleans, then up the Mississippi with the Old State Capitol at Baton Rouge (1847) which with its battlemented towers looks for all the world like a medieval castle, standing on a hill over this Southern city.

But the Garden District's architectural currency was classicism. No matter how modest the dwelling, it was built in temple form. As if ordained by some unspoken law, the style spread with infinite and infinitesimal variations throughout the suburb producing a perfect serenity of sameness. And so it was to continue, through slumps and booms, even after the Civil War, no jarring note was added to interfere with its harmony. Here was a little classical democracy where rich and poor lived side by side behind pillared porticoes, built by architects or by the owners themselves. Besides the vast mansions they built a quantity of tiny homes: the shotguns, so-called because a bullet could be shot clean through their modest proportions without hindrance, and the camelbacks, with a single hump of a roof over a tiny double dwelling.

After the Civil War many Garden District houses were graced with a lace-like abundance of cast-iron balconies and railings. For example, the house built by Degas's Creole uncle, at 1331 Third Street, was festooned with such ironwork by 1884. Such galleries gave a lighter, livelier air to the façades and therefore to the whole suburb. Most charmful of all is the corn-stalk fence that surrounds a house built for a Colonel Short in 1859, at 1448 Fourth Street, with its iron leaves writhing round fat, iron cobs.

Colonel Robert Henry Short was a man who had behaved disreputably during the Civil War, fleeing New Orleans with the pretence of having to see a doctor in Philadelphia and thus escaping the horrors of General 'Beast' Butler's virulent eight-month occupation of the city. According to Frederick Starr, 'Even today, over a century later, the very mention of this walrus-faced leader can evoke sneers in New Orleans.'

Butler's successor was General Nathanial 'the Bobbin Boy' Banks – so-called because he had started life in a mill – and he occupied Short's house with style. His wife wrote an account of those times, when, with the Civil War raging in the North, the Union occupiers took to the elegance of the Garden District as if it was their natural due. She described giving a reception that was both 'pleasant and brilliant…

crowded with elegantly dressed people and with fine performers on the piano and many excellent singers… your dear wife, darling children, the beautiful flowers elegant rooms – altogether it was a picture for a painter'. At one party a fountain spewed forth cologne! Here life was 'all gay and exciting… with every pulse throbbing with exhilarating emotions'.

And so, remarkably enough, those social pulses still throb away today, in the same rooms that were built for those vast receptions, and in houses that have been lived in by the same families for well over a hundred years. The Walter Robinson House is one of the biggest and the best, and here lives a Southern friend of mine, Dolly Jordan, along with her five dogs.

Walter Robinson was an entrepreneur *par excellence*. One of the few native Southerners in the Garden District, he was a cotton and tobacco broker as well as a banker who built up a vast financial empire. After the Civil War, with his businesses in ruins, he collapsed from 'nervous prostration' and cirrhosis of the liver leaving 'his brother to go to the courts to claim so much as one horse'. His legacy though lives splendidly on in the great house that was designed for him by Henry Howard, at 1415 Third Street, in 1859.

As with many of these buildings, you start back at the shock of its gigantic proportions, with its door and window cases soaring so high that you feel as though you have suddenly shrunk. Not only have you shrunk, but you are also made drunk by the intoxicating smell of the cypress wood, borne down the Mississippi to build these homes. While outside the house is decked out with elaborate wood and ironwork, inside there is the bonus of a dining room of banqueting hall proportions, built onto the house by the Irish architect, James Gallier.

Yet another layer was added when Dolly's father covered the walls with 'Scenic America' – a French paper designed for Zuber's in 1834, as startling a social document as it is an aesthetic surprise. Described when

A French view of Manhattan in the 1830s, Zuber's Scenic America wallpaper.

it was designed as 'views of the cities and landscapes greatly appreciated by travellers... [with] scenes and people... from authentic sources', it reveals all the idealism of France's view of New World democracy and egalitarianism with both blacks and whites decked out in equal and extravagant finery. Of immense interest too are the cityscapes of 1830s Boston and Manhattan. Boston, 'bristling with steam boats... [which] ply the oceans of the world'; whilst New York – Oxford-like with soaring spires – is seen from the 'Weehawk Hill... a meeting place for fashionable parties'.

And so we are led around early nineteenth-century America, past military manoeuvres at West Point 'with its fine situation on the Hudson River' and on into the Allegheny Mountains where our black and white travellers are enjoying the spectacle of 'Indian chiefs of the Windbag tribe... performing a Red Indian "Pipe of Peace" Dance'.

Standing in this room, where, I was told by Dolly's courtly white-suited Southern friends that they have 'no more hope of changing than a crustacean does of escaping death when tied to a railroad track', Dolly still dreams of her 'debut ball when the house had seemed lit up like a love cake'.

THE CRITERION THEATRE

I had read that the Criterion Theatre at Bar Harbor in Maine was an undone-up Art-Deco delight. The first clue that it was going to be more than an architectural adventure came when I rang to find the cinema's programme times. It seemed as if Lauren Bacall had answered the telephone. Here was a period piece, the sound of gravel rolling through gin, aerated only by the inhaling of nicotine, obviously through an elegant cigarette holder. For many minutes it held forth, giving views and reading reviews on the film to be shown that night (*Saving Private Ryan*), with snippets from the *New York Times*, and many other personal flourish besides.

It was Betty Morrison, the cinema's owner and self-styled film reviewer, who later told me that since falling in love with 'Bogie' as a young girl, she had indeed modelled herself on Bacall. It is thanks to this septuagenarian beauty – and crime writer to boot – that the Criterion Theatre was saved from demolition. Her husband had bought it in 1966 and died three years later. Rather than sell it to developers who firstly wanted to turn it into a parking lot (and then into a multiplex) she hung on to the place, scrubbing the floors on her hands and knees, and cleaning it up throughout, while being mocked for keeping such a 'dingy old place' alive. It was then, she says, that a young woman walked in, 'heaven knows who she was, maybe an angel' and told her what a perfect example of Art Deco she had on her hands. 'Wait a minute, I thought. I grew up with the style, why didn't I realize what we have?'

Wittingly or unwittingly, the cinema-going audiences of the 1920s and 1930s were, in fact, experiencing the very cutting edge of American popular architecture. The movie houses were the meccas for Mr and Mrs America, and the Criterion is one such living example of a 'neighborhood palace' built on behalf of 'His Excellency the American Citizen'. These cinemas were scaled-down versions of the downtown extravaganzas, the vast auditoriums which had been hit by the Depression and by the surge towards suburbia. All the glamour and excitement of the movies was distilled into these little buildings, with its marvellous magic-made-miniature.

Queue for a show at the Criterion and you are given your marching orders with innumerable hand-written notices: to 'have the exact change ready', as 'everyone gets in much faster and we start on time'; to buy the 'world-famous "real-buttered" popcorn', 'Movies Bites' and 'home-baked sweets'; and sweep down through the foyer, with lighting that was described when it opened as 'flattering to women patrons'. Here today the theatre's saviour marshals her flock – on a high director's chair, with a dog on a lead – ensuring that nothing escapes her eagle eye (I saw one man forbidden to go in with his own paper beaker of water). Before you stands an old popcorn-warming machine, and the 'Candy Counter' – invented by Charles S. Lee, an architectural colossus of American cinema design.

The Criterion Theatre, Bar Harbor, Maine, where the cinema-going audiences of the 1920s and 1930s experienced the very cutting edge of popular architecture and design.

Straightway you see that nothing has been altered since 1932 when the Criterion was built for George McKay, with his revenues from rum running, by Augusta architects, Bunker and Savage. Here is the style of the time, as was seen at the time: chevrons slice throughout, zigzagging their way across the ceilings, walls and floors, giving form to the lights, mirrors, doorways and corridors.

The night this little cinema opened it was cheered to its Art-Deco rafters by 'scores of surprised and pleased people' making it a 'big night for Bar Harbor'. Telegrams were read out from Greta Garbo, Joan Crawford, John Gilbert and John Barrymore, who was starring in the first film to be shown there, *Arsène Lupin*, one of the first 'talkies', with 'too much talk' according to the critics! That night the 'vaudeville ran off smoothly and was a well-balanced and cheerful part of the program'; altogether it was 'a lively and impressive evening'. The carpets are 'thick and give with pressure' wrote one enraptured first-nighter. It had 'the air of Broadway, of the Big Time'.

So great was the success of Art Deco throughout America during the 1920s and 1930s that, like a declaration of independence in both architecture and design, it became a style that was truly America's own. It is startling to discover therefore that the term was in fact first coined by an Englishman, Bevis Hillier, as late as 1968 – long after the style had died an unjust death – when describing how its roots had grown from the *Exposition des arts décoratifs et industriels moderne* of 1925 in Paris. This multi-rooted European style, the result of Germany, France, Austria and Italy forging futuristic lines, was brilliantly transmogrified into the modern America of the machine age. With such sleek materials as aluminium, stainless steel, plate glass and Vitrolite (an opaque structural glass), its success was assured.

For many, Art Deco came not a moment too soon, with everything but architecture hitherto seeming to join in America's modernizing march. In 1920 the critic Richardson Wright captured the mood of the moment: 'We live in an age of motor cars, radio and air transportation, and yet we are satisfied to have houses that suit ages when none of these improvements were dreamed of. We listen to a radio in a Louis XVI living room, drive our motors up to early Italian villas and land our airplanes in gardens that might have been laid out by Le Notre. Why not chuck the whole bundle of ancient sticks and create styles of our own, suitable to the age in which we live?'

And so Art Deco took off, slicing into the swag-ridden styles of the past. Everything, from water towers to toasters, from dams to gleaming diners, was to be cut through with its geometric abstractions, setting off in umpteen invigorating directions. Skyscrapers were, of course, prime targets for Art Deco's skyward soaring designs, but also in the cinemas where the fantastical forms of the buildings became as much part of the adventure of going to the movies, as seeing the films themselves. During the Depression both the films and the buildings in which they were shown feasted on one another with ever more extravagant designs: as the architecture became part and parcel of the fantasy of the films, so the film sets, in turn, fuelled the flames of real architecture.

The wonder of the style was of course to wane and it was largely thanks to an American heroine, Barbara Capitman, that America now reveres its home-grown architecture once again. It was she who popularized the term 'Art Deco' in America, and in the 1970s and 1980s she alerted her countrymen to the importance of the movement. She spearheaded the salvation of Miami Beach, and in an almost lone crusade, the chronicled Art-Deco buildings throughout the country, waking everybody up to the wonders of a style that had become so indigenous it was scarcely noticed.

The Criterion Theatre is a perfect example of how the style had crept under the architectural cover of the country, being lavishly applied to some hundreds of thousands of buildings, however modest

The flying loges at the Criterion.

they might be, with its heavy-as-liquid-lead drapes of bright orange velvet – now curiously aged to the touch – flanked by glowing puce torcheres, walls of silken panels and bronzed and silvered chevrons. A small cow bell hangs on a chain to warn the proprietor of non-paying 'sneakers in'! To parade to your seat is to parade down an Art-Deco avenue, with the end of every row emblazoned with chevrons in iron relief. Overhead, zigzag-decorated beams radiate out, sunburst-like from a central light, with the ceiling painted, according to Betty Morrison, by Italian artisans 'brought over here to lie on their backs like Michelangelo but with paint-soaked Turkish towels to do their work'.

Upstairs the flying balcony does indeed fly forth, filled with the *loges* – seats divided off from each other in sections by sharp chevron-shaped and dec-

orated partitions. All about you the same orange velvet hangs heavy – to be pulled aside to enter the loges, or to be draped about each door. 'The curtains hide little nooks and corners that are mysterious and fascinating' wrote the *Bangor Daily News* in 1932, and so they do today. Most notable of all is the original carpet that still stretches throughout the entire upper floor. Designed with countless overlapping chevrons, in violent hues of black and yellow, orange and green, it is a threadbare but triumphant survivor. Over all, a silver frieze of yet more chevrons pierce, teeth-like, around the auditorium walls.

Sink into the velvet seats, and the original 1930s camera will start to whir 'that delicate promissory whir…' as John Updike so pleasingly put it, and enjoy an evening out at the tiny, unsung and unrestored Criterion Theatre in Maine.

NOTTOWAY

Nottoway— otherwise known as the White Castle – is a sensationally swell house on the banks of the Mississippi. It was designed by Henry Howard – he who was responsible for Walter Robinson House and so much of the Garden District of New Orleans. With its grand seigniorial aspect, surrounded on all sides by moss dripping oak trees, banana trees and magnolias, and with the Southern air always heavy with humidity, Nottoway never fails to drench you with the delights of Old World America. Furthermore, and hard to believe, it is a 'bed and breakfast' allowing you to stay in surreal splendour, sleeping in towering four-posters. The memory of standing alone in the vast white ballroom at midnight is no mean one; nor is creaking away on the rocking chairs on the upper gallery, watching the Mississippi shining by in the moonlight. Suddenly, in the silence, you will hear the throb of an engine, as slowly, very slowly, a single red or white light glides into view and for many minutes the entire horizon is filled by the black outline of a gigantic and heavily-burdened barge; with its odd lights here and there it looks for all the world like a small town being borne down the Mississippi to New Orleans.

Nottoway – the word is Algonqian Indian for rattlesnake – is the largest plantation house still standing in the South. It was built in 1859 for John Hampden Randolph, who was born to English parents in Virginia, and about whom it was said 'When justice lays the wreath of nobility of character, she will lay it upon the grave of this one.' Having been almost ruined in the cotton trade, Randolph was to make such a fortune with sugar that there were said to be few to rival his wealth between Baton Rouge and New Orleans. Like the entrepreneurs of the Garden District, he was one of 'those men who build up a country and make it great and prosperous. By his energy and industry, under his skilful hand the soil yielded its riches'.

However it was not, I fear, by *his* 'skilful hand' that such riches were tilled, but rather by the 500 slaves he owned – although Randolph seemed to be a conscientious master, employing a doctor and a priest on the plantation. According to his daughter, Cornelia, in her novel *The White Castle of Louisiana* based on Nottoway, Randolph was offered $200,000 in gold for his slaves by a Cuban dealer. In 1866 he had taken them to Texas during the Civil War so that their presence would not antagonize the Union troops; after the hostilities were over the offer was made. They were assembled and 'before their dazed minds could plunge from the hope of freedom to the abyss of Cuban captivity' he told them 'that he had never broken his word to any man… and that he would not sell'.

It took Randolph six years to plan and four years to build Nottoway, but he was to enjoy its splendour for only three years before the Civil War put an end to it all.

As befitted their affluent lives, the Randolphs conceived of Nottoway on the grand scale in the Italianate style with twenty-two enormous Doric-with-a-Moorish-flourish columns rising the full height of the building. A hybrid of the raised Creole cottage, as well as the Greek-Revival style – with an exotic twist or two on its tremendous scale, Nottoway is unique.

Two floors of elaborately ornamental iron railings embrace the body of the house and flank either side of a double stairway that sweeps up to the gargantuan front door setting an awe-inspiring tone

The white ballroom with its two white marble fireplaces, lorded over by white Corinthian columns on a snow-white floor, Nottoway Plantation, Louisiana (1859).

which predominates throughout. With the 'handsomely trimmed' doorways of double height leading from one immense room to another, and with all the windows – many with panes of the original 'rippling' hand-blown glass – stretching from floor to ceiling, through which you may stroll out onto the balconies there is, all in all, a most pleasurable sense of loftiness and space. There are sixty-four rooms altogether, many of them of palatial proportions. The back hall alone was made large enough to be a ten pin bowling alley! All are richly-scented with the cypress wood from which they were built, cut down from the plantation and cured underwater for four years

before being used. Some 4,200 yards of plasterwork enriches the house.

Most remarkable of all the rooms at Nottoway is the white ballroom with its two white marble fireplaces, lorded over by white Corinthian columns that stand in state on a snow-white floor made of maple – the most durable type of wood for a dancefloor. No matter how richly carved the wooden capitols, they are matched, twist for turn, by an abundance of plasterwork. Made from a mixture of mud, clay, horsehair and Spanish moss, they were all created by Jeremiah Supple from Co. Cork in Ireland. He and Nottoway's architect, Henry Howard (also from Co. Cork), were to go off to the Civil War together where they would fight, side by side, in the same regiment.

It was largely due to Supple that Nottoway's interior has all the appearance of a luscious wedding cake. He eventually became a prosperous plantation owner in his own right, although the Mississippi all but flooded away his land. Where it failed in his lifetime, it succeeded after his death – sweeping away the cemetery in which he had been buried. His son rescued his tomb, but now, out of the frying pan and into the fire, he lies forever roasting in the New Orleans hinterland, in the miserable heat of a grim cemetery crisscrossed over and through by interstates and highways.

Walk up the grand mahogany staircase and you will see that here there is no 'bragging button' on the newel post. This was either a brass or ivory button that signalled that the mortgage had been paid. John Randolph had needed no mortgage, but instead paid every cent as the bills came in.

The best bedroom in the house is the Randolph's guest bedroom. It is bold and beautiful with its original four-poster and armoire; floor-to-ceiling windows look out over the Mississippi. In the corner stands a child's bed in which all eleven Randolph children – seven girls and four boys – slept.

During the Civil War Mrs Randolph was alone in this great house, except that is, when forced to give shelter to Union troops, with several hundred of them camped about the place. 'The Yankees have served Ma rather badly' her son, Hampden, wrote to his father in Texas. When the enemy gunboats hove into view, she showed her full mettle standing on the porch, dagger in belt, ready to confront the troops. The house was shelled twice and, as with rest of Nottoway where no nuance of its past is ignored, the indentation of one of those shells can still be seen on the pillar, whilst the shell itself is preserved in the house. Three Randolph sons were old enough to fight in the Civil War. The youngest Sidney was not, but he had enlisted nevertheless and it was he who

was killed, aged seventeen, at Vicksburg.

In the music room, gold glints on a harp and other instruments. It was here that the Randolph children were prepared for the outside world. A French master was hired to 'teach the Terpsichorean art', as well as a German master for music. For the younger ones though, it was the English governess who ruled over all, with John Randolph holding dear the habits of his forbears. As a one-generation-removed English grandee in the midst of Cajun country, he and his friends would still observe such rituals as 'rising with the ladies after dinner and re-seating themselves to exchange thoughts over their wines and crack jokes with their nuts after the ladies had passed into the parlour'!

The dining room still shines away today with its seventeen-foot-long American Empire table. 'In the good old days', wrote Cornelia, 'the owners of plantations were mostly travelled, intelligent and well read… [and] having an abundance of time to such culture they were social and fond of giving dinners, in which they excelled; fish, ice, and oysters in season being sent from New Orleans regularly'.

Not only was Nottoway created as a shrine to the aesthetic aspirations of the Southern grandee, but it was also a triumph of up-to-the-second technology with hot and cold running water, baths and flushing water closets. Most innovative of all, there was gas lighting shining from wall sconces in every room and in the many ornate chandeliers – all provided by Randolph's private gas plant. So as not to sully the marble fireplaces, smokeless coal was specially shipped down the Mississippi to the house.

When Charles Dickens first saw the great waters of the Mississippi in 1842, he despaired, describing it as 'the great father of rivers, who (thanks be to Heaven) has no children like him'. The old river has done a good deal of aesthetic harm to Nottoway over the years, robbing it of a full six acres of its gardens. Where once were planted hundreds of orange and lemon trees, as well as magnolias, roses, strawberries

Nottoway: a hybrid of the raised Creole cottage, as well as the Greek-Revival style – with an exotic twist or two on its tremendous scale, Nottoway is unique.

and a 'reflecting pond', there is now only grass between the embankment and the house. Sugar cane still grows both behind and on either side of the building, although in Randolph's day there was also a corn crop – planted to entice marauding bears away from the sugar crop. The Randolphs were to exact vile revenge on poor bruin, however, when they enjoyed the delicacy of roasted bear's paw – said to be 'good with a capital G' when cooked in hot coals in the ground.

After the Civil War, few fortunes flourished and Nottoway was never again to have the life for which it was so extravagantly created, save, that is, for the ballroom where five of Randolph's daughters were married to the manor born. Thus was established a tradition which has continued to this day, and often, as if by divine justice, it is a black bride in this white plantation ballroom. In 1999, for example, I saw Heaven Jackson being married to Eric Gunnel by the Revd Johnny Williams – a pastor who was born and raised on this old plantation land.

Wander alone through these great rooms at night and before sinking into sleep in this spellbound world, pull up the vast landing window and step out onto the gallery, high over the Mississippi. For it is here, thanks to the great waters moving before you, and thanks to the thickly humid, cicada-chattering-filled air about you that the Old New World becomes most palpably alive.

THE WAGNER
FREE INSTITUTE

Head for the grimmest area in all Philadelphia and you will be in for a grand surprise. In the midst of a sorry swathe of inner city decay you will find a learned nineteenth-century institution, which, by its revered and treasured survival, puts all equivalents in Britain to shame. It is the Wagner Free Institute of Science, built by William Wagner, merchant, gentleman scientist, philanthropist and most importantly of all, the Philadelphian force for free education. Here, set down on a greensward is his temple of learning: a severe, classical building with an interior that, in terms of scientific, social and historic interest, must have few equals in the world.

The sad district in which it now stands, with its surrounding streets of rotting and burnt out 'row houses', is the original site of Wagner's country estate, with its eighteenth-century farmhouse, Elm Grove, that was already being described in the nineteenth century as a curiosity of 'ancient days'. It was here that Wagner first put his collection of specimens on public view. Since boyhood he had amassed many thousands of minerals, fossils, plants and shells and he was determined that all should benefit from his 'cabinet', as such private collections were then called.

Hitherto it had been only the specialist swells – the 'gentlemen scientists' – who studied such subjects and who, in their private academies and societies, were the incubators of scientific study and research. William Wagner was determined that the working man too should benefit from these all-important discoveries. He gave lectures, to which people poured; but the crowds soon became so vast that it was said they quite 'exceeded the capacity of the cabinet'.

And so Wagner set about creating his Free Institute. It was built between 1859-65, with the Civil War somewhat interrupting proceedings, and the architect, John McArthur, being required to design several Union hospitals during the conflict. (A man of many parts, McArthur also built the ornate Philadelphia City Hall, with its teeteringly-top-heavy tower.)

Designed, as was stipulated, to be 'of light, beauty and utility', the Free Institute stands well back from the streets so as to let the light flood through the round, arched windows, showing off the full wonder of the Exhibition Hall's interior and contents.

Having hauled open the handsomely-heavy main doors, you walk in wonder through the library, lined with rare books, their cases complete with footplates and handles so as to allow you to reach to those at the top. Already the air is heady with age, but when you step through to the lecture theatre the smell positively stirs up your sensibilities as to what has gone before.

During the first half of the nineteenth century, America looked to Europe for its sages of science, medicine and natural history. But as the century developed, so too did the stature of the American scientist. 'The New World', it was said 'began to alert the Old World that the child was becoming a man.' It was a child furthermore, with vast virgin lands to explore. To see this room is to see America at the dawn of that understanding.

The Free Institute offered two lectures a night, every night, for six days a week. Philadelphians flocked in their thousands, with the men first ensuring that their bowler hats were safely secured in the wire racks

– designed specifically for that purpose – beneath the lecture theatre seats. They would sit down to hear such notables as the eminent palaeontologist and evolutionist, Edward Drinker Cope. It was he, along with Othniel Marsh, who made the first significant discoveries of dinosaur skeletons, in Colorado and Wyoming, in the 1870s, thus triggering the First Great Dinosaur Rush in North America. Although initially friends, Drinker Cope and Marsh were to become bitter rivals, with stories surrounding them of armed field parties, spying, and the intercepting of one another's shipments of fossils.

Sombre portraits hang heavy on the walls and the iron and wooden seats march in decreasing tiers around three sides of the lecture theatre. A tall, narrow cupboard reveals a skeleton, thought to date from the earliest days of the Institute, it appears somewhat home-made, and not the gleaming white and bright of its professionally-polished successors. Glass-doored cupboards give an enticingly-dim view of their contents, which, on closer inspection, turn out to be sensational: a crowd of uncommon instruments dating from the dawn of American science and before. One 'astrological arrangement' was invented in the eighteenth century in England by George Graham, and was made in 'cabinet form' at the behest of Charles Boyle, the Irish Earl of Orrery, after whom it was then named. Described as 'the most complete planetarium… in which the motions of the celestial bodies were demonstrated with great accuracy', it survives today in Philadelphia, spider's web-like in its frailty.

Taking centre stage among these rarities is the terrifying laboratory table, used for demonstrations and experiments. With its rusted and corroded drains and 1880s brass gas-jet fittings standing proud, it

A bowler hat safely secured in the wire rack – designed specifically for that purpose, in the lecture theatre of the Wagner Free Institute of Science, Philadelphia (1859-65).

looks sinisterly and suspiciously like a cadaver's slab.

According to the US National Register of Historic Places, the Institute is 'an unparalleled survivor of a virtually extinct institution' – the philanthropically-supported Scientific Society of the nineteenth century. True to the Deed of Trust decreed in 1864, the Wagner Institute has continued to provide free education in the sciences; there are now extensive programmes for children – a concept that was not even considered in the nineteenth century.

During the 1940s and 1950s, the great anthropologist Margaret Mead lectured here. Specializing in the study of the people of the Pacific Islands and New Guinea, she described one tribe as 'superficially agreeable... but they go in for cannibalism, headhunting, infanticide, incest, avoidance and joking relationships, and biting lice in half with their teeth'.

The palaeontologist, Joseph Leidy, described as 'the prototype for a scientist in a young emerging nation', also gave talks here. 'Large and rather awkward' with his 'dark rich chestnut brown hair... a kindly bearded face and a subdued smile' he would 'lumber to his feet' to deliver a mere fraction of his encyclopaedic knowledge. He was the foremost human anatomist in America and the leading authority in anthropology, pathology, entomology and zoology, as well as protozoology, botany and geology, mineralogy, histology and helminthology – the study of parasitic worms. Indeed he was the founder of parasitology in America. He was also the father of forensic pathology, and, to boot, he was an expert on gems. To put it in a nutshell, his was a complete inventory of nature! 'How' he said 'can life be tiresome so long as there is a new rhizopod undescribed?' He had mountains named after him, as well

as capes, lakes and creeks. He was, according to Leonard Warren in his excellent biography of Leidy, 'The last man who knew everything'.

It was Leidy, who, on Wagner's death in 1885, took over the Institute, and who was responsible for enlarging and re-ordering the remarkable museum in the lofty iron-columned Exhibition Hall. In this evocative room, so surreally set in its time, you are jolted back some hundred years to the days when the fast-developing successes of scientific inquiry made the world truly seem your oyster. Hitherto, the collections at Wagner had been described as 'shameful clutter, dust and disorder'. Three centuries before, Francis Bacon had described its European equivalents as: 'the shuffle of things... In small compass the model of universal nature made private... whatsoever nature has wrought in things that want life and may be kept... shall be included'.

Leidy though, was to systematically re-order Wagner's specimen collection, following the order of Darwin's theory of evolution. Visitors could – and still can – walk through geological time: 'From the inorganic to the organic, from the simplest organism to the most complex and to the culmination of man!' Charles W. Johnson was the Institute's first curator, and it is his meticulous hand that wrote many of the still-surviving labels for over 100,000 specimens – a task that took him a toilsome fifteen years.

There are an infinite number of pinhead size insects and their various parts in an array of dignified display cases, including the 'Mouth Parts of the House Fly' – an exhibit with which I have particular affinity. Years ago in a tiny country museum in Cambridgeshire I ran to ground 'The Lips of a Fly' as well as a 'Fly's Kneecap'. I then read of a bracelet made out of the 'Thighs of Indian Flies' on show in eighteenth-century London!

By way of contrast at Wagner, dinosaur bones discovered by Drinker Cope are heftily on view, together with the first known fossil of the sabre-toothed tiger in the world, discovered by a Leidy-sponsored expe-

Opposite: *The lofty, iron-columned exhibition hall of the Wagner Free Institute – so surreally set in time that you are jolted back some hundred years to the days when the fast developing successes of scientific inquiry made the world truly seem your oyster.*

The still-surviving labels of over 100,000 specimens, all in the curator, Charles W. Johnson's meticulous hand, c. 1880s.

dition to Florida in 1886. A 'Human skull exploded – study specimen' is also on show. Incidentally, when Drinker Cope's own brain was removed from his corpse and weighed – as was fashionable to do at the time – it turned out to be precisely the same weight as Joseph Leidy's – 1.545 grams.

On the uppermost floor in an area closed off to the public, the very foundations of the Institute stand in rows, with William Wagner's original cabinets of the 1840s, along with alarming nineteenth-century plaster-casts taken from cadavers – one with the 'skin' folded back to reveal the brain. Human bones used for the teaching of anatomy are piled in cardboard boxes to the ceiling: legs and arms stick gloomily forth by the dozen. Here too is a box of elephant bones belonging to a poor creature that came as a curiosity from India and perished in America. His skull is on slightly more

dignified display in the Exhibition Hall below.

Whereas most, if not all scientific museums throughout the world, have been bought up to date, the Wagner Free Institute has remained a vision of the nineteenth-century view of the universe. Wagner wrote that he based his schemes on the Jardin Des Plantes in Paris, which has itself since been changed (although recently returned to its original layout!) No such travesties have tainted Wagner; it is a museum of a museum. The Victorian spirit of science has permeated the Wagner Institute, indeed you feel as if you are breathing that self-same air of discovery, until that is, you look out of the window: when, by now being so keenly immersed in the nineteenth century, it shocks you senseless to suddenly see the modern world, with the grim twenty-first century streetscape but yards away.

PENN'S STORES

Of all memories in this great adventure few are as magical as coming upon Penn's Stores at dusk. For it is the American country store, more than anything else, that confirms the plain unassailable fact that America thrives on tradition, that the New World is often more entrenched in its past than is the Old. Where better to go therefore than to the oldest continuously-operated-by-the-same-family store in America, to Gravel Switch in Kentucky?

I had discovered that it was run by three generations of Penns – eighty-five-year-old grandmother Alma, her daughter Jeanne and her twin singers-in-harmony granddaughters, Dava and Dawn – and that they were descended from William Penn. What more desirable baits to entice you from England, most especially for one who lives three miles from where Penn lies buried, by the old Meeting House at Jordans in Buckinghamshire?

Nevertheless I was little prepared for what awaited me at Penn's Store, where, at the junction of two rivers – the North Rolling Fork and the Little South Creek – there stood the very symbol of all that I was seeking. It had taken hours to find, but when I did I could scarcely believe what I saw: for there, at the end of a long dusty road, stood a shack that you felt would blow down with a mere puff of air – 'kinda swaggy, kinda settled in its own way' as Alma Penn was later to put it. What seemed like a mirage from afar was no less magical as I drew near. I well remember that I had to touch it to believe it, stepping round the heaps of gourds and pumpkins as well as six kittens, two cats and a dog. The Stars and Stripes hung on softly weatherworn wooden walls, the notice boards were full, and peering through the

window you could see that this was obviously a working store. Here was a scarcely believable example of the old-fashionedness of America.

It was founded in 1845 by twenty-one-year-old William Spragens and in 1850 it was sold to Gabriel Penn, whose descendants still run it today. It has been open every day for 150 years including Christmas Day, Thanksgiving and Independence Day, with a Penn unlocking the door on every one of them.

Martin Wilson 'Dick' Penn, son of Gabriel, was the next to take over. He was a master of all trades, as was often the case with the country-store owner, being a surveyor, as well as a dentist – pulling teeth there and then in the store. He was also a pharmacist who became a doctor when granted the right to practice medicine by the Governor of Kentucky. There are startling claims, with witnesses to prove it, that he discovered an effective treatment for skin cancer. He died on the front porch of the store on 4 July 1913, with his formula unrecorded. Alma, his granddaughter and one of ten children – runs the place today, ruling empress-like from behind the counter, along with her daughter and granddaughters who are all dead set on preserving the store: 'It never changes and that is what is wonderful in this world where everything changes so fast, in a blink of an eye. Here you come back to something that has never changed and that is a very nice feeling.'

They did change one thing, once: they substituted their 'cash box' cigar box for a modern metal one, 'but the people didn't like it'.

With its unaffected atmosphere, where a print of William Penn is plonked amongst the washing powders and where people wander in and out barely noticing that the twins are playing their guitars and

It is the American country store that confirms the plain unassailable fact that the New World is often more entrenched in its past than the Old. Penn's Store at Gravel Switch, Kentucky (1845) is still run by the Penn family.

singing away in harmony by the 'Warm Morning Model 521 Stove', you feel embraced by the very spirit of America.

And what an odd distillation of America we made together that day. Along with the locals drinking their beer, there were the New World descendants of William Penn (who are also descended from the Scottish Earl of Wigton, whose son was married to a descendant of Pocahontas – in other words we were kin!) Both Old and New World descendants of the Indian Princess – by whose intervention the first English settlers were saved – jammed together in a tiny Kentucky country store.

The Penns have published *The Family Cookbook* of all their old recipes such as 'Mammy's Clabbered Milk' and 'Evelyn's Country Ham... cooked in a spe-cial way which enhances the flavor' with instructions to 'cover kettle with coats, blankets and quilts to hold in heat... let sit for 12 hours or so'. What too about 'Hog's Head Souse', with its unpromising starter's orders to 'Scrub and clean an uncooked hog's head, cut off the nose and snout'. A recipe for squirrels' brains is to be in the new edition.

In 1992 the Penns built an outside lavatory – the first 'rest room' that the stores had ever known. The singer, Chet Atkins, performed at the opening cere-mony and the Penns organized 'outhouse races' between teams of five, with two pulling and two

---

Opposite: *Eighty-five-year old Alma Penn ruling empress-like from behind the counter of Penn's Store.*

pushing an outhouse and one sitting 'on the hole' inside! Such was their success that by 1996, the World Outhouse Olympics were established with a total of ten teams competing from as far afield as Canada and Hungary, as well as Kentucky, Virginia and Arkansas, with one team from the 'White House Outhouse'. All this to the score 'I'm Just a Pig for Your Love', written by Jeanne Penn and sung by her daughters:

> *Root hog or die*
> *Gonna make you mine*
> *We'll live in hog heaven*
> *Til the end of time-e-im*
> *Render me helpless*
> *Throw me some slop*
> *Whatever you're giving*
> *Just keep giving and giving*
> *Don't… Stop*
> *Cause…*
>
> *I'm just a pig for your love*
> *Umm Just a hog for your love*
> *I just want all of your love*
> *Yeah yeah yeah yeah…*

Establishments such as Penn's are being determinedly hung on to – from Massachusetts to California – as a beloved part of the very culture of American country life. At Tracy City in Tennessee, for example, there stands 'Henry Flury's Staple and Fancy Groceries'. Established in 1905 and run by the founder's grandson today, it has the best collection of decorated American flour sacks of the early 1900s – every one a work of art – that I have ever seen. Hanging in rows from the ceiling, they have been added to since the store first opened. Tracy City is a tiny, half-a-horse town – yet at its Dutch Bakery, founded in 1902, you can find cakes as good as any in the world, still made to thigh-tinglingly delectable recipes. Then there is the 'Brick Store' in New Hampshire, which has flourished since 1804. Such survivals thrive at Seneca Rocks in West Virginia, at Becket in Massachusetts, at Leavenworth in Indiana and in Valle Crucis in North Carolina. Despite this embarrassment of riches, Penn's Stores is, to me, the most supremely evocative of days gone by, when such buildings were the very backbone of small town rural America.

The road to Penn's has long since been diverted on to a new and modernized route but not so these three generations of heroines: the Penns. By setting an example of selflessly serving the sparse local community, they are honouring the efforts of their forefathers: 'It's almost like a duty, like something that has been bestowed upon you, handed down, you really do not have a choice… We are stewards. The store is its own entity,' says Alma Penn.

In one way or another the Penn family are keeping the wolf from the door. As Jeanne says 'Sometimes it's a struggle to keep the doors open, there are hard times and you think in your mind, should we give up the boat? Then it is no, I wouldn't want to be the last Penn to close the door.'

A. SCHWAB

In the 1920s W. C. Handy wrote the blues song 'Beale Street'. It was to make this mile-and-half-long Memphis thoroughfare famous throughout the world as the 'Birthplace of the Blues'. Elvis Presley drew on its music and it is mainly thanks to that fame that the street has survived where most of downtown Memphis has floundered.

'If Beale Street could talk' wrote Handy... It was first laid out in 1838 by Robertson Topp and with the Mississippi being a mere third-of-a-mile away, it straightway became the haunt of roustabouts, hucksters, hustlers, peddlers, merchants, travellers and preachers, as well of course of innumerable musicians. Jazz and the blues were played night in and night out, while gospel singing rang forth from the churches by day. 'Aristocrats' filled the saloons with their liquor, wines, women and gambling. Farmers set up market stalls and fortune-tellers set up booths. There were grand mansions too, as well as wharf warehouses, theatres, an opera house and dance halls, bordellos, shops, restaurants and hotels, funeral parlours and pawn shops – all in all it was a hive of humanity. It was also thanks to the Mississippi that Memphis became a great centre for cotton, where drays piled high with bales would pass by. Processions of as many as two hundred mules would proceed through Beale Street to and from their stables.

Race riots raged in Memphis in 1886 when two dray drivers, one African-American the other white Irish, collided: the Irishman was killed and his fellow countrymen retaliated, slaying scores of Beale Street residents.

Yellow fever struck the city twice after Beale Street was built, with the epidemic of 1878 infecting over 17,500 people and bankrupting the city. A black man, Robert Church, was one of the first to invest in its recovery. He built the first park for blacks and he opened the auditorium to the Beale Street Baptist Church, where Booker T. Washington and Theodore Roosevelt were among the many to speak.

The Depression of 1937 hit hard and deep and by the 1950s a good deal of Memphis was ready to be raised. And so it was – to its wretched detriment – save for precious few buildings in the stately downtown, such as the imperious Peabody Hotel where, for the last seventy years mallard ducks have lived on the roof, and have been daily brought down in the elevator to waddle across the Aztec foyer along a red carpet rolled out for their benefit, to a marble fountain – and to a thundering rendition of the 'King Cotton March'.

Beale Street may have been saved thanks to the mystique of its music, but it has only been by the skin of its teeth. It now stands in a wasteland, sliced off from the rest of downtown. At last though, the revival of Memphis is underway, and it will soon be rejoined to the rest of the town, via a quantity of glitzy modern developments.

Throughout all these reversals there has been a lone bastion at Beale Street, a bulwark against time and its varying fortunes; at one point it was the only building not boarded up. A. Schwab dry goods store, established in 1876, is still run by the Schwab family today, Abe and Elliott, father and son, who both radiate their pleasure in the place and their determination to leave every inch of it unmolested by modernization.

'If you can't find it at Schwab's then you're better off without it!' has been the rallying cry with rousing good reason. To step inside A. Schwab's is, to

use a saying of Mark Twain's, 'enough to stir the vitals of a cast iron dog'. Never, ever, have I seen such a selection of 'dry goods' and 'fancy notions'. Here are two storeys of thousands of brain-bashingly-old-fashioned goods, all reminders of America's past – many of them sold here since the store opened in 1876, the year of Custer's last stand and the same year that Twain finished *Tom Sawyer*. 'When you walk in our front door,' says Abe, 'you step into history with its old-fashioned atmosphere and its odour, the merchandise has an odour of… it's almost like time'.

The gents' wear section is mountainous, piled high along the long wooden counters, seemingly as far as the eye can see. Gentlemen's overalls go up to size 70 and trousers go to size 84, as do the underpants – all made by a firm that has been producing them for over sixty years. There are belts that are two yards long. After size 66, I am told, the customers tend to send their wives, girlfriends or daughters. Spats 'to keep the ankles warm in wintertime' are no common sight today, yet they are stacked high at Schwab's. Alongside sit a vast variety of gentlemen's celluloid collars in stout cardboard boxes and sixty-three varieties of gentlemen's braces and suspenders. All-in-one vests and long johns, or 'Union suits', are still strong sellers here after a hundred years as are the short-legged and -sleeved version, 'BVDs'– originally made by the Boston, Vest and Drawer Company. Union suits are for winter, BVDs for summer.

Abe Schwab is at the heart of the place. The very sight of him sends you spinning through time with his green visor, white starched shirt and long green apron tied with its strings around his tiny stooped form. He sits on a high wooden stool at a high wooden desk where he keeps the books always with a pencil – it is as if a painting by Norman Rockwell

Opposite: *Abe Schwab is at the heart of the place, overseeing ladies' hats and aprons; the very sight of him sends you spinning through time.*

has come to life. He was ten-years old and in knee pants when he began working in the store and he has ruled the roost from this selfsame spot, overseeing ladies' hats and aprons (the like of which I can dimly remember in the North of England in the 1950s) for forty-five years. Behind him, ledgers dating back to the early 1900s stand on shelves up to the ceiling, while lording it over all is a photograph of his grandfather, Abe Schwab, the founder of the firm. It was said that Abe Snr. knew his store 'as intimately as Charles Lindbergh knew the narrow confines of his cockpit'.

As with the gents' wear, so too with the ladies', handsome proportions are provided for, with dresses going up to size 80, and while sizes are magnificent, prices are modest: skirts and trousers go for $1 and there are gents shoes to be had for $4. Zippers cost a dime.

Cut prices began with a bang, when in the 1890s Schwab's did battle with 'a sure swell fellow' next door. Schwab's hats were priced at 49 cents and so his rival sold his at 39 cents. Schwab's sank to 29 cents, the rivals to 19 cents. 'So' wrote Sam, in *My Life on Beale Street*, 'we put out a sign "A free hat with every purchase"'. Today there are Italian bowlers, derbies and top hats side by side with raccoon 'Davy Crocketts' as well as three-foot-wide sombreros and tweed trilbeys – stack after stack of them, all teetering away into the distance.

So much of the past of this place is so much of America's past. Elliott Schwab, son of Abe, laughs and talks as much as he breaths, he never stops. Exploding with the excitement of telling you about the store like a series of sparkling fireworks on the Fourth of July, he stresses how important it is that 'kids don't loose touch with their parents, grandparents and great-grandparents. We must keep this store alive. Today there are so few kids that know what it is like to go into a store that is not perfectly done up in a package, where they can't touch anything… fantastically awful.'

Cash registers that have been working since 1911

can still be heard ringing throughout the store; beside them are giant rolls of brown paper on nineteenth-century iron contraptions that enable you to tear it off to size. Abe's great-grandfather had some new counters built 'to spiffy up the place', but they were only temporary. His three sons soon asked if they should be replaced: 'My great-grandfather said no,' says Elliott, '"lets stick it out another year to see how business is." Well 1913 came along "lets stick with them another year" then 1930, 1940 1960, 2000. Daddy, I says, as a standing joke, do we get some new counters? "No lets stick it out another year". Those counters speak to you, the store speaks to you; it moans, it creek and it groans. People ask me if I enjoy working here. Well no, I don't enjoy working here, I enjoy *being* in here. This ain't a job.'

In the ladies' department you can buy a 'Jac-o-Net Nylon Hair Net', still in its 1960s packaging, for 49 cents. Here too are snuggies – vests and knickers, some cut above the knee and some below. 'Luckily the Amish and Mennonites still wear them, otherwise I wouldn't be selling them, they'd have gone,' says Elliott Schwab. Then there are the heavyweight, cotton stockings for the old to keep their legs warm. 'Only one person in the country makes them. He's in his eighties and when he dies, they ain't going to be making them no more. What we gonna do?' says Elliott. They can no longer find makers of 'lap hand-kerchiefs' for church, so people come to Schwab's and buy a 9-inch square of material, as well as lace trimmings, and make them for themselves.

Not only has Schwab's run many manufactures to ground – it has also, in its bustling busyness, tri-umphantly proved that they are all still needed today. Tin bathtubs, for example, are still sold at Schwab's. 'New apartment blocks are fitted with showers rather than baths,' Elliott says indignantly, 'old people don't like showers, they like tubs.' Washboards for clothes washing are still sold here too, as even in the land of plenty there are those who do not have a washing machine.

What too about long and thin 'well buckets' – complete with the ropes on their handles? 'As long as people still use wells, we're okay' says Elliott. Step along the smoothly-worn wooden floor and you will see, say, piles of bars of 'Grandpa's Wonder Soap' alongside heavy-duty knee pads, rakes, ostrich-feather dusters, wooden ice-cream makers, rolls of chain, bugles and black iron dinner bells. Bulging pot-bellied stoves stand beneath rows of brass spittoons and china chamber pots. Elvis is, of course, very much in evidence, along with such gifts as pearlized logs inscribed with 'Mother'.

Schwab's is selling the last surviving 'pot menders': if you have a hole in your cooking pot, you fill it with this screw and washer, tighten it up and it leaks no more. 'There was no profit in them though,' says Elliott, 'so they were no longer made. We bought about a thousand and people come from all over, looking for them. We have a lot of stuff that does not make a profit. It is fairness to everybody, being honourable, that is what's important'.

As if this was not enough to show Schwab's appreciation of old America, half way up the stair-way there is a dusty display of the history of Beale Street. School children come on field trips to see this 'museum collection'. Faded photographs of Elvis Presley and old wooden shoe trees are jumbled together with 1920s bottles as well as a pecan nut picker, alongside toys, knife grinders and gramo-phone horns and pile upon pile of unidentifiable machinery. Trigger – 'The Smartest Horse in the World' – makes a surprise and welcome appearance. A framed notice tells of the only time the store was closed, by the yellow fever epidemic of 1878.

The oldest continuous sellers in the store are *Macdonald's Farmers Almanac* and *Aunt Sally's Policy Players Dreambook*. The *Almanac* has been published,

Opposite: *At Worthmore's store in Rayne, Louisiana, the merchandise is barely believable.*

Gentlemen's overalls go up to size 70 and trousers go to size 84, all made by a firm that has been producing them for over sixty years: A. Schwab, est. 1876, Memphis, Tennessee.

unchanged in its design and selling yearly since 1897; it is still reverently referred to by farmers. Under the heading 'The Proper Time to Plant and Harvest' we read that it is 'when nature has the earth ready and man has prepared the soil for crops as indicated by the signs of the heavens'. The headings for each month are so extraordinarily old-fashioned that your jaw drops at the sight of them. For July – celebrating Independence Day – Edwardian children set light to a toy cannon, lit by the heavenly rays of the bald American eagle. Advice on astrological livestock management, such as 'Ranching by the Moon in West Texas', is sent in by readers. There is a report indicating that '…moonlight influences the foraging activity of fruit bats'. While under 'A Little Nonsense

Now and Then is Relished by The Wisest Men' we read: 'Never try to teach a pig to sing; it wastes your time and annoys the pig'. J. Macdonald himself reigns resplendent on the cover, his profile in a roundel, flanked by encircled farming scenes and a colonnade of Corinthian columns.

Aunt Sally too appears on the cover of her *Dream Book* – a black mammy with curly white hair, a kerchief and a shoulder cape. Since the 1800s her followers have read of such wisdom as: 'If you dream of seeing a fairy you will meet a woman who will seduce you from the path of propriety and make your life vexatious.' 'To dream of fainting,' apparently 'shows you are wanton'. While to dream of walnuts, we read, 'signifies the fulfillment of your most sanguine wishes'.

Then there is *The Master Book of Candle Burning* – a hot seller since 1942, advocating rituals 'based upon practices described by mediums, spiritual advisors, evangelists, religious interpreters, neologists and others who should be in a position to know'. All part of an unexpectedly exotic element of Schwab's is the mojo department, started seventy years ago, selling oils, incense, herbs, unguents and 'Old-Fashioned Love Potions' or otherwise 'Stay Away Powder' if that is your plan. Then there is the 'Dragon's Blood' potion, with instructions to 'pour half a bottle into the tub. Read Psalm 23 while mixing and concentrate on your desires when bathing'. This is white magic with African roots which has had a large following in the Southern states since it was brought up the Mississippi in the early 1920s.

Although a bewildering example, Schwab's is by no means the only example of such survivals in America – although there cannot be many that are as merry. In Kidron, Ohio for example, Lehman's Hardware Store still sells hand-cranked butter churns, kerosene-powered fridges and gas-powered washing machines. Similarly in South Carolina there is the Thomas Store of 1885, and at Lagrange in Tennessee the Cogbill family are running their store that was founded in 1838 and rebuilt in 1901 after a tornado. At Worthmore's at Rayne in Louisiana, the merchandise is barely believable. I am now the proud owner of a box of lace trimmings made by Wright's, sporting an oval photograph of supposedly Mr Wright himself – stiff collared and proper – surrounded by a floating array of ladies wearing 'fancy goods' trimmed with his lace. Then there are the 'Universal Plastic Bowl Appliance Covers – the practical household helpers' of 1957 – pink polka-dotted vinyl protectors for kitchen appliances.

Spats are no common sight today, yet they are stacked high at Schwab's, alongside a vast variety of gentlemen's celluloid collars in stout cardboard boxes.

On the packet, a high-heeled housewife invites you to buy one; they are still sold by the dozen in Louisiana.

Like the country store, the old general store is still very much part and parcel of American life. With these survivals alone, I rest my case that much of the New World is now more old-fashioned than the Old.

ROOTS AND OFFSHOOTS

THE LIVINGSTON TRAIL

Whereas many Americans go to Europe to find their family roots and their offshoots, I went to America to find mine – and ragingly romantic ones they turned out to be. I had always heard scarcely credible tales of my American great-grandmother, Helen Margaretta Livingston, who, when in England, had been seduced by an English lord. He had promised to marry her when she returned home, but instead he wed an heiress, leaving my great-grandmother alone and humiliated. For years, I was told, she attempted to purge her shame by looking after those struck by leprosy, on Ellis Island in New York harbour, caressing their limbs, in the hope that, by way of punishment, she too would catch the same dread disease.

So it was, that on this curious circuitous route, I too was to set off to Ellis Island, to trace my ancestors, to where three out of four Americans can successfully embark on this self-same quest. Here, at the mouth of the Hudson River, lit by the lamp of Liberty, the 'Mother of Exiles', is a vast domed immigration hall, built in the French-Renaissance style by architects Boring and Tilton in 1899-1900. On a single day in 1907 11,747 immigrants passed through its portals. Between 1892-1924 only 2 per cent were turned away (an alarming 250,000 no less). On the 'Isle of Tears', within swimming distance of Manhattan, there were 3,000 suicides.

Ten steps from the tourist trail – the immigration hall has been recently restored with spanking success – and you can sense all too acutely the agonies that were suffered, when suddenly and surreally you come upon the hospital buildings that have remained untouched since the day that they were abandoned in 1954. Here, in the words of the Federal Immigration Law 'persons suffering from a loathsome or a contagious disease' were treated. An extraordinary sight is the all-but-sunken hull of the last immigrant ferry, *The Ellis Island*, with the entire sweep of the top of its deck rail a mere half an inch above the water. Sometimes seagulls sit all around it, seeming as if by magic to be forming the exact formation of a boat's prow in the water. It is docked at the hospital's mournfully evocative entrance hall. Here then were the wards of wretched suffering, in which people who had endured the hardships of steerage would stay, having been marked with a blue chalk on their first, frightening line inspection: C for conjunctivitis, G for goitre, SC for scalp, K for hernia, S for senility and X for insanity. TC stood for the most dreaded trachoma, the eye disease that forced thousands to return to Europe – under the chilling rule 'to keep out a class of persons from whom so large a proportion of the inmates of institutions for the blind and recipients of public dispensary charity are recruited'. There is no record of L for leprosy, but my great-grandmother always told my father that those were the patients under her care.

A mere spit from the shining skyline of New York and writhed through with undergrowth, these are sensationally strange sights. A single shoe lies in six-inch deep dust, the crematorium looms large and

---

Opposite: *Within sight of the Statue of Liberty, the immigrant hospital on Ellis Island in New York harbour.*

132

there are the countless corridors, thick with encroaching greenery and many of them a quarter-of-a-mile-long. Either side of their great length are the grim paint-peeling wards from which, through the windows the sick would see the sadly symbolic Statue of Liberty,

> *'Keep your ancient lands, your storied pomp'*
>   *cries she with silent lips.*
> *'Give me your tired, your poor,*
> *Your huddled masses yearning to breathe free,*
> *The wretched refuse of your teeming shore.*
> *Send these, the homeless, tempest-tost to me,*
> *I lift my lamp beside the Golden Door'!*

Eventually Helen Livingston did marry an Englishman – my great-grandfather, Granville Farquhar (known as 'Granny'). He had made his money on the Stock Exchange and henceforth her shame would be shielded by his riches, with the wealth that enabled him to rent vast estates in 'good hunting country' so that the neighbours would be obliged to speak to his fallen wife! My father can remember her with white hair to her waist.

The family she left behind in the New World were far grander than that which she married into in the Old. In 1835, Harriet Martineau wrote that the Livingston family, 'one of the oldest, most numerous and opulent in the United States', has been 'faithful to its democratic principles. In Boston it seems a matter of course that the "first people" should be federalists; that those who may be aristocratic in station should be aristocratic in principle. The Livingstons are in evidence that this need not be.'

Indeed two Livingstons were responsible for drafting the Declaration of Independence. Robert was unable to be present at the signing of the great document, as he was away fighting the British, but his cousin Philip was at the ceremony in 1776, 'Amid jocular remarks by the signees, the pealing of the Liberty Bell and the joyful hallelujahs of the populace

freed from insufferable tyranny'. (The same week as discovering all of this, like a trumpet voluntary, I was to find that I had an maternal ancestor who was also a signatory; one Charles Carroll, a great revolutionary leader who was written of in 1829 as 'the sole survivor of an assembly of as great men as the world has witnesses'.)

It was Robert Livingston, though, who was to pave the path of true greatness. At twenty-nine he was the youngest delegate at the Continental Congress – a man, it was said, whose 'appearance would not impress a stranger favourably'; stick thin, he was known as the 'whipping post'. It was he who administered the Oath of Office to George Washington in 1789. He was also the first Chancellor of New York State and it was he, who, in partnership with Robert Fulton, produced the world's first successful steamship, which set off up the Hudson River, from New York to Albany, in 1807, appearing to the fishermen and farmers 'like a weird craft from Pluto's realm – a transfiguration of Charon's boat into a living fiend from the infernal regions'.

Most central of all to the fortunes of the new nation, it was Robert Livingston, who, as Thomas Jefferson's minister to France between 1801-4, was responsible with James Munroe, for negotiating the Louisiana Purchase, the deal of 1803 that in one fell swoop doubled the size of the United States. With $10 million to spend on the land rights of New Orleans – the port on which the Western states depended for their development – Chancellor Livingston and Munroe were astounded when Napoleon's foreign minister, Talleyrand suggested 'somewhat abruptly' that they could have the whole of Louisiana for a mere $5 million more. Accepting without hesitation, they increased the size of America by 825,000 square miles, gathering in the whole of the mid-West – the richest agricultural land in the world – from the Mississippi to the Rocky Mountains. The deal was negotiated at the Tulleries the next day; Livingston, Munroe, Tallyrand and the Emperor Napoleon, dined together, drinking toasts to their deal.

The architectural triumphs of the Livingstons were also legion, building dozens of houses, which, like a giantess's necklace of jewels, are strung along the bosom and banks of the Hudson River in Upstate New York.

The classically-plain Clermont was built by the first lord of Livingston Manor in the 1600s and rebuilt by his descendants after being burnt by the British in 1777. Robert Livingston's sister, Janet, built Montgomery Place in 1804, which was then fancied up to the nines, during the 1840s and 1860s. Urned and domed balustrades bulge along the skyline. Stone swags swoop. Ornate columns march around a semi-circular entrance portico and there is an arcaded porch of 1847 – thought to be the first formal structure for outdoor living in America. The brick Oakhill dates from 1790 and then there is Wildercliff of 1799. Federal without and sombrely Gothic within, it was built by Catherine Livingston and her husband, the Revd Freeborn Garretson, who brought Methodism to America. The Pynes was built in the Federal style in 1790, as was Callender House, in 1794, although it is now most graciously appointed with Greek-Revival columns. Edgewater is a chaste temple dating from 1821-24. Another most curious jewel was added to the bounty in the twentieth century, with Orlana, the brilliant Persian palace south of the Hudson. Screeching with polychrome brick and tiles, as well as with towers and spires and Moorish details galore – one, rather fancifully, is a teapot on the roof – it was built by the great Hudson River artist Frederic Church, whose descendant is now married to a Livingston.

Vastly ostentatious is the brightly white, beaux-arts neoclassical confection is Staatsburg – now known as Mills Mansion – designed by McKim, Mead and White, in 1896. It was built on what was already Livingston land, by Ruth Livingston Mills, great-great-great-granddaughter of the founder of the family. Parade up its icing-sugar-like steps –

shining away whatever the weather – and peer through the dining-room window. I defy anyone not to start back in surprise at the marbled and tapestried, frenziedly-French interior. A gleaming symbol of the Gilded Age, this is the 'Bellomont' of Edith Wharton's *The House of Mirth* – the house that so gratified poor Lily Bart's 'craving for the external finish of life'. Further south, at Hyde Park, is Springwood, where Franklin D. Roosevelt was born, lived and died. This too became part of the Livingston empire, when he married Eleanor, the great-great-great-granddaughter of Chancellor Robert Livingston.

High over the Hudson River near Rhinebeck, laced through with Livingston lore, stands Wilderstein, a house that retains every ounce of the emotional attachment that was so obviously breathed into its walls.

Having wanted to see the house and its venerable owner for years, but having just heard that she had died, I respectfully trespassed, on tiptoe, up the long front drive. There before me was a decaying Queen-Anne sensation; a proudly-towered pile built in the style that had been brought from England to the Philadelphia Centennial Exposition of 1876, injected with American jubilation and dash.

Like a structural melting pot, every style bristles and bulges forth from these buildings, which stand in their many millions throughout the United States. From 'Medieval England' to the Orient, from Rheinish gloom to French frippery, all styles are blended into one exhilarating whole. With their towers, domes, spires and finials, as well as their richly wrought 'belly porches', verandas and decorative woodwork, they send your spirits soaring, from sea to shining sea. Rearing up before me was such a house, one furthermore that was romantically rotting.

Shielding the light, I pressed my nose against the glass and, as you read is done in such moments, I 'rubbed my eyes in disbelief'. There before me, in a state of faded splendour, was a richly-plastered, white and gilded room, hung from ceiling to floor with shredded golden silk.

The Rhinebeck land was bought during the 1850s by Thomas Suckley and his wife, a Livingston. Suckley's father originated from Sheffield and had made his fortune as an agent for such hardware as the terrifying-sounding 'toupee pinching irons'. Together they built a severely modest Italianate villa that still lurks within the walls of Wilderstein today. It was attired in the Queen-Anne style by the next generation–their son, Robert, and his wife Bessie, in 1888. Their architect was Arnout Cannon from nearby Poughkeepsie. He added two floors and gave the house a tower with a 'jaunty candle-snuffer roof', as well as a wraparound porch and a port *cochère* of magnificent proportions. All this, set down upon grounds newly-landscaped in the Romantic style by the fashionable designer Calvert Vaux – (who was also responsible for the great green mall that sweeps away from the Capitol Building in Washington).

Walk through its doors and your senses are whacked by the wonder of a wall-to-wall explosion of eclecticism – created by the designer, Joseph Burr Tiffany, in a mere four months. The Aesthetic Movement is richly represented here: a lustrous metal-painted frieze of fruit sparkles around the leather-hung walls of an English-Jacobean hall. Jewel-like bulging and bent, stained and leaded Gothic windows illuminate a somewhat sombre smoke-blackened library designed in the Medieval-Flemish style. The saloon, designed as 'a complete specimen of the Louis XIV period', seems alight with its golden shredded-silken walls and upholstery. The painted canvas ceiling of cherubs, amid billowing clouds, protecting a dove from a hawk, is by H. Siddons Mowbray, (who was later to paint the dazzling Italian-Renaissance decoration at the Pierpont Morgan Library in New York).

That all this has survived is thanks to Margaret 'Daisy' Suckley, Robert's eldest daughter, who was born in the house in 1891 and died in it one hundred years later. As the family fortune dwindled

so Daisy supplemented it as an archivist at the Franklin D. Roosevelt Library in New York. That she was a friend of Roosevelt was generally known: it was she who had given the president his famed black Scottie, Fala – having first taught the little dog a host of tricks that were to amuse Churchill and other big noise politicians the world over. Once, to the scandal of the nation, the president dispatched a fully-manned warship to rescue Fala, who had been mistakenly left behind in the Aleutian Islands.

What was not realized until after Daisy's death was how close their friendship had been. An old suitcase was found beneath her bed full of some thousands of pages of diaries and letters to and from the president, revealing a chaste and clandestine love affair. She was with him when he died, and she wrote of Fala at his funeral giving 'a sharp bark' after each gun volley, 'an unconscious salute of his own, to his master'. Daisy Suckley told no-one about Roosevelt, but she wrote everything down and saved it all. The sale of these papers have, in turn, helped to save the house, enabling the founding of the Wilderstein Preservation Corporation to care for this grand old pile.

Not only did the Livingstons build fine houses, but they were to a great extent responsible for preserving the land that surrounds them – land that is superbly seared into the mind by the Hudson River School of painting, with artists such as Thomas Cole, Frederic Church and Alfred Bierstadt who so exquisitely captured its beauty. In his 1893 forward to Washington Irving's *Rip Van Winkle*, George Boughton wrote: 'There was always something in the very air and nature of the place, that seemed to film over the landscape with a hazy atmosphere of romance… the distant lines of the Kaatskill Mountains seemed as rhythmic as a hymn to the eternal'. Washington Irving himself wrote of those river views, with the 'magical hues and shapes of these mountains… swelling up to a noble height and lording it over the surrounding country'. Andrew Jackson Downing added an extra dimension to the

The parlour at Wilderstein hung with feathery, fine and fading yellow silk.

beauty of it all, designing many of the gardens and grounds of the houses. Great were the landscapers, architects and patrons and guardians of the Hudson Valley, who have masterminded its miraculous survival to this day.

How pertinent too were the prophesies of the nineteenth-century essayist Nathanial Parker Willis, as he cheered on the improvements to the Hudson Valley: '"The opening down the middle" of the Empire State's robe of agriculture will soon be edged with velvet. A "class who can afford to let the trees grow" is getting possession of the Hudson… With bare fields fast changing into wooded lawn, the rocky wastes into groves, the angular farmhouses into shaded villas, and the naked uplands into waving forests, our great thoroughfare will soon be seen (as it has not been for many years) in something like its natural beauty.'

This paradise was realized and astonishingly, has survived intact, beginning a mere ninety miles north of New York City.

Of all the gems in the Livingston architectural legacy none shines brighter than Rokeby. Commanding grand views of the Catskill Mountains, the house stands on skirts of land that sweep down to the Hudson — land that was given to the Livingston family by James II in 1688. By the early 1800s it had been inherited by Alida Livingston who married General John Armstrong; together they built a house here between 1811–15, which has remained with their descendants to this day.

The discovery of Rokeby and its owners, the Aldriches, was a brilliant bull's-eye on the Livingston trail! As New York State's deputy commissioner for Historic Preservation, Winty Aldrich masterminded the saving of Wilderstein and he and his brother Ricky and sister Rosalind's preservation of the house is no less heroic. Although they are not, as he puts it, 'financially equipped to carry the burden', their passion and duty for protecting this stretch of land

Rokeby, Upstate New York (1895). By the banks of the Hudson River, Rokeby has a hanging-on-for-dear-life splendour.

and all the houses that stand on it, knows no bounds. 'There was never any question that this was a sacrifice… you just keep going, it is more important to us than anything else'.

The house was originally called *La Bergerie* – the sheepfold. Like his brother-in-law Chancellor Livingston before him, General Armstrong had been US ambassador to France; when he returned to America he was presented with a flock of merino sheep by Napoleon. In their honour, the house's porch still sports a faint mural of the creatures with Napoleon, tricorn hat aloft, handing them over to Armstrong, both men amid a sea of fat white sheep.

In 1818 the Armstrongs's daughter, Margaret, married William B. Astor, the son of John Jacob Astor – founder of the Astor fortune. In the high tide of Romanticism (much of which was infused into the American mind by Sir Walter Scott), Margaret Astor renamed the house after his poem 'Rokeby' and enlarged it to forty-five rooms. With its richly glowing nineteenth-century wallpaper and its hanging-on-for-dear-life splendour, it has an atmosphere of conviviality that has few equals in America. Not only that, with its every object held onto since the day it was built, Rokeby is, as one of its present owners, Winty Aldrich, puts it: 'A repository of the whole American story.' What a happy contrast to the Astor homes in England today, Clivedon and Hever Castle, so glitzed up to the corporate nines.

Rokeby's Gothic octagonal library would do credit to the glories of Scott's own gothicary at Abbottsford in Scotland. With a plaster ceiling painted to imitate wood, its forms radiate out in deep rounded relief with arches leaping round the angled walls, splendid with the spines of eighteenth-century books. Here are the books that had belonged to Armstrong in Paris, although he could not speak a word of French, a fact which incurred the wrath of Napoleon, when he presented his credentials in 1815. About-to-be-crowned Emperor, and already

Looking out over the Hudson Valley and the Catskill Mountains from Rokeby.

bored by Armstrong's brother-in-law, Chancellor Livingston who had gone prematurely deaf, and realizing that he could exchange no word with Armstrong, Napoleon turned to Talleyrand in despair: 'What strange people these Americans are. First they sent me a man who is deaf, now they send me one who is dumb.'

Roman emperors and marble men of letters add lustre to this Gothic enclave. Portraits stand thick on the tables. One is of Julia Ward Howe, great-great aunt to the Aldriches, who – glory, glory, hallelujah – wrote 'The Battle Hymn of the Republic'. A fervent abolitionist, a social reformer, as well being as co-founder of the American Woman Suffrage Association, she was as poetic and patriotic a women

The octagonal library at Rokeby.
Opposite: *The parlour at Rokeby with a bust of Julia Ward Howe on the radiator. She is the great-great aunt of the house's owners and, of course, wrote 'The Battle Hymn of the Republic'.*

141

Ricky Aldrich and bust by the Polish sculptor, Bartîomiej Kurzeja.
Opposite: *The drawing room at Rokeby with its flamboyant nineteenth-century wallpaper. Amongst the photographs on the mantelpiece is one of Roosevelt's dog, Fala.*

barely looking at the paper. 'I had learned to do this' she later wrote 'when attacks of versification had visited me in the night and I feared to wake the baby.' After writing the immortal words she returned to bed saying to herself 'I like this better than most things I have written'.

She appears again in the parlour, her life-size head and shoulders in marble, plonked down on an old ornamental radiator, overlooking the gentle harmonious riches of the house

Throughout Rokeby there is evidence of the most curious phase in its history, when towards the end of the nineteenth century it was lived in by eight Astor orphans. By 1877 both their parents, Margaret Astor Ward and John Winthrop Chanler, had died: 'They had had eleven children in their fourteen years of marriage, none of them twins, no wonder they died exhausted' says Winty Aldrich.

To relate their lives is like trying to describe in detail ten thousand exploding fireworks. Willie Chanler, for example, headed off West with Butch Cassidy before leading an armed band of tribesmen against Italian colonists in Africa. He also became the military advisor to the 'Mad' Mullah of Somaliland. After working at a copper mine in Santiago, he brought back the recipe for the local rum concoction, thereby introducing the daiquiri cocktail to America. Both Willie and his brother, Wintie, fought in the Spanish-American War of 1898 in which their sister, Margaret, tended to the wounded by the hundred and set up her own hospitals; she became known as 'The Angel of Puerto Rico'. She then went on to found the US Woman's Army Nursing Corps as well as the National League of Woman Voters.

as ever lived. Give me three finer lines than these: 'He has sounded forth the trumpet that shall never call retreat/ He is sifting out the souls of men before His judgement seat/ Oh be swift my soul to answer him, Be jubilant, my feet/ Our God is marching on.'

I was delighted to discover that she had 'scrawled' these lines in the 'grey light of morning twilight'

The eldest orphan sibling was Archie who claimed he possessed the 'X-faculty', enabling him to change the colour of his eyes as well to write reams of automatic writing. He would go into a 'Napoleonic trance' during which, with lurid accuracy, he would 're-enact the death-bed scene of Napoleon'. So constant were these forays that his siblings had him committed to an asylum, for a miserably unjust three years and eight months. Unable to convince anyone of his sanity, one day he simply sauntered out of the gates leaving a note: 'My Dear Doctor, You have always said that I was insane… that I believe I am the reincarnation of Napoleon Bonaparte… you therefore will not be surprised that I take French leave.' He fled to the Southern states where he established his reputation and sanity. Having first been committed 1897, Archie was finally declared sane in July 1919 'freed from the incubus which he has borne these many years.' For eighteen years he campaigned against the sanity laws of New York State which had committed him, with their 'foul odour masquerading as law', writing and lecturing copiously and travelling throughout America in his blue-and-white striped, seven-seater Pierce Arrow limousine which was fitted out with a field kitchen. As for his 'former family' – as he referred to his siblings – 'Hell' he said 'would be frozen tight and I'll be skating figure eights on it before I have anything to do with a single one of them'.

His brother Bob Chanler was an artist of alarming note. He had been married to Natalina Cavalieri, a prima donna who sang with Caruso and Manon Lescaut. Before the wedding she forced him to relinquish his fortune; two days after, she announced that he would board with her gratis and be granted $20 a week. Soon she took up with an old lover. From his elder brother, Archie, came the telegram: 'Who's loony now?' Leaked to the world, the phrase became the catchword of the moment, hurled from the stage by comedians, intoned from

The hallway at Rokeby: the scene is redolent of an ancient European pile.
Opposite: *The attic at Rokeby.*

the pulpit by preachers; it was, according to Lately Thomas in his delightful biography of the Chanlers, *The Pride of Lions*, 'the most widely heard three-word ejaculation since "Et tu, Brute?". The phrase was set to music and "Who's loony now?" became better known than the national anthem.'

After such humiliations Bob Chanler plunged into his art, wildly working away in his extraordinary 'House of Fantasy' on East 19th Street in New York, where both painting and parties were permanently on the boil. It was from here, wrote Ethel Barrymore, that 'I entered… in the evening as a young girl, and came away early the next morning an old woman'. Bob's painted animals roamed the walls with porcupines and hippopotami, boa constrictors and buffalo. His bedroom was a forest of foliage through which detached eyes peered forth. One of his legacies to Rokeby is a screen on which is painted a slit-eyed black creature (Natalina Cavalieri) gnashing its sharp teeth into the neck of a white hart (the artist himself!)

Such are a mere sprinkling of details of the lives of the Chanler siblings who were raised at Rokeby. Here was a land so beautiful that when the later-to-be-great English actress Fanny Kemble first saw it in 1832, she wrote that 'the beauty and sublimity of what I beheld seemed almost to crush my faculties… I could have stretched out my arms and shouted aloud – I could have fallen on my knees and worshipped – I could have committed any extravagance that ecstasy could suggest'.

Two hundred years later she would see no change. Thanks to Winty Aldrich's crusading, the land is now preserved in perpetuity.

Although unaltered, Rokeby is still zingingly alive. Ricky Aldrich and his Polish wife, Anya, live there today – Ricky permanently coated with the filth that comes from keeping the old house on its feet. Rokeby is now owned by two generations with the five daughters developing a flourishing business producing puppets and other paraphernalia for New York pageants.

'It is dynamic' says Winty, with each generation making their own mark. A house, he says, is best enjoyed 'not as a museum or a mausoleum, but rather as a living place that does undergo changes but nevertheless retains enough of the past so that each generation can recover, move around and bring things down from the attic, things that are then of interest to them. Part of the pleasure of Rokeby is that it is all still here. It's an accretion of family tastes and objects over many generations and the total effect is a pleasing one that does in fact illuminate this sense of a continuity of ownership'. His job, he says, 'is to be the transmitter, making sure that nothing gets lost… then it is up to destiny'.

LAMBTON WITH A 'P'

Pocahontas, my seven-times-great-grandmother.

Discovering the American Lamptons was an adventure which I can unreservedly say was the most extraordinary experience of my life. It all began when a letter arrived from a total stranger, a Louis Lyell from Jackson, Mississippi, who had come across a book by a Lucinda Lambton in a catalogue of the swell London bookshop, Heywood Hill. He wondered whether I would mind signing a copy for his new grandson, just born to his daughter Louise, who was married to one Lucius Lampton of Magnolia, Mississippi? Furthermore, he wrote, did I know that Mark Twain's mother was a Lampton?

Did I know that Mark Twain's mother was a Lampton? It was like a bolt from the blessed blue, a shiveringly exciting, shimmering with promise, bolt from the blessed blue. Having discovered years ago that Pocahontas was my seven-times-great-grandmother, I felt that my cup of American happiness had already, and dramatically, overflowed. Completely unaware of any connection with Twain, I had called my son Huckleberry over thirty years earlier; to have found this link with the 'Lincoln of Literature' was, therefore, sensational news.

I happened to be going to New York, (as advisor on British sanitary history to the American Sanitary Plumbing Museum in Worcester, Massachusetts!) and I determined to set south, on a trail-blazing mission to find my American kith and kin.

A mere hint of the enormity of what lay ahead was at Brookhaven in Mississippi, my first stop on the Lampton-Lambton trail. There, cut into stone above the robust columns of New World classicism was 'Mary Jane Lampton Auditorium'. To see that name incised above bright white Corinthian capitals, against the bright blue American sky, was enough to make a slug sing. Whooping and cheering I punched the Mississippi air with joy. Here was a quite terrifyingly tangible link with the Lamptons and the land that I so loved.

The New World Lamptons, it turned out, had left a veritable treasure trail for this Old World Lambton to follow, leading me from Mississippi to Kentucky and on up to Missouri. Furthermore, in the course of this great adventure, I was to discover that most of Twain's life, as well as the lives of many other American Lampton's besides, had been instilled with the 'legend' that the inheritance of the Lambton family in Durham, England should be rightfully theirs.

Three Lambtons had originally come to America from the north of England. Mark Lambton was the first – a recusant Catholic, he had fled from Durham in 1664. Samuel and William Lambton, elder sons of the English family, departed for the New World in the mid 1700s, disgusted at what they considered to be 'the foolish fraud of hereditary aristocracy'. Twain (whose real name was, of course, Samuel Clemens) always claimed that it was because of this disdain that they 'corrupted' the name. One more cheerful explanation of the interchange of the 'p' and the 'b' was that 'the hump simply went up and down the pole'. A most elegantly-curved 'p' appears in Lampton on a seventeenth-century map of north-east England, while in a Kentucky census of 1810, Benjamin Lambton, Mark Twain's maternal grandfather, had a 'b' firmly planted in the middle of his name.

Soon after the Lambton brothers arrived in the New World, they were fighting in whiplash reaction against the British in the Revolutionary War. By the time their father died in England the two American brothers – by now prospering farmers in Virginia – were thought to have perished. 'This has always been the way with our family' wrote Twain. 'They always die when they could make anything by not doing it.' The younger sons in north-east England were left to reap the rewards of the inheritance that had been the right of their elder siblings. The vast yields of coal – 'black diamonds' for the Lambtons – had never disappointed. In 1834 the Earldom of Durham was conferred on my great-great-great-grandfather, the great 'Radical Jack' Lambton. It was then, according to Twain, that 'the great tribe of American Lamptons began to bestir themselves'.

Twain never met his English kinsmen, indeed he once purposefully avoided it, leaving a London hotel when he heard the startling news that Lady Durham was also within its walls!

So much I had discovered. Now at long last, in

the tiny town of Magnolia, Mississippi, a Lampton of the New World – Lucius Lampton, was to meet a Lambton of the Old – Lucy Lambton.

Lucius is a doctor and we were to meet in his clinic. It was slick steel and sterile – no less suitable spot could be countenanced. Nearby, raised upon a greensward, was a clapboard church, with green Gothic shutters and a bell-towered steeple. There was no time to lose; I raced in, 'had a word' with Mark Twain telling him – in case he had no notion – of what was about to happen and composed myself on the grass outside. With eyes almost shut, I could just see a white coat emerging from the clinic. I implored it to climb onto the greensward; then by dextrous 'blinkering' all that was in view was the church and a tree. I waited for that white coat to be there, full square. Suddenly it was and we leapt into each other's

Lucius Lampton and Lucy Lambton at China Grove, Mississippi.
Opposite: *Lucius Lampton amid the Lampton-Lambton lore in Magnolia, Mississippi.*

arms, embracing for all we were worth, with the years of Lampton-Lambton torment flowing off in a torrent!

Lucius is also a scholar, poet, conservationist and proprietor/editor of the local newspaper, the *Magnolia Gazette*. I have seldom, if ever, met a man whose combination of cheery sweetness and scholarship is so happily mixed, as he passionately propounds the Lampton-Lambton saga – in paroxysms of excitement and laughter – with each breath he takes. He has, for as long as he can remember, been pursuing every written word on the tale, as well as writing several weighty tomes on it himself. So vast indeed is his collection that it has had to be crammed into a huge house of its own, while Lucius lives more modestly nearby. The books lord it at Hedge Hill – a shingle-hung, belly-porched Gaudi-like, china embedded building where every inch of the floor

is stacked teeteringly high. Here in Magnolia, Mississippi, you find umpteen books on the Durham miners, as well as Hutchinson's *History and Antiquities of the County Palatine of Durham* (1785). Here too is *The Life and Letters of Lord Durham* (1906) in two volumes – a dry read. Every book written by my father is there too, as well as mine, seeming to hail me from the shelves. The last find was the best find of all: a seventeenth-century map of County Durham, showing 'Lamton' with neither a 'b' nor a 'p' – the last division downed!

As we left, past the stained-glass windows over the vast carved newel post at the foot of the grand stairs, a passing mile-long American freight train howled its way into my heart. It took a deal of control not to collapse.

The house is handsome, but a ruin, and will be restored by Lucius, as will the tiny Italianate palazzo

China Grove Methodist Church, Mississippi, (1861), the slaves gallery looms overhead.

of a newspaper office. He has schemes too for the nineteenth-century railroad station and the grain store. Magnolia, like hundreds of other small towns in America that have not positively prospered, has declined into a state of sympathetic grace. Now Lucius will ensure that this is arrested and diverted from doom.

Then it was off down Lampton Lane – its sign of rickety thin tin – to meet Lucius's father, Bob Lampton, who had imbued his four sons and daughter with the Lampton-Lambton saga from the day that they were born. Every night, before they went to sleep, he would hurl the words of 'The

Lambton Worm' into the air. This, a nineteenth-century music hall refrain, written in a Geordie accent and still belted out in north-east England today, is based on a legend – dating from the 1200s – of a 'feorful worm' that ravaged Durham's countryside, killing 'calves an' lambs and sheep' and swallowing 'little bairns alive when they lay doon to sleep'.

Lucius's father had neither known the accent nor the tune, but instead would orate it to his children in his most terrifying tones. Now this once flaming, now sadly fading man was on his deathbed and Lucius wanted me to sing the song so that he could hear it before he died. 'I'm sure' said Lucius 'that if he can hear you, it will add a day or two to his life.'

He seemed unconscious when we went into the room, with medical paraphernalia in grim abundance. His automatic bed was cranked into sitting position and he opened his eyes. I gave him a smacker of a kiss. 'My that was a kiss' he said and I gave him another.

'This is Lucy Lambton from Durham, who has come to Mississippi' cried Lucius.

His eyes flashed. 'It can't be, not after two-hundred-and-fifty years, it can't be.'

Then he was off, hell for leather, with tales of the Lampton-Lambton lore. 'She is going to sing "The Lambton Worm"' said Lucius. And so I most willingly obliged, filling the air with words that they had known for so long but which they had never heard in the rightful tongue or set to their rightful tune. There was not a dry eye in the room.

Lucius and I then set off into the country, to China Grove, where the force of what awaited me is still hard to fathom. Here, far from any habitation, was a little clapboard Methodist church, built, in part, by the Lamptons, in 1861. Severely simple, it is painted white with green shutters without, and white edged with pink within, with the slaves gallery looming separated overhead.

With the sun setting we walked into the cemetery and there, seemingly screeching out of the stone, was a grave to 'LUCY LAMPTON' whose husband, William Lampton – lying at her side – I was then told to my stupefied delight, was the model for Twain's literary hero Huckleberry Finn! Here then, beneath my feet, lay Mark Twain's mother's favourite cousin, William, who had fled hearth and home in Kentucky, after being sent out 'to fetch the calves' by his mean stepmother. Instead he had 'kept on going' down the Mississippi on a flat boat, arriving in these parts in the early 1800s.

His great adventure became a legend within the family, and to cap it all, he had been known as 'Buck'

– discoveries that defied belief to an English Lucy Lambton who had called her son Huckleberry over thirty years before.

I staggered on, only to be stopped short by the grave but yards away to 'LUCIE LAMPTON'. Further on a vast plot proclaimed itself 'LAMPTON' in big, bold letters of white stone. 'LUCINDA, WIFE OF JOHN CONERLY', lay nearby; she had been born Lucinda Lampton in 1834. Another stone was inscribed with 'LUCY L. LAMPTON', who died in 1915. This was of no mean moment, it was of alarmingly momentous moment, to find yourself in a tiny and far-flung cemetery in Mississippi, realizing that your roots are so deeply dug into American soil.

The temperature was in the nineties and the humidity likewise. Thank God for that air, alive with cicadas and so thick with the spirits of the place that it would be easier to inhale syrup. It kept me propped up on my pins! It all felt like an illusion, but there they all were: Lucy, Lucie and Lucinda Lampton, cut into the stone, before my very eyes. 'Do you realize' said Lucius 'that all those buried in the ground around us perceived themselves as members of the house of Lambton – always a little different because of being from Durham in England?' We stared round at this tiny enclave in Mississippi. 'Every one of them here have consistently thought of your family throughout their lives.'

There has never been another Lucy or Lucinda in the English family. It was a dream come true, to find this heavenly host of Lamptons.

As night fell we drove on to another small town, called Columbia, where the last of the Lampton Stores was in its final week before closing forever – a victim of the collapse of America's main street and the far mightier forces of the shopping mall.

The stores were founded in the nineteenth-century by Benjamin, son of William 'Huckleberry Finn' Lampton, and were passed on to his sons, Walter, Lucius, Iddo, Eddie, Thad and Frank, in whose hands six Lampton Company stores were to

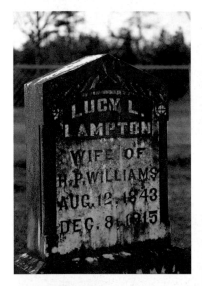

China Grove and Columbia graveyard – 'William Huckleberry Finn' Lampton lies next to his wife Lucy (bottom left).

flourish throughout the state. Indeed they were so highly valued that once one had been built, a town would grow around it.

An Art-Deco building, it was once the pride of the place. Its neon sign 'The Lampton Company' is no longer ablaze, but mosaics advertising the store's wares still decorate the surrounding pavement: 'LAMPTON'S DRY GOODS' 'LAMPTON'S SHOES', 'LAMPTON'S FURNITURE' and 'LAMPTON'S MEN'S DEPT', while the family name is wrought into decorative ironwork above each door. The Lampton Company even had its own fleet of steamboats that plied the Pearl River, supplying the cotton farmers with their clothes, food and furniture. Everything could be put on credit and paid for once yearly, when the cotton crop came in. If the yield was poor, then the stores suffered.

Inside, there are survivals galore, all locked away

© Alex Harvey

Above: The five Lampton brothers: Thad, Eddie, Iddo, Lucius and Walter.
Paraphernalia from the Lampton store, Columbia, Mississippi.

in a handsome, classically porticoed iron safe, emblazoned with the name 'Lampton'. Of particular delight was the lavishly-headed paper displaying the Lampton steam packet, *The Earl*, full steam ahead; there are account books, coat hangers and coupons; newspaper advertisements proudly proclaimed 'First with the latest since the 1880s' and 'More than a Century of Honourable Service'.

Darkness had almost engulfed the little cemetery in Columbia, and a uniformed man was shutting the gate. 'State trooper' cried Lucius, 'please let us in, this lady has come from England to find her kin.' Here in the gloom I could just make out a name carved beneath a marble child: I knew before I saw it: 'LUCIE LAMPTON'. She had died of consumption, as had her English cousin, the famed 'Red Boy' painted by Sir Thomas Lawrence. His two half-sisters had perished likewise, as had their father, 'Radical Jack' – the 1st Earl of Durham.

Thirteen months later I returned to Mississippi to take the photographs for this book. It was to be the day that Bob Lampton died. Standing over all those Lampton bones, it was all but intolerably moving to dwell on Bob's death only hours before. But for him and his interest in keeping the story alive and instilling it into his son Lucius, the Lamptons and the Lambtons might never have met.

To alight on any American Lampton past or present is to thunder off down every avenue of American life, surrounded by a galaxy of characters, places and buildings that can not be ignored. One of them, W. J. Lampton, would dress in a full suit of armour to honour his English kinsmen. Photographed in the *American Magazine* as 'a fine example of a descendant giving an imitation of his ancestors', it was said that 'not one critic or connoisseur in ten thousand would dispute the date if this portrait were labelled 1640 instead of 1913'. Describing himself as the 'plain poet of the people', he was the creator of yawp verse – poetry that he popularized throughout America, which he

Colonel W.J. Lampton, yawpist – 'a fine example of a descendant giving an imitation of his ancestors'.

explained, 'was nature's own expression… it rhythms when it rhythms, and it rhymes sometimes, but whether it does or not, it gets there just the same'. Remarkably, this Lampton contemporary kin of Twain's was judged by one critic to be 'the most characteristic of American writers of his day', whilst another described him as 'the most refreshing of contemporary writers'. He was loved by all. When he died in 1917, the *New York Times* reported that he was 'a freelance of the heart as well as of the pen'. He had tried many times to change the 'p' to a 'b' in Lampton, 'but the newspapers wouldn't let it stay changed'.

Twain's maternal grandfather was Benjamin Lampton. He was a brick mason, a mercantile man and a lieutenant colonel in the Corn Stalk Militia during the Revolutionary War. His great-great-uncle was President Monroe. His aunt-in-law gave birth to the first white child in Kentucky, William Logan, who was born in Harrodsburg in 1776 (founded in 1774 by one James Harrod, kin to my son Huckleberry, whose surname is Harrod!)

Here, one of his daughters, Patsy Lampton, would give Twain his happy childhood holidays on her farm in Missouri, cooking him 'sumptuous meals' which when he was an old man, made him 'still cry to think of'. It was here too that he was regaled with tales by 'Uncle Dan' – the slave who was to be immor-talized as 'Jim' in *Huckleberry Finn*! Patsy Lampton was married to John Adams Quarles, whose sister in turn married William Snodgrass – a name that tickled Twain into creating three characters: Quintus Curtius Snodgrass, Thomas Jefferson Snodgrass and Zylobalsamam Snodgrass. Quarles also had an aunt who married a descendant of William the Conqueror. Would that all these threads could be woven into one fantastic raiment!

Twain's mother, Jane, was the eldest of Benjamin Lampton's daughters; a beautiful fiery redhead who smoked a pipe, she was considered the finest dancer in the state. Twain wrote that 'to the very day of her death… she felt a strong interest in the world and everybody and everything in it'. She had 'a heart so large that everybody's grief and everybody's joys found welcome in it and hospitable accommodation'. Every animal too found harbour in her heart, in 1845 there were nineteen stray cats in the family home in Hannibal – each one having been welcomed as the prodigal son. All were without character, all without merit, wrote Twain 'except the cheap and tawdry merit of being unfortunate. They were a vast burden to us all – including my mother – but they were out of luck, that was enough, they had to stay'.

Jane Lampton gave birth to Samuel Clemens on 30 November 1835 in a two-roomed cabin in Florida, Missouri – a tiny hamlet on a tributary of the Mississippi at the fork of the Salt River. He was

born six months after the family had arrived in Florida. 'I was postponed' he wrote, 'postponed to Missouri. Missouri was an unknown new state and needed attractions.' When he was an old man he was sent a photograph of the house. 'Heretofore' he wrote 'I have always stated that it was a palace but I shall be more guarded now.'

Today, in a modern Missouri limestone building that slices into the sky, you find the tiny dwelling where the great man came into the world, complete with the curvingly carved and spindled bed on which he took his first breath.

How magical is this transatlantic tale – from the soaring grandeur of an Old World castle – Lambton Castle looms majestically over the River Wear in Durham – to the extreme modesty of this New World cabin, culminating with Twain, forever elevated in the marble halls of fame.

Twain wrote of enjoying mocking his mother's 'weak spot', her pride in what he called her 'gilded ancestry' of the 'feudal lords of Lambton Castle… holding the high position of ancestors of hers when the Norman Conqueror came over to divert the Englishry'. He argued 'cautiously and with mollifying circumlocutions, for one had to be careful on that holy ground and mustn't cavort – that there was no particular merit in occupying a piece of land for nine hundred years… she was merely descended from an entail and she might as well be proud of being descended from a mortgage'.

Jane Lampton Clemens died in 1890 but she lives on in the minds of millions, she is Tom Sawyer's Aunt Polly!

Another Lampton kinsman, Jesse Leathers – great-grandson of Samuel Lampton, the eldest son who had come to the New World in 1740 – determinedly called himself 'The American Earl', and with his self-proclaimed 'princely looks' he set out to claim the family honours 'that my keen sensi-bilities… have particularly fitted me to enjoy'. Twain – no doubt thanks to the roots with which he was

Mark Twain's birthplace, Florida, Missouri. A tiny two-room cabin placed within a vast 1970s building.

raised – was entranced by the idea of this 'rightful Earl'. He was convinced that this cousin could produce an autobiography 'that would make a cast iron dog laugh' and with his encouragement Leathers wrote *An American Earl*. But despite such promotion, it was deemed unpublishable.

Leathers doggedly pursued his obsession, imploring many American Lamptons to help him, including Twain. Time and again Twain's interest was rekindled and time and again it died. In 1878, for example, he reflected in his note book that he, Twain, 'was descended from the Earls of Durham through my mother… Mr Leathers is the rightful Lord Durham, not I'. When in England during the Titchborne

Claimant trial, Twain pasted up six scrapbooks of cuttings on the case and even proposed paying for Leathers to cross the Atlantic so as to set him up as the Durham claimant. In the end though poor Leathers was to die – unheralded by his English kin – of complications related to tuberculosis. He was buried with military honours in Cypress Hills National Cemetery in Brooklyn. Twain wrote: 'There was something very striking, and pathetically and grotesquely picturesque… about this long and hopeless, plucky, foolish and majestic fight of a foghorn against the fog. (Or, reverse that figure, perhaps).'

Twain's works are riddled through with the

romance of the tale of his forbears: of how English grandees could, by coming to the New World, be cheated of the fortune due to them in the Old. The very body of *The American Claimant* is based on the Lampton-Lambton lore (most particularly on Leathers's aspirations), with the so-called Earl of Rossmore being assailed for years, first by Simon Leathers of Arkansas, then Mulberry Sellers of Washington, in turn laying claim to the earldom in England. He tells his son: 'The truth is, the rightful heir did go to America, but disappeared somewhere in the wilds of Virginia… he wrote no letters home, was supposed to be dead; his younger brother softly took possession, presently the American did die, and straightway the eldest product put in his claim… successor after successor has done the same down to the present idiot… morally the American tramp is the rightful Earl… legally he has no more right than a dog.'

Such a saga is the essence too of *The Prince and The Pauper*. It stirs through *A Connecticut Yankee in King Arthur's Court*, as well as *The Gilded Age*. In his play 'Colonel Sellers as a Scientist' it is the Earldom of Dover on which the Colonel has set his sights. With *Life on the Mississippi* we read of a night-watchman who, with tears dripping, tells Twain that he is 'a wronged man' – the son of an English earl, whose mother had 'hated him from the cradle'. In *Huckleberry Finn* our hero runs into trouble on the Mississippi when he meets 'the rightful Duke of Bridgewater', a vagrant trickster, who claims that his great-grandfather was the eldest son of an English duke who had fled to America 'to breathe the pure air of freedom'. He had died leaving a son – 'I am the lineal descendant of that infant' declared the 'low down hum-bug'. The 'title and estates were seized in England.'

But it is in his essay 'Mental Telegraphy' that Twain himself is the central player. He writes of lying 'under a tree thinking of nothing in particular, when an absurd idea flashed into my head, and I said to a member of the household, "Suppose I should live to be ninety-two, and dumb and blind and toothless, and just as I was gasping out what was left of me on my deathbed" – "Wait I will finish the sentence" said my wife: "Somebody should rush in with a document, and say 'All the heirs are dead, and you are the Earl of Durham.'" 'That', wrote Twain, 'is truly what I was going to say.'

He wrote too of being upbraided by his cousin Sherwood Clemens, for cavorting with Northern Republicans, who had, he said 'swept away the old aristocracy of the South with fire and sword… it ill became [Twain], an aristocrat by blood, to train with that kind of swine. Did he forget that he was a Lampton?'

Twain grew up in Hannibal, Missouri. The Clemenses lived in several houses there and although they are now all too cleaned up for comfort, you can blinker yourself from the terrible Twain tourist trap with delightful results. Stand in front of the Pilaster House on the corner of Hill and Main Street and have a good laugh at the plight of Twain's brother, Orion Clemens, who arrived there late one night, at what he thought was home. Unknown to him, the family had just moved up the street and the house was now lived in by Dr Meredith as well as his two 'ripe old-maid sisters' who were asleep in Orion's old bed. Unsuspecting of the calamity ahead, he undressed and climbed in as well, to be welcomed by an explosion of shrieks: 'It's a man!' Fleeing with what clothes he could grab, he was all but felled by the good doctor – also naked and armed with a butcher's knife!

Twain's step-uncle, Dr James Lampton, was another who lived in Hannibal. He had studied under the alarming Dr Joseph McDowell who owned a labyrinth of caves nearby, in one of which he kept his embalmed daughter who had died aged fourteen. Wishing to see how she would petrify, he laid her in an alcohol-filled glass cylinder enclosed by another of copper, all suspended from a rail, in one of the fantastically-formed limestone passage-ways. To add insult to this already grievous injury, steamboats would stop along the Mississippi so that the passengers could flock to view the corpse. Twain recalled that 'loafers and rowdies used to drag it up by the hair and look up at the dead face'.

These, of course, are the caves immortalized in *Tom Sawyer*. (A 'sawyer', incidentally, was a tree which had fallen from eroding river banks into the water and had continued growing at the angle at which it fell.)

The Mississippi – 'Mother of Rivers' – some 4,300 miles long, was 'discovered' by Hernando de Soto in 1594. 'The discovery of the Mississippi' Twain wrote 'is a datable fact which considerably mellows and modifies the shiny newness of our country and gives it a most respectable aspect of rustiness and antiquity.' Here then are the waters that he plied when working as a pilot on the steamboats – a job in which he took 'measureless pride... loving the profession more than any I have followed since – a pilot being the only unfettered and entirely independent being that lived on the earth'. It is generally known that his pen name came from the Mississippi leadsman's call, 'mark twain!' – the line on the boat for two fathoms deep of safe water. What is not realized by many is that he was not the first writer to use the name. Those laurels should be laid at the feet of a venerable river boat captain, a certain Isaiah Sellers who, in the course of his life, travelled over a million miles of the Mississippi. 'A high-minded man', according to Twain 'handsome, stately... with hair as black as an Indian's in his old age', he was held in awe by his fellow pilots as the 'genuine Son of Antiquity'. This added 'some trifle stiffening to his natural dignity, which had been sufficiently stiff in its original state'.

An assiduous recorder of river life, Sellers would send dispatches 'of plain and practical information about the river' to the *New Orleans Picayune*, signing them 'Mark Twain'. They were inoffensive, save in

Detail from the funerary monument of Captain Isaiah Sellers, the original Mark Twain, Bellefontaine cemetery, St. Louis.

one regard: that of constantly reminding the reader that his knowledge of the mighty Mississippi was without parallel. He was mercilessly mocked in the public prints, most painfully by the fledgling journalist, Samuel Clemens. 'Captain Sellers did me the honour to profoundly detest me from that day forth' wrote Twain. 'I am not using empty words. It was a very real honour to be in the thoughts of so great a man as Captain Sellers... he loved scores of people but he didn't sit up at nights to hate anybody but me.'

When the old man died Clemens adopted his name as his nom de plume, 'a warrant,' he wrote that 'whatever is found in its company may be gambled upon as the petrified truth'.

The mournfully eroded form of Captain Isaiah Sellers, hauntingly portrayed in stone at the ship's wheel, stands in Bellefontaine cemetery in St Louis. Sellers designed his own funerary monument long before his death and would take it with him wherever he went! 'He stands on duty at the pilot wheel' wrote Twain 'worthy to stand and confront criticism, for it represents a man who in life would have stayed there till he burnt to a cinder if duty required it.'

Nor was this the only honour paid to the old riverboat captain; Twain gave his name to his most consistently endearing hero Colonel Mulberry Sellers, whose character had in fact been based on his cousin Major James Lampton and whose grave – with the long arm of coincidence as always looming large – is within sight of Seller's own memorial. Twain's first cousin, James Lampton, was also his favourite cousin, and was made a pivotal figure throughout many of his works. It was he above all others of Twain's characters who warmed to the idea of his 'English ancestry – a grand old line… a sublime old line. It is a more enviable thing to be an English Earl than to be materialized Solomon, with all his unapproachable paraphernalia of wisdom including his eight hundred materialized wives'. When James Lampton died his family were too impoverished to buy him a burial plot and it was left to Lucius Lampton, 113-years later, to have a granite memorial put over his remains in Bellefontaine cemetery in St Louis.

In 1870 Twain had married Olivia Langdon; they were to have four children: Langdon a son, who died when he was only twenty-two-months old; Clara, Suzy, and last of all Jean. Twain blamed himself for his son's death and in a curious paragraph in his autobiography – written some forty years later – claimed that this was probably the first time that he had the courage to confess to the 'treacherous mornings work' of having allowed his son's covers to slip off whilst out on a freezing winter's drive.

Of all traces of Twain throughout America, none is more tremendous than 351 Farmington Avenue, Hartford, Connecticut, a lavish house that spikes off in the Stick style with a proliferation of fanciful woodwork – balconies, porches, spindles and brackets – all painted in brilliant scarlet. Red brick, lofty chimneys soar out of the body of the building, adorned with patterns painted in vermilion and black. Further encrustations of brick are overlaid at odd angles. With its blue slate roofs and striped awnings it must have seemed like a giant firework when it first appeared, although one critic lent a more structured voice when he described it as 'part cathedral… part steamboat, part medieval castle and part cuckoo clock'. A reporter on the *Hartford Daily Times* was so startled when he first saw the house in 1874, that he wrote of it as 'one of the oddest looking buildings in the State ever designed for a dwelling, if not in the whole country… The novelty, the oddity of its internal arrangement, and the fame of its owner, will conspire to make it a house of note for a very long time.'

Twain loved this house, writing that 'it had a heart and a soul, and eyes to see us with, and approvals, and solicitudes, and deep sympathies, it was of us, and we were in its confidence, and lived in its grace and in the peace of its benediction. We never came home from an absence that its face did not light up and speak out its eloquent welcome – and we could not enter it unmoved.' He also penned a poem on the place:

These are the bricks of various hue
And shape and position, straight and askew,
With nooks and angles and gables too,
Which make up the house presented to view,
The curious house that Mark Built.

Its architect was Edward Tuckerman Potter and the richly-appointed interiors were designed by the equally richly-named Louis Comfort Tiffany,

The hall of Mark Twain's house, 351 Farmington Avenue, Hartford, Connecticut, 1874, painted to simulate mother-of-pearl.

Hartford: the library with mantelpiece salvaged from the demolished Ayton Castle in Scotland.
Opposite: *Hartford: the curious view over the drawing-room fireplace into the hall.*

Lockwood de Forest, Candace Thurber Wheeler and Samuel Colman. When summoned to enhance the Tudor front hall in 1881 they excelled – smothering the woodwork with tiny shimmering triangles of aluminium paint, giving all the effect of inlaid mother-of-pearl. Stand in the drawing room and you get a delightfully curious view of it all: where over the fireplace there would usually be the chimney breast, sporting say, a mirror, here instead is a great opening, allowing you to look straight through into the shining hall.

The library too groans under the weight of glories with a carved overmantel which the Clemenses salvaged from the demolished Ayton Castle in Scotland. When Twain left Hartford in 1903 he took it with him to Redding, Connecticut where

he was to die seven years later. That house burnt to the ground in 1923, but the overmantel was salvaged yet again. After years of lying in pieces in a barn it was returned to Hartford in 1958.

Now, as in the Clemenses' heyday, pictures and bric-a-brac abound around and on this mantelpiece. Twain's daughters would regularly insist that he spun tales about the objects – always in the same order and without a moment's preparation permitted. He wrote 'In the course of time these bric-a-brac and pictures showed wear… they had had so many and such tumultuous adventures in their romantic careers.' *The Prince and the Pauper* was first aired in this room, when it was 'performed' by the girls. It was here too that Olivia Clemens insisted on a refinement to *Huckleberry Finn*, that the hero should not be 'combed all to hell' but rather 'all to thunder'. The course of American literature was thus polished rather than pruned – Twain never changed anything that he did not want to – by 'Livy's' delicate sensibilities. 'My darling little mentor' as Twain called her, subtly edited his works throughout their married life.

Of all the decorative and architectural details, it is the billiard-room ceiling that is most pleasing of all, painted with crossed cues and with pipes at each corner. Twain relished the game, often playing through the night 'to rest his head', as his daughter Clara put it, although the room would be blue with the smoke of his incessant puffing. He said that the game had destroyed his naturally sweet disposition.

Olivia had been born in the Langdon House in Elmira, Upstate New York – a vast porticoed, towered and columned Italianate mansion that had been an important safe house on the underground railroad – the slave escape route to Canada and freedom. But due to one of the most glaringly ghastly acts of vandalism that I have ever seen – and I have seen enough to make Pevsner puke – it is no more. Where once stood a 'beautiful and impressive' house there is now a most wretched example of a 1960s mini mall – called, if you please, the 'Langdon Plaza'.

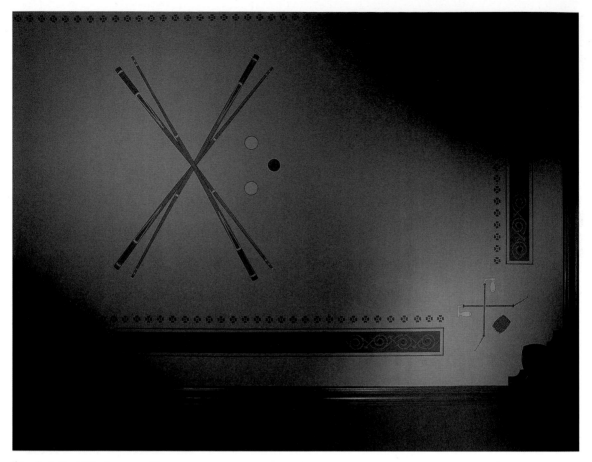

Hartford: the billiard-room ceiling.

Where, in the richly-hung, furnished, chandeliered, gilded and painted great parlour Twain was married, and, after his death had lain in state – to the mournful notes of the orchestrelle's 'Nearer my God to Thee' (as had his wife before him), we now ponder on 'Picnic Pizza'. And where, according to Twain's daughter Clara ,'wide mahogany staircases belonged in an eventful romance' we are now faced with the 'Subway Sandwich Shop'.

It was on the lawns of Langdon House that Twain lounged under a shady tree with his friend the Revd Thomas Beecher (uncle of author, Harriet Beecher Stowe). It was here too that the young, and as yet unknown, Rudyard Kipling and Twain first met;

when two hours of talk built the foundations of a firm friendship between them. The Englishman wrote an ecstatic account of that 'golden morning'. At one point Twain put his hand on Kipling's shoulder:'It was an investiture of the Star of India, blue silk, trumpets and diamond-studded jewels, all complete. If, hereafter… I fall to careless ruin, I will tell the superintendent of the workhouse that Mark Twain once put his hand on my shoulder, and he shall give me a room to myself and a double allowance of paupers' tobacco.'

The last named Lampton in Twain's line was his third daughter, Jane Lampton Clemens, always known as Jean. She was born at Olivia's sister's house, Quarry

Mark Twain in his octagonal study at Quarry Farm.   (© *Elmira College, Mark Twain Archives*)

Farm, high on the hills above Elmira in 1880, where the Clemens family came for twenty summers. It was here that Twain's sister-in-law built an ornate octagonal house in which he could write 'on top of an elevation that commands leagues of valley and city and retreating ranges of distant blue hills'; where, according to Clara, the air in the summerhouse was 'permeated with tobacco smoke'. Twain had smoked since he was 'a shade past eleven' – and 'that it was almost stifling… No exercise, little fresh air, constant inhaling of cigar smoke – all contributed to keep him in good health.' He felt that he wrote with 'red hot interest' within the walls of this octagonal den.

By 1952 Twain's octagonal den had been vandalized and was in a state of gradual deterioration, and so was moved – most mistakenly in my view – to the campus of Elmira College below. With traffic roaring by, it sadly lacks the 'complete isolation' that so delighted Twain.

It was in this little building that, joy of joys, Tom Sawyer and countless others of Twain's characters were created. Beating a path to where it once stood was no paltry pilgrimage. How I hollered from that hilltop that this is where Huckleberry Finn was 'born'.

Quarry Farm itself is still intact – a simple gabled wood house with its great porch on which the whole family would gather every evening to listen to the latest exploits of what Twain called 'Huck Finn's Autobiography'.

What a pretty kettle of fish it is, to realize that the first and greatest democratic writer of the New World should have as his blood mainspring the ancient swanks of the Old. With his free and funny,

Dinwiddie Lampton, the flamboyant hero of Kentucky.

family are modest. Twain's memorial stands exactly twelve feet – two fathoms high ('mark twain') – at the head of the Langdon and Clemens clans. There are twenty-three graves in all, including one to 'Jean Lampton Clemens – a most desolate father sets this stone'. The whole family lie together at Elmira, where more than anywhere else, Twain was inspired to write. He always said that it was 'a foretaste of Heaven'.

William 'the Pioneer' Lampton had died in 1790, having battled into the wilderness of Virginia that was to become Kentucky – 'the dark and bloody ground' of the new frontier, so bitterly fought over with the Shawnee tribes. It had proved to be a land lush with blue grass, with fertile meadows and with forests. Generations after generations followed this first New World Lampton to Kentucky. Like my kinsmen before me I too headed West, to seek out a direct descendant of William Lampton – the octogenarian Dinwiddie Lampton, a figure whose reputation thundered before him: a terrific and

easy and breezy language flowing forth so brilliantly on to the page reflecting the golden horizons of the New World, Twain forever cast off the shackles of Old World literature – and yet, it turns out, much of it is a Lambton legacy! While it is one thing for me to have the genius of the man impressed upon my mind, it is quite another to find to what an extent the Lambtons were impressed upon his.

Twain and his family would always leave something behind when departing the farm at the end of each summer, thereby ensuring their return. Olivia bestowed her 'heart's content' whilst the children left kisses on the gates. By way of a sad salute before I left Quarry Farm, I waved an imaginary sheet to the town in the valley, where the Langdon House had once stood. The Clemenses would often send sheet-waving signals to the Langdons below (although when Mrs Langdon died, Alexander Graham Bell contrived an apparatus by which Olivia could listen to her mother's funeral service at the church in Elmira).

On 21 April 1910 'the grand old fellow peacefully breathed his last'. The graves of Twain and his

BENJAMIN
LAMPTON

MAY 24 1770
MARCH 18 1837

GRANDFATHER OF
SAMUEL L CLEMENS
(MARK TWAIN)

trumpet-tongued character who was as handsome as hell, with eyebrows that sprouted a foot from his face.

Suddenly there was a roar as, like an approaching fireball, Dinwiddie's progress could be heard as it combusted its way up the stairs. Diamonds flashed and he was there, sporting a crimson velvet and jewel-encrusted fez, hollering 'Miaaaah cousin!'

He is one of the most spirited carriage drivers in all America. If he fails to win – which is seldom the case and he won his first ribbon in 1924 – the crowd will ignore the winner and instead cheer Dinwiddie to the skies. He is the proud owner too of some dozens of rare carriages as well as some dozens of horses to pull them. To find yourself in the Southern states of America, climbing aboard the Windsor and Egham mail coach of 1820 is odd indeed, as is seeing the Maharaja of Jaipur's carriage, dating from 1875, under the Kentucky skies.

With Dinwiddie's topper shining and cape coat flying, we hurtled along the banks of the Ohio River in a late nineteenth-century German hunting Studbaker drawn by six skewbalds, with their creaking harness making a music all of its own.

There are more, no doubt hundreds more illustrious Lamptons throughout America – those who wisely went off to the New World, to abandon the hereditary principle of the Old. I could go on until the cows come home. Or rather the Earldom of Durham comes home, home to America!

The Lambton brothers had left England in the seventeenth and eighteenth centuries. They had divided in the nineteenth century, when William 'Huckleberry Finn' Lampton fled down the Mississippi. In what remains of the hamlet of Florida, Twain's birthplace, there was to be a dedication for a new gravestone to mark the burial place of Twain's grandfather, Benjamin Lampton.

I flew from England, Lucius flew from Mississippi, and Dinwiddie flew from Kentucky. The two branches of the New World Lamptons had never met and it was with immense pride that a Lambton from the Old World was able to bring them together once again – over the grave of the grandfather of Mark Twain – he who was the greatest Lampton of them all.

SELECT
BIBLIOGRAPHY

Ailenroc, M. R., *The White Castle of Louisiana* (John P. Morton and Co., 1903)

Baigell, Matthew, *Thomas Cole* (Watson-Guptill Publications, 1981)

Ballard, Sandra L., and Hudson, Patricia L., *Smithsonian Guide to Historic America: The Carolinas and Appalachian States* (Stewart, Tabori and Chang, 1989)

Barker, Sister Mildred, *The Sabbathday Lake Shakers: An Introduction to Shaker History* (Shaker Press, 1978)

Brachey, Doug, and Brachey, Dawn, *Rugby Tennessee's Victorian Village* (Historic Rugby, 1995)

Bradbury, Malcolm, Introduction and afterword to Wilson, James D., *The Oxford Mark Twain* (Oxford University Press, 1996)

Brandt, Clare, *An American Aristocracy: The Livingstons* (Doubleday, 1986)

Brooks, John Graham, *As Others See Us* (Macmillan Co., 1908)

Bultman, Bethany Ewald, *Compass American Guide to New Orleans* (Fodor's Travel Publications Inc., 1996)

Burgess, Larry E., *Mohonk, Its People and Spirit* (Purple Mountain Press, 1993)

Calhoun, Charles C., *Compass American Guide to Maine* (Fodor's Travel Publications Inc., 1997)

Cantor, George, *Historic Festivals: A Travelers Guide* (Visible Ink Press, 1996)

Capitman, Barbara K., Capitman, Michael, D., and Wilhelm, Dennis. W., *Rediscovering Art Deco USA* (Viking Studio Book 1994)

Carr, Sister Frances A., *Growing Up Shaker* (United Society of Shakers, 1995)

Carver, Richard A., *A History of Marshall* (The Donning Co., 1993)

Casewit, Curtiss, *Off the Beaten Path, A Guide to Unique Places: Colorado* (Globe Piquot Press, 1987)

Chernow, Ron, *The House of Morgan* (Touchstone/Simon and Schuster, 1990)

Colbert, Judy, *Off the Beaten Path, A Guide to Unique Places: Virginia* (Globe Piquot Press, 1986)

Commager, Henry Steele, *America in Perspective* (Random House, 1947)

Crockett, Albert Steven, *When James Gordon Bennett Was Caliph of Bagdad* (Funk and Wagnalls Co., 1926)

Curtis, Wayne, *Off the Beaten Path, A Guide to Unique Places: Maine* (Globe Piquot Press, 1992)

Delano, Patti, and Johnson, Cathy, *Off the Beaten Path, A Guide to Unique Places: Missouri* (Globe Piquot Press, 1990)

Dickens, Charles, *American Notes and Pictures From Italy* (Macmillan, 1893)

Donzel, Catherine, Gregory, Alexis, and Walter, Marc, *Grand American Hotels* (Thames and Hudson, 1989)

Dore, Susan Cole, *The Pelican Guide to Plantation Homes of Louisiana* (Pelican Publishing Co., 1971)

Dow, George Francis, *Whale Ships and Whaling: A Pictorial History* (Dover Publications, 1985)

Du Fresne, Jim, *Off the Beaten Path, A Guide to Unique Places: Michigan* (Globe Piquot Press, 1988)

Duncan, Alastair, *American Art Deco* (Thames and Hudson, 1986)

Dunn Jnr, Jerry Camarillo, *Smithsonian Guide to Historic America: Rocky Mountain States* (Stewart, Tabori and Chang, 1989)

Durham, Michael S., *Smithsonian Guide to Historic America: The Mid-Atlantic States* (Stewart, Tabori and Chang, 1989)

Eliot, Samuel, *The Oxford History of the American People, Volumes 1 and 3* (Meridian Books, 1965)

Emerson, Ralph Waldo, *The Complete Writings, Volumes 1 & 2* (Wm. H. Wise and Co., 1929)

Fensom, Rod, and Foreman, Julie, *Off the Beaten Path, A Guide to Unique Places: Illinois* (Globe Piquot Press, 1987)

Festschrift., Theodore, *Stempfel's Fifty Years of Unrelenting German Aspirations in Indianapolis, 1848-98* (German American Centre, 1991)

Fischer, David, *Albion's Seed* (Oxford University Press, 1989)

Foerster, Norman, (ed.), *American Poetry and Prose* (Houghton Mifflin Co., 1925)

Franci, Giovanna, Mangaroni, Rosella, and Zago, Esther *A Journey Through American Art Deco* (University of Washington Press, 1997)

Free Serbian Orthodox Church, 'Serbian Heritage of Kosovo Booklet of Truth' (Serbian Orthodox Free Diocese of the United States of America and Canada, 1990)

— *Gracanica Consecration, 11-12 August 1984* (Serbian Orthodox Free Diocese of the United States of America and Canada, 1984)

Lord Sawyer, Priscilla, and Clegg Gamage, Virginia, *Marblehead: The Spirit of '76 Lives Here* (Chilton Book Co., 1976)

Garret Wendell, *Victorian America* (Rizzoli, 1993)

Gebhard, David, *The National Trust Guide to Art Deco in America* (John Wiley and Sons, 1996)

Gilborn, Craig, *Adirondack Furniture and the Rustic Tradition* (Harry N. Abrams Inc., 1987)

Gilmartin, Gregory, Stern, Robert A. M., and Mellins, Thomas *New York 1930: Architecture and Urbanism Between The Two World Wars* (Rizzoli, 1987)

Gunther, John, *Inside the USA* (New Press, 1946)

Gurko, Miriam, *The Lives and Times of Peter Cooper* (Thomas Y. Crowell Co., 1959)

Hamlin, Talbot, *Greek Revival Architecture in America* (Dover Publications, 1994)

Hughes, Thomas, *Rugby Tennessee* (Macmillan and Co., 1881)

Huntingdon, James Lincoln, *Forty Acres* (Hastings House Publishers, 1922)

Hutner, Gordon (ed.) *Immigrant Voices* (Signet Classic Penguin Group, 1999)

Huxtable, Ada Louise, *Kicked a Building Lately?* (University of California Press, 1998)

Jerome, Robert D., and Wisbey Jnr, Herbert A., *Mark Twain in Elmira* (Mark Twain Society, 1977)

Kelly, Franklin, with Gould, Stephen J., Ryan, James Anthony, and Ringe, Debora, *Frederic Edwin Church* (Smithsonian Institution Press, 1989)

Kennedy, Roger G., *Greek Revival in America* (Stewart, Tabori and Chang, 1989)

Ketchum, Richard M., *Faces from the Past* (American Heritage Press, 1970)

Kidder Smith, G. E., *Source Book of American Architecture* (Princeton Architectural Press, 1996)

Kostyal, K. M., *Compass American Guide to Virginia* (Fodor's Travel Publications Inc., 1994)

Lampton, Lucius Marion, M.D., *The Genealogy of Mark Twain* (Diamond L. Publishing, 1990)

Lane, Mills, *Architecture of the Old South: Virginia* (Abbeville Press, 1984)

— *Architecture of the Old South: Mississippi* (Abbeville Press, 1989)

Lately, Thomas, and Aldrich, John Winthrop (ed.), *The Astor Orphans, A Pride of Lions* (Washington Park Press, 1999)

Laughlin, Clarence John, *Ghosts along the Mississippi: The Magic of The Old Houses of Louisiana* (American Legacy Press, 1958)

Leibling, A. J., *Back Where I Came From* (Fourth Estate, 1938)

LeMaster, J. R., and Wilson, James D. (eds.), *The Mark Twain Encyclopaedia* (Garland Publishing, Inc., 1993)

Logan, William Bryant, and Muse, Vance *Smithsonian Guide to Historic America: The Deep South* (Stewart, Tabori and Chang, 1989)

Loveday Jr, Amos J., *The Rise and Decline of the American Cut Nail Industry* (Greenwood Press, 1983)

Lowe, David Gerrard, *Stamford White and New York in the Gilded Age* (The New York School of Interior Design, 1994)

McAlester, Virginia, and McAlester, Lee, *A Field Guide to American Houses* (Borzoi Books, 1984)

Mack, Edward C., *Peter Cooper, Citizen of New York* (Duell, Sloan and Pearce, 1949)

McLean, Alex, *Great American Houses and Their Architectural Styles* (Abbeville Press, 1994)

Mandell, Patricia, *Off the Beaten Path, A Guide to Unique Places: Massachusetts* (Globe Piquot Press, 1992)

Martin, Gay, *Off the Beaten Path, A Guide to Unique Places: Louisiana* (Globe Piquot Press, 1990)

Melville, Herman, *Moby Dick* (J.M. Dent and Sons, 1907)

Minks, Louise, *The Hudson River School* (Crescent Books, 1989)

Mitchell, Joseph, *McSorley's Wonderful Saloon* (Blue Ribbon Books, 1938)

Mulligan, Tim, *The Hudson River Valley* (Random House, 1981)

Muse, Vance, *Smithsonian Guide to Historic America: Northern New England* (Stewart, Tabori and Chang, 1989)

Neblett, Nathaniel Palmer, 'Christ Church, Lancaster County' (VA Historic Structure Report)

Neider, Charles (ed.), *The Autobiography of Mark Twain* (Harper Perennial, 1959)

O'Brien, Tim, *Off the Beaten Path, A Guide to Unique Places: Tennessee* (Globe Piquot Press, 1990)

Pachter, Marc (ed.), *Abroad in America: Visitors to the New Nation 1776-1914* (Adison-Wesley, 1976)

Penn, Jeanne, *A History of Penn's Stores* (Lane, 1993)

— *The Penn's Stores Friends Book of Sharing* (1996)

Pitzer, Sarah, *Off the Beaten Path, A Guide to Unique Places: Pennsylvania* (Globe Piquot Press, 1989)

Randall, Monica, *Phantoms of the Hudson* (Overlook Press, 1995)

Reeves, Pamela, *Ellis Island: Gateway to the American Dream* (Crescent Books, 1991)

Rifkind, Carole, *A Field Guide to American Architecture* (New American Library, 1980)

Ritchie, David, and Ritchie, Deborah, *Off the Beaten Path, A Guide to Unique Places: Connecticut* (Globe Piquot Press, 1992)

Roberts, Bruce, and Jones, Ray, *American Country Stores* (Globe Peqot Press, 1991)

Roberts, Bruce, and Keddish, Elizabeth, *Plantation Homes of the James River* (University of North Carolina Press, 1990)

Roth, Leland M., *A Concise History of American Architecture* (Harper Row, 1979)

Rousmaniere, John, *The Luxury Yachts* (Time Life Books, 1981)

Russell, John, and Pierce, Charles E., Forewords to *In August Company: The Collections of the Pierpont Morgan Library* (Harry N. Abrams Inc., 1993)

Scheller, William G., and K., *Off the Beaten Path, A Guide to Unique Places: New York* (Globe Piquot Press, 1994)

Seitz, Don C., *The James Gordon Bennetts* (Bobbs-Merrill Co., 1928)

Sibley, Marlo, *Off the Beaten Path, A Guide to Unique Places: Mississippi* (Globe Piquot Press, 1997)

Skjelver, Mabel Cooper, PhD thesis, 'Nineteenth-Century Homes of Marshall, Michigan' (Marshall Historical Society, Michigan, 1971)

Smith, A. I., and Frazer, A. J., *White Pillars: The Architecture of the South* (Bramhall House, 1949)

Smith, Gregg, *Beer in America: The Early Years, 1587-1840* (Brewers Publication, 1998)

Smith, McKelden (ed.), *The Great Estates Region of the Hudson River Valley Historic* (Hudson Valley Press, 1998)

Stahl, Jasper J., *History of Old Broad Bay and Waldoboro, Volumes 1 & 2* (Bond Wheelwright Co., 1956)

Starr, Frederick S., *Southern Comfort: The Garden District of New Orleans* (Princetown Architectural Press, 1998)

Stein, Stephen J., *The Shaker Experience in America* (Yale University Press, 1992)

Stern, Robert A. M., Gilmartin, Gregory, and Massengale, John, *New York 1900* (Rizzoli, 1983)

Stewart, Cecil, *Serbian Legacy*, (Harcourt, Brace and Co., 1959)

Strecker, Zoe'Ayn, *Off the Beaten Path, A Guide to Unique Places: Kentucky* (Globe Piquot Press, 1992)

Tauranac, John, and Little, Christopher, *Elegant New York: The Builders and the Buildings, 1885-1915* (Abbeville Press, 1985)

Thomas, Phyllis, *Off the Beaten Path, A Guide to Unique Places: Indiana* (Globe Piquot Press, 1985)

Tuckerman, Henry T., *America and Her Commentators* (Charles Scribner, 1864)

Twain, Mark, *Adventures of Huckleberry Finn* (Charles L. Webster and Co., 1884)
— *Mississippi Writings* (Library of America, 1876)
— *Adventures of Tom Sawyer* (Library of America, 1876)
— *The American Claimant* (Chatto and Windus, 1892)
— *A Connecticut Yankee in King Arthur's Court* (University of California Press, 1984)
— *The Guilded Age* (Chatto and Windus, 1873)
— *Hartford* (Connecticut Printers Finlay Bros Inc., 1958)
— *The £1,000,000 Bank Note And Other New Stories* (Oxford University Press, 1996)

Valentine, Maggie, *The Show Starts on the Sidewalk* (Yale University Press, 1994)

Vanzant, Roland, *Chronicles of the Hudson* (Black Dome Press, 1992)

Velimirovich, Bishop Nikolai, and Popovich, Archimandrite Justin, *The Mystery and Meaning of the Battle of Kosovo* (The Free Society Orthodox Diocese of America and Canada, 1989)

Wall, Joseph Frazier, *Andrew Carnegie* (University of Pittsburgh Press, 1970)

Ward, Geoffrey C., *Closest Companions* (Houghton and Mifflin Co., 1995)

Warren, Leonard, *Joseph Leidy: The Last Man Who Knew Everything* (Yale University Press, 1998)

Welland, Douglas, *The Life And Times of Mark Twain* (Studio Editions, 1991)

West, Amanda B., *Main Street Festivals* (Preservation Press National Trust Guide, 1998)

Wiencek, Henry, *Smithsonian Guide to Historic America: Southern New England* (Stewart, Tabori and Chang, 1989)
— *Smithsonian Guide to Historic America: Virginia and the Capital Region* (Stewart, Tabori and Chang, 1989)

Winckler, Suzanne, *The Great Lakes States* (Stewart, Tabori and Chang, 1989)
— *Smithsonian Guide to Historic America: The Plains States* (Stewart, Tabori and Chang, 1990)

Zukowski, John, and Stimson, Robbe Pierce, *Hudson River Villas* (Rizzoli, 1985)

INDEX

A

Abbotsford, Scotland 139
Adams
  John 10, 32
  John (New Orleans) 102
  John Quincy 80
  Samuel 11
Aesthetic Movement 136
Aldrich
  Anya 146
  Ricky 138, 146, *143*
  Rosalind 138
  Winty 138-9, 143, 146
Alison & Sons, Ralph 31
Alka-Seltzer Company 72-3
Allen
  Abel 21
  Max 58
Alliance 79
America
  Civil War 6, 23, 25, 37, 39,
  46, 49-50, 53, 76, 104, 110,
  112-14
  Declaration of
  Independence 11, 134
  War of Independence
  ('Revolutionary War') 4, 6,
  8, 10-11, 19, 49, 53, 80, 95
American Magazine 58
American Sanitary Plumbing
  Museum 147
American Woman Suffrage
  Association 139
An American Earl (Leathers)
  157
Anacreonic Society 60
Angelina, Sister 68
Anheuser, Eberhard 60
Anheuser-Busch Brewery, St
  Louis, Missouri 59-64, *61*,
  63, *64*
Architectural Review 84
Armstrong
  General John 138
  Margaret 139
Arnold, Sarah Rotch 36
Art Deco 70, 106-9, 152
Astor
  Archie 145
  John Jacob 83, 139
  orphans 143, 145
  William B. 139
Astor Ward, Margaret 143
Atkins, Chet 120
Autry, Gene 56

Ayton Castle, Scotland *162*

B

Bacon, Frances 117
Baker, Sister Mildred 23
Bakewell
  Elizabeth 47
  Robert 23
Bangor Daily News 109
Banks, General Nathanial 104
Barry, Uncle George 31
Barrymore
  Ethel 145
  John 108
Basil, Bishop 65
Bates, Issachar 21
'Battle Hymn of the
  Republic' 139
Beale Street, Memphis 123,
  125-6
Beecher
  Henry Ward 17
  Revd Thomas 162
Belcher, Governor 4
Bell, Alexander Graham 40,
  165
Bellefontaine cemetery, St
  Louis 159
Bellomont *see* Staatsburg
Bennett, James Gordon 84-7
Bertz, Edward 27-8
Bevo Bottling Plant 62
Bierstadt, Alfred 136
Black Joe 11
Blacklock
  Mary 31
  Revd Joseph 31
Blackstone, Sir William 32
Boal
  David 19
  Mathilde 14, 17
  Pierre 17
  Theodore Davis 14-15, 17,
  19
Boal Mansion, Boalsburg,
  Pennsylvania 15-19, *16-18*
Bolivar, Simon 17
Boone, Daniel 55
Booth
  Edwin 43
  John Wilkes 43
  Junius Brutus 43
Boring & Tilton 132
Boston 3, 8
  Court House 10

Boston Sunday Globe 43
Boughton, George 136
Bourke-White, Margaret 83
Boyle, Charles (Earl of
  Orrery) 115
Brick Store, New Hampshire
  122
Briggs
  Charles 102
  Ephraim and Barnabas 21
Broad Bay *see* Waldoboro
Brooks, Harold 73-4
Brown, John 17
Buck, William 70
Bullfinch, Charles 77
Bunker & Savage 108
Burke, Edmund 32
Burroughs, John 93
Busch, Adolphus 60, 159
Busch III, August 60, 62
Butler, General 'Beast' 49, 104

C

Calhoun County Historical
  Society 74
Callender House (Livingston
  house) 135
Camisard 20
Cannon, Arnout 136
Cape Isobella, Santo
  Domingo 17
Capitman, Barbara 108
Capitol Building, Washington
  136
Capone, Al 58
Carnarvon, Lord 19
Carnegie, Andrew 87
Carroll, Charles 134
Carter
  Ann *see* Lee, 'Light Horse
  Harry'
  Ann (mother) 47
  Charles 47, 49
  Howard 19
  John 45, 47, 53
  Robert 'King' 45-7, 51-4
Cassidy, Butch 143
Castle Tucker, Wiscasset,
  Maine 77-82, *78*, *80-2*
Cavalieri, Natalina 145-6
Centennial Exposition 22
Chanler
  Bob 145-6
  John Winthrop 143
  Margaret 143

Willie 143
Chicago World Fair 62
China Grove, Methodist
  Chapel, Mississippi 150-1,
  150, *152*
Christ Church, Lancaster
  County, Virginia 51-4, *52*,
  54
Church
  Frederic 135-6
  Robert 123
City Hotel, New York 55
Clairk, Zeruah 21
Clark
  General William 159
  Guy Gaylord 43
Clay, Henry 76
Clemens
  Clara (Twain's daughter)
  160, 165
  Jane Lampton 156
  Jane Lampton (Jean, Twain's
  daughter) 160, 164
  Langdon (Twain's son) 160
  Olivia Langdon (wife of
  Samuel/Twain) 160, 166
  Orion 158
  Samuel 148, 156, 159, *see
  also* Twain, Mark
  Sherwood 158
  Suzy (Twain's daughter) 160
Clermont (Livingston house)
  135
Cleveland, Grover 76
Clinton, Bill 56
Clivedon, UK 139
Coburn, Joe 39
Coffin, Levi 74
Cogbill family 129
Cogbill's, Lagrange, Tennessee
  129
Colby, Mr (builder) 82
Cole, Thomas 136
Colman, Samuel 160
Columbus, Knights of St 15
Columbus, Christopher 14,
  17
Columbus Chapel,
  Pennsylvania 14-19, *15*
Comstock Jnr, Dr Oliver
  Cromwell 72, 74
Continental Congress 134
Cooly, Ebenezer 21
Cooper, Peter 40, 42-3
Cooper Union 40, 43

Copley, John Singleton 10
Corrie, William 88
Corsair Compact 88
Corsairs I, II, III, SS 87
Cranch, Isaac 21
Crary, Isaac 74
Crawford, Joan 108
Creehan, James 86
Criterion Theatre, Bar
  Harbor, Maine 106-9, *107*,
  109
Crosby, Bing 70
Crosswhite
  Adam 74
  Ben 76
Cuyler, Revd Theodore 93
Cypress Hills National
  Cemetery, Brooklyn 156

D

Daily Crescent 102
Das Deutsche Haus-
  Athenaeum 57
Davis
  Roger 56
  Theodore 19
Degas (uncle of) 104
Dempsey, James 39
Derby, Revd 54
Dickens, Charles 56, 112
Dinosaur Rush, First Great
  115
Dobovich, Sebastian 67
Donnell, Annie 81, 82
Dorchester (troopship) 36
Dorsey, Tommy 58
Downing, Andrew Jackson
  136
Drinker Cope, Edward 115,
  117-18
Dunton, Ammon G. 54
Durham (UK), Earldom of
  148
Dutch Bakery, Tracy City 122

E

Edgewater (Livingston
  temple) 135
Ellis Island immigrant
  hospital 132, *133*
Elmira *see* Langdon House;
  Quarry Farm
Equine Palace, St Louis 62
Everett
  Elaine 38
  Revd Noble 95

F

Fala (Roosevelt's dog) 136
Falmouth, USA 5
Family Cookbook, The (Penn)
  120
Farquhar, Granville 'Granny'
  134
Farrington, Nathan and
  Mehetabel 21
Fitch, Ebenezer 95
Fitzgerald, F. Scott 56
Forest, Lockwood de 160
Fowles, John 24
Fox Theatre 70
Frances, Sarah 93
Franklin D. Roosevelt Library
  136
Frederick, Christina 82
French, Virginia 27
Fugitive Slave Law 76
Fulton, Robert 134

G

Gallier, James 104
Garbo, Greta 108
Gardiner, Washington 76
Garfield, President James A.
  40
Garnier, Charles 83
Garretson, Revd Freeborn
  135
Gates, John W. 88
German immigration 2-4,
  55-60
Gerry, Elbridge 11
Gilbert, John 108
Gilded Age 83, 135
Gilliat, John and Barbara 31
Gilmour, Thomas 102
Gleason, Jackie 39
Goetz Hotel, Frankenmouth
  57
Goodrich, Elizur 21
Goodyear, Charles 40
Gormanghastian brewery, St
  Louis 60
Gracanica, Illinois 65-8, *67*, *68*
Grace, F.A. 71
Graham, George 115
Great Gatsby, The (Fitzgerald)
  56
Greeley, Horace 96
Griffin, Norbert 37, 44
  (Griffen p 44)
Grinnan, Robert 102
Grose, Miriam 11
Gross, John Martin 6
Gunnel, Eric 113
Guyot, Arnold 89

H

Hale, Edward Everett 92
Hammond, Hezekiah 21
Hancock, John 11
Handy, W.C. 123
Hanson, Tony 99
Harper's Ferry, Boston 17
Harrigan and Hart 43
Hartford, Connecticut (351,

Farmington Avenue, Twain's
  home) 160-2, *161-4*
Hartford Daily Times 160
Harvard Club 83
Havel, Hippolyte 39
Hawthorne, Seth 77
Henrietta (yacht) 84
Henry Flury's Staple and
  Fancy Groceries 122
Hever Castle, UK 139
Heyer, Conrad 6, 7
Heywood Hill (bookshop)
  147
Hill
  Colonel Edward 45
  Elizabeth 45
Hill-Carter II, Charles 45, 47,
  49, *46*
Hill-Carter III, Charles 47, 49
Hillier, Bevis 108
Hilton, Ebenezer 77
Historic Places, US National
  Register of 117
Holmes, Josiah 21
Honolulu House, Marshall
  70-6, *71*, *73*, *75*
Hoosier Kitchen Cabinet
  'Want List' *82*
Hotckins, Amerin 159
House of Mirth, The (Wharton)
  135
Howard, Henry 102, 110-11
Howe, Julia Ward 139, 143,
  140
Hudson River
  Livingston houses 135-6
  preservation 138
  School of painting 136
Hughes
  Madame 28, 30-1
  Thomas 25-8, 30-1
Hussey, Erastus 74
Huston, John 33
Huxtable, Ada Louise 94
Hyer, Tom 39

I

Ingersoll, George 74
International Court of Justice
  92
Ireland, Shadrach 21
Irney, Metropolitan 65-6
Irving, Washington 136

J

Jackson
  Andrew 76
  Heaven 113
Jahn, Friedrich Ludwig 57
James I 45
James II 8
Jardin Des Plantes, Paris 118
Jefferson, Thomas 32, 59-60,

95, 134
Jensen, Jens 74
Johnson
  Charles W. 117
  Lois Walker 31
Jordan, Dolly 104-5
Joy, Dr 72
Jungenfeld, E. 60

K

Kast, Revd Dr 4-5
Keaton, Buster 72
Keith, Linus 74
Kelly, Barney 43
Kemble, Fanny 146
Kinglsey, Charles 27
Kipling, Rudyard 164
Kirwan, Mrs 44
Kneller, Sir Godfrey 47
Kurst, Revd Dr 4-5

L

La Bergerie *see* Rokeby
Ladd, Alan 56
Lafayette, Marquis de 8, 11
Lagarde, Mathilde *see* Boal
Lambton 147-67
  Huckleberry 147
  Lucinda (Lucy) *149*, *153*
  Mark 147
  'Radical Jack' 148, 152
  Samuel 147-8, 156
  William 147-8
Lambton Castle, Durham
  (UK) 156
'Lambton Worm, The' 150
Lampton
  Benjamin 155, 167
  Bob 149-50
  Dinwiddie 165-6, *166*
  Dr James 158
  James J. 159
  Jane, 155, *see also* Clemens
  Lambton inheritance 147,
  151
  Lucie (China Grove) 151
  Lucie (Columbia,
  Mississippi) 152
  Lucinda 151
  Lucius 147-52, 159, *149*
  Lucy 151
  Lucy L. 151
  Thad, Eddie, Iddo, Lucius,
  Walter 151, *154*
  William 'Huckleberry Finn'
  151, 165, 167, *152*
  William J. 152, 155, *155*
  see also Leathers, Jesse
Lampton Company Store
  151, *154*
Langdon, Olivia 159-60, *see
  also* Clemens
Langdon House, Elmira,

Upstate NY 160-2, 165
Latrobe, Benjamin 55
Lawrence, Sir Thomas 152
Lazar, Tsar 66
Le Notre 108
Le Vau, Louis 11
Leathers, Jesse 156
LeBrun, Napoleon 94
Lee
  Ann 20-1
  Charles S. 106
  Christopher 15
  Jeremiah 8-13
  'Light Horse Harry' 49
  Robert E. 49, 51
  Silas 77
Lehman's Hardware Store,
  Kidron, Ohio 129
Leidy, Joseph 117-18
Lewis
  Jerry 70
  Meriweather 159
Lexington 11
Lincoln, Abraham 43, 76
Lincoln Intelligencer 77
Lindbergh, Charles 125
Livingston
  Alida 138
  Catherine 135
  Chancellor Robert 134,
  139
  Helen Margaretta 132-3
  Janet 135
  Philip 134
Livingston Mills, Ruth 135
Livingston Trail 132-46
Livingstone, Dr David 87
Llamas Del Mouro 14-15
London Gazette 39
Longfellow, Charles 84
Lonsdale, Henry 102
Louis XIV period 136
Louisiana Purchase 134
Louisville Waterworks 166
Low, Captain Ned 33
Lutherans 2, 5-6
Lyell, Louis 147
Lyndhurst, Lord 10
Lysistrata, SS 86

M

McArthur, John 114
MacDonald, J. 128
McDowell, Dr Joseph 158
Mack, Edward 42
McKay, George 108
McKim, Mead & White 83,
  87, 135
McKinley, President 40
McSorley
  Bill 38, 40
  John 37-8, 40, *41*
McSorley's Old Ale House,

Manhattan 37-44, *38, 41,*
  42
Maddox, Joseph 102
Madison, Dolley 17, 166
Magnolia Gazette 148
Maher, George 83
Mahon, Mathew 39, 44
Mapple, Father *see* Mudge,
  Revd
Marblehead, Massachusetts 4,
  8-13, *9, 12*
Marcella, Miss 58
Mariners' Home, New
  Bedford 36
Marsh, Othniel 115
Marshall, Michigan 70-6, *71,*
  73, 75
Martin, Dean 70
Martineau, Harriet 134
Mature, Victor 56
Mead, Margaret 117
Meade, Bishop 52
Medieval-Flemish style 136
Medomak River 4-5
Melville, Herman 32-3, 35
Menotomy, Massachusetts 11
Meredith, Dr 158
Merton, Thomas 23
Michigan Bell telephone
  company 74
Miles, David 53
Miller, Glen 58
Milutin, King 65
Mitchell, Joseph 43
Mittelberger, Gottlob 2
Moby Dick (Melville/Huston)
  32-3
Modern French style 83
Mohonk Mountain House,
  Upstate NY 89-94, *90-1,*
  93, 94
Mont Ferrat 11
Montgomery Place
  (Livingston house) 135
Morgan, J. Pierpont 83, 87-8
Morrison, Betty 106
Morton, John 8
'Mother Fresh Roasted' 37
Mowbray, H. Siddons 136
Mudge, Revd Enoch 35
Munroe, James 134
My Life on Beale Street (Sam)
  125
Myrick, Elijah 21

N

Namouna (ship) 86
Napoleon, Emperor 134, 139
Nastich, Barnoda 67
National Historic Landmark
  70, 94
National League of Woman
  Voters 143

New Bedford, Massachusetts
  32-6, *34*
New Orleans Garden District
  100-5, *101, 103, 105*
New Orleans Picayune 158
New York Herald 84, 86-7
New York Morning Post 39
New York Times 38, 106, 155
New York Tribune, The 96
New York Yacht Club 83-8,
  85, 6
Northern Neck News 54
Nottoway Plantation,
  Louisiana 110-13, *111, 113*

O

Oakhill (Livingston house)
  135
O'Connell, Daniel 44
Oglethorpe, Governor James
  59
Onderdonk, Cornelius 31
O'Reilly, Revd Bernard 80
Orlana (Livingston palace)
  135
Orne, Azor 11
Othello (ship) 79

P

Paine
  Thomas 11, 89
Paley, Frederick Apthorp 35
Pannini, Giovanni 8
Paris Exposition 60
Peabody Hotel, Memphis 123
Peck, Gregory 33
Penn
  Alma 119, 122, *121*
  Dava 119
  Dawn 119
  Gabriel 119
  Jeane 119, 122
  Martin Wilson 'Dick' 119
  William 2, 59, 119-20
Penn's Stores, Gravel Switch,
  Kentucky 119-22, *120-1*
Pershing, General 17
Peter, Bishop 65
Peterman, Hiram A. 72
Philadelphia Centennial
  Exposition 135
Pierce, John D. 74
Pierpont Morgan Library 87,
  136
Pilgrim Fathers 8, 59
Pitt, William 10, 32
Pitt Packet 10
Pleasant Hill, Kentucky 21, 23
Pocahontas 120, 147, *147*
Potter, Edward Tuckerman
  160
Pratt
  Abner 70-1

Bellona 74
Isaac 95
Jared 95
Presley, Elvis 123, 126
Pride of Lions, The (Thomas)
  145
Purchas, Samuel 32
Pynes, The (Livingston house)
  135

Q

Quakers 2
Quarles, John Adams 155
Quarry Farm, Elmira, Upstate
  NY 162, 164-5, *165*
Queen Anne (style) 2, 45, 70,
  135-6

R

Raft, George 56
Rand, Eleazar 21
Randolph
  Cornelia 110, 112
  John Hampden 110, 112-13
Rathbun
  Amos 21
  Reuben 21
Ratskeller *see* Seelbach Hotel
Read, Nathaniel 96
Rebecca (schooner) 84
Red Boy (Lawrence) 152
Redd, Wilmot 11
Reiser, Major 5
Remington, Frederick 166
Rhumus, George 58
Rip Van Winkle (Irving) 136
Rivera, Diego 70
'Robber Barons' 83, 87
Robinson, Edward G. 56
Rockwell, Norman 125
Rogers, Roy 56
Rokeby (Livingston house)
  138-9, 143, 146, *138-42*
Rookwood Pottery,
  Cincinnati 58
Roosevelt
  Franklin D. 56, 136
  Theodore 123
Root, Elihu 92
Royal Hospital, Greenwich
  (London) 10
Rugby, Tennessee 25-31, *26,*
  28-9
Ruth, Babe 39

S

Sabbathday Lake, New
  Gloucester, Maine 20
Sabbathday Lake Shakers 20-
  4, *22-3*
St Francis (tribe) 4
Sala, Augustus 55
Salem Trials 11

Sam 125
Sayer, Robert 77
Schaeffer, Dr 5
Schuler's Restaurant, Marshall
  76
Schwab
  Abe 123, 125-6, *124*
  Elliott 123, 125-6
Schwab's, Memphis 123-30,
  124, 128-30
Scott
  Hugh Lennox 93
  Sir Walter 102-3, 139
Seaman's Bethel, New
  Bedford 32-6, *35*
Seelbach, Louis and Otto 55
Seelbach Hotel, Louisville,
  Kentucky 55-8, *57*
Sellers, Captain Isaiah 158-9,
  159
Shakers 156
  Sabbathday Lake, Maine
  20-4, *22-3*
Sharpsteen
  Dr Henry 72
  Verne 72
Shaw, Dr Moses 77
Shirley Plantation, Virginia
  45-50, *46, 48, 50*
Short, Colonel Robert
  Henry 104
Sinatra, Frank 70
Sloan, John 39
Slosson, Eliphalet 21
Slout, Salome Amie 72
Smiley
  Albert 89, 91-3
  Alfred 89
Smith
  Captain John 32
  John Stafford 60
Smith, Parson 5
Society for the Preservation
  of New England Antiques 82
Soto, Hernando de 158
Soule, John 96
South Carolina, SS 79
Spragens, William 119
Springwood (Livingston
  house) 135
Staatsburg (Livingston house)
  135
Stagg, Brian 31
Stamp Act 10
Stanley, Henry Morton 87
Starr, Frederick 100, 104
Stephens, Leslie 28
Stevens, Uriah 74
Stokes, John Festus 89
Stowe, Harriet Beecher 162
Stuart, Frank 72
Suckley

Margaret 'Daisy' 136
  Robert 136
  Thomas 136
Sullivan
  Barnabas 77
  Louis 159
  Yankee 39
Supple, Jeremiah 111-12

T

Taft, Howard 56
Talleyrand (-Périgord),
  Charles-Maurice, Prince de
  134, 139
Taylor, Zachary 76
Teasdale, Sarah 159
Tennyson, Alfred 28
Thayer, Cornelius 21
Thomas
  Elisha 21
  Lately 145
Thomas Store, South
  Carolina 129
Thompson, Jared 'Yankee' 74
Tiffany
  Joseph Burr 136
  Louis Comfort 160
Tillotson, Zenas 74
Tom Brown's Schooldays
  (Hughes) 25
Topp, Robertson 123
Toribius of Astorga, St 14
Tremont House Hotel,
  Boston 55
Tremont Nail Factory,
  Wareham, Massachusetts
  95-9, *96-8*
Trobriand, General James de
  17
Troutman, Francis 74
Truman, Harry S. 56
Tucker
  Jane (granddaughter) 79-82,
  81
  Jane (mother & daughter)
  77, 81-2
  Richard Holbrook 77,
  79-81
  see also Castle Tucker
Turnvereins 57
Twain
  Mark
  see also Clemens, Samuel
  books
  *A Connecticut Yankee in King
  Arthur's Court* 156
  Huckleberry Finn 157, 160,
  164
  Life on the Mississippi 100,
  157
  model for Huckleberry
  Finn 151

The American Claimant 156
The Gilded Age 157
The Prince and the Pauper 43,
  156, 160
Tom Sawyer 125, 158, 164
Tom Sawyer's Aunt Polly
  156
chair 166
commenting on
  Captain Isaih Sellars 159
  cats 155
  Hartford house 159-60,
  161-3
  his birthplace 155, *157*
  his cousin 158
  his son 159
  Sir Walter Scott 102-3
death 162, 165
essay, 'Mental Telegraphy' 157
Lambton connection 147-8,
  155-8
Langdon House 162
McSorley's playbill 43
meets Kipling 162
octagonal den (Quarry Farm)
  162, 164, 165
pen name 158
play, 'Colonel Sellars as a
  Scientist' 157
sayings 125
smoking 162

U

Underground Railroad 74
University Club, Manhattan
  83
Updike, John 109
US Woman's Army Nursing
  Corps 143

V

van der Rohe, Meis 166
Vanderbilt, William 83
Vaux, Calvert 136
Vernet, Claude-Joseph 8
Villa, Francisco 'Pancha' 17

W

Wagner
  Martin 71-2
  William 114, 117-18
Wagner Free Institute,
  Philadelphia 114-18, *115-
  16, 118*
Wainwright Tomb,
  Bellefontaine 159
Waldo, General Samuel 3-4
Waldoboro, Maine 2-7, *3, 6*
Walter Robinson House,
  New Orleans 104, *101,
  103, 105*
Walton, Sarah Kellogg 30

Wardley, John and Jane 20
Ware, James 94
Warren
  Leonard 117
  Whitney 84
Washington
  Booker T. 123
  George 6, 10-11, 60, 134
Wells, Freegift 21
Western Brewer, The 60-1
Wetmore, Charles 84
Wheeler, Candace Thurber
  160
Whipple, Henry Benjamin
  93, *92*
White, Stamford 87
White Castle *see* Nottoway
White Castle of Louisiana
  (Randolph) 110
Whittaker, James 20-1
Wigton, Earl of 120
Wilder, Shubal 96
Wildercliff (Livingston house)
  135
Wilderstein (Livingston
  house) 135-6, 138, *137*
Wilderstein Preservation
  Corporation 136
Wilkinson, Jeremiah 96
'Will Wimbles' *see* Rugby
Williams, Revd Johnny 113
Williamsburg Foundation's
  Library 47
Willis, Nathanial Parker 138
Wilson
  Uncle Samuel George 31
  Woodrow 56
Winfrey, Oprah 23
Wollaston, John 47
Wood
  Abiel 77
  Samuel 95
Wooster, Abijah 21
Working Men's College,
  London (UK) 25
World Outhose Olympics
  122
Worthmore's store, Rayne,
  Louisiana 129, *127*
Wren, Christopher 47, 53
Wright, Richardson 108

Y

Yeats, W.B. 39
Young, Howard F. 73-4

Z

Zuber's 104, *103, 105*